HACK ON!

4·18·18

HACKING INNOVATION

JOSH LINKNER

PUBLISHED BY FASTPENCIL PUBLISHING

Table of Contents

To my new little hackers, Avi and Tallia.

May you grow healthy and change the world.

≈

Part 1
HACKING FOUNDATIONS

CHAPTER 1: INTRODUCTION

$7.2 billion. Gone in an instant.

The Year: 2013

The Target: Target

As shoppers stocked up on holiday gifts, a more sinister plot was underway. While point-of-sale systems and Internet checkouts inhaled the credit card numbers of unsuspecting consumers at Target stores around the country, hackers were enjoying their own holiday cheer as they silently breached the security of this cyber-naïve retail giant. At least 40 million credit card numbers were stolen along with the theft of the personal information of nearly 110 million customers.

As the news broke in the subsequent weeks, Target's performance plummeted. Revenue was down 46.2% compared to the same period the year before, and their stock price crashed. The market cap of this powerhouse company shriveled by $7.2 billion, bringing once insulated executives to their knees. Target eventually agreed to pay victims a total of $10 million. Disastrous publicity ensued, customer loyalty was eradicated, and this shiny brand was forever tarnished. CEO Gregg Steinhafel was forced out, leaving a giant crater of scorched value in the ashes.

Meanwhile, the hackers profited to the tune of $53.7 million. The deviants behind the hacks have never been identified, caught, or tried. They exist in the ether, lurking in the shadows. Hackers represent no one country, yet a top security expert told the *Wall Street Journal* that they are the single biggest threat to our national security.

And their approaches are your best model for innovation, growth, and success.

To be clear, I'm not endorsing cybercrime. But if you put their sinister motives aside and simply study their techniques, hacking is nothing more than an unorthodox problem solving methodology. In the Target scheme, hackers established their prey, surveyed the obstacles, generated a number of creative approaches, discovered vulnerabilities, exploited their adversary's weakness, and generated outsized results. Compare that to the lackluster performance of many bureaucratic companies, and you'll quickly wish your team embraced the mindset of hackers to drive better, more creative outcomes.

Since the classic 1983 movie *War Games*, hackers have been a global fascination. They are feared, glamorized, and hated. Rarely does a day go by without headline news coverage of the wreckage left behind by malicious hackers. They hack corporations, governments, and individuals. It's been said there are only two types of organizations: those that have been hacked and those that don't know they've been hacked.

Hacking is big business, and it's taking a big toll. In 2014, the FBI received 269,422 complaints of cybercrime. The annual cost of hacking is estimated at over $100 billion in the United States, and more than $300 billion worldwide. Over 60,000 websites are hacked each day, and 47% of adult Americans had their personal information exposed within the last 12 months. MyDoom, the most expensive virus of all time, began in 2004 and has racked up an estimated cost of $38.5 billion. Cybercrime targets 556 million people each year, and 68% of funds lost to these attacks are deemed unrecoverable. No wonder the mere mention of hackers makes the hairs on the back of our necks stand up.

Hackers come in all shapes and sizes. There are government-sponsored hackers, looking to perpetrate espionage on behalf of their mother countries. There are lone-wolf hackers who pursue their craft for financial gain, revenge, social status, or simply to prove that they can. There are bands of hackers, loosely organized affiliates, who team up to deliver vigilante justice, like hacking into ISIS accounts or using hacking to expose criminal acts. There are "white hat" hackers who use their skills for good, "black hat" hackers who perpetrate evil, and hundreds of shades of gray in between.

Some hackers use their skills for positive impact. Startups in Silicon Valley deploy a specialized set of techniques known as "growth hacking" in order to grow massive audiences quickly. That's how Twitter, FourSquare, and Instagram grew so big, so fast. There are also biohackers who leverage hacking techniques to cure disease, solve healthcare problems, and improve environmental quality. There are life hacks (7 Simple Ways To Eliminate Plaque), educational hacks (How To Read With 50% Greater Speed), and even parenting hacks (Reverse-engineering Temper Tantrums To Create A Peaceful Household). With all these seemingly disconnected uses and groups, what commonalities exist?And why should you care?

We often define hacking as a criminal act using computer software to violate cybersecurity defenses. We envision a pimple-faced young man in a hoodie, guzzling energy drinks in a dimly lit basement, perpetrating malicious deeds for illicit gain. While there certainly are individuals that fit this stereotype, hackers are a much wider and more diverse group than this unimaginative caricature.

Hackers, in fact, are not good or evil. Some master software while some have never turned on a computer. Hackers are foreign and domestic, young and old, educated and improvised. Hackers are not defined by their ability to crack code, but by their specialized approach to problem solving.

Hacking does not ascribe a specific intent, and nothing about the skillset itself is right or wrong. In fact, hacking is a tool, an approach. In the same way a knife can be used for evil (to murder) or to heal (a scalpel used to perform a life-saving surgery), hacking can be used to destroy or rebuild. While hacking can clearly be used for wrongdoing, it can also serve as a powerful model of growth, innovation, and success.

The purpose of this book is to share the ideas, mindsets, and techniques of hackers to empower you to use them for legitimate purposes. You won't learn how to rob a bank or take down a power grid. Instead, you'll discover the most powerful model to crush your challenges, foster creativity, and harness what's possible. You'll learn to topple your competitors, drive growth, and ensure long-term success. Hacking is the cutting-edge leadership model to help you to excel and elevate your company's performance.

You are a hacker. You have the ability to unlock potential and solve the most intimidating problems you face, both personally and professionally.

A DORK FINDS HIS MUSE

Back in the early '80s, I got my first taste of hacking. Full disclosure, I was a nerd of epic proportion. As a socially awkward teen with few athletic skills, I spent my days practicing guitar or in front of a computer screen.

Using my Atari 800 computer with 48k of memory and a dial-up modem that transmitted slower than I could type, I had a sinister idea. A mischievous plan to conquer the world.

Sort of.

Back in the day, when long-distance calls cost nearly as much as a luxury vacation, calling cards by MCI, Sprint, and AT&T were a status symbol. Using a special number, along with a 5-digit code, you could speak to someone in a different country. This sounds lame now, in the age of live video streaming from your watch, but back then it was wicked cool. Since I didn't have any money, I decided to use hacking to see if I could score some free codes.

My approach was pretty basic – I wrote a very simple software program to do the dirty work. At the time, AOL was the gateway to the online world and they actually had a phone number rather than a website. You could dial their number from your modem and you'd hear the famous screechy noise, alerting you that you'd reached a computer and not the local pizza joint. So my software did the following: dialed MCI's toll-free calling card number, entered a five-digit code (it started with 00000), and then tried to connect to AOL. If the call went through and AOL's computer tone connected to my machine, my software would record the 5-digit code as valid. If it didn't work, my system would hang up and try the next sequential number (00001). So I'd go to bed each evening, run the system all night, and wake up to 10-15 fresh and valid long-distance codes to use.

Thankfully, I was never caught and am not on any watch lists, as far as I know. At the time, I thought this was the coolest thing ever. I had no intention of selling these codes, or even using them myself. Sadly, I didn't have anyone to call in Paris or São Paulo. I didn't brag about my exploits, and until now, never shared the scheme with anyone. So why did I do it? To see if I could. It was the allure of the challenge, and the euphoric fix of outsmarting the big boys. I felt like I was important, someone of consequence.

I've been hacking ever since. Though that was the end of my cybercrimes, I've used the same unconventional tenets of hacking to craft a fairly interesting life. I started my career as a jazz guitarist, hacking my way onto stages throughout the world. Jazz itself is a form of hacking: it relies on defying rules and using non-traditional routes to bring the art form to life.

Then, in 1990, I started my first company as a hack. At that time, buying a discount computer was nearly impossible. Traditional retail outlets were expensive and time consuming, so I hacked a different approach. I found that I could mail order individual computer components and assemble them in my college apartment for a fraction of the going retail rates. This led to a company – Gator Computer Systems – which I built and sold over the next two years.

Ready for a new project, in 1995, I launched an Internet company that built websites and e-commerce solutions for corporate clients. This was pretty cutting-edge stuff at a time when only 2% of companies even had a website. I deployed hacking techniques in the way we hired, sold, and produced our work. This strange approach helped me build the firm fast and ultimately sell it to a public company.

By the time I sold the company in 1999, Internet adverting had become all the rage. I briefly thought about starting an Internet ad company, but quickly realized I'd be too late to that party. Instead of following the herd, I launched the first Internet promotion company, ePrize. Promotions is a large category of the marketing mix, but online, it was largely dormant back then. Taking this oppositional approach made all the difference as we scaled the company to nearly $100 million in revenue and 500 employees before selling it in 2012. Hacking our product offerings, corporate culture, sales methodology, and even fundraising led to terrific outcomes. The company's success was fueled by a renegade, unorthodox approach.

Next, my partners and I decided to launch a venture capital fund in my hometown of Detroit, Michigan. Sure, we hoped to make some money, but more importantly we wanted to make a difference. Once an international center of innovation, Detroit has suffered for years, largely because it stopped innovating and became complacent. We set out to use venture capital investing as a mechanism to drive social change, to help rebuild our beloved, though troubled city.

Instead of investing in manufacturing companies, we focused our efforts exclusively on tech startups – social media, mobile apps, e-commerce, Internet of Things, cloud computing. People thought we were nuts, but we forged ahead with a hacker-like approach. Today, Detroit Venture Partners is thriving, helping to create jobs, diversify our economy, and foster an exciting work/live/play environment in downtown Detroit.

Recently, I co-founded Fuel Leadership, a company focused on disrupting professional growth and development. My partners and I are passionate about helping people perform better, which leads to successful communities and a vibrant economy. Traditional learning approaches have become stale, boring, and ineffective, and we know there's a better way. Using the principles of hacking, we've set out to disrupt a tired industry and help professionals throughout the world perform better. It's early on, but the traction we've enjoyed is directly related to our non-traditional approach.

But this book isn't about me, it's about you. I only share my background because the principles of hacking drove my success. I didn't call it that throughout my journey, but looking back, there's no mistaking the hacking patterns that were my foundation over the last 26 years in business. To be clear, I have more shortcoming than assets. I stink at details, don't have an MBA, have the patience of a toddler, and never passed calculus. My secret weapon has been my willingness to hack, and it can be yours as well.

Today, I can't write a lick of code. But I proudly consider myself a hacker. Hackers are change agents. They stick their finger in the eye of conventional wisdom. They break and then rebuild things. They imagine. They create.

NOT IMPOSSIBLE

Daniel's life changed with the thunderous crash of an explosion. A boy living in the Nuba Mountains in war-torn South Sudan, Daniel lost both his arms when bombs fell near his village. Life in his situation was hard enough, but with no arms he needed constant help for even the most basic tasks. In a *Time* interview, he tearfully said, "If I could die today, I would, so I will not be a burden to my family."

Struck by Daniel's profound and heartbreaking remarks, Mick Ebeling decided to start hacking. More than 8,000 miles away in Venice Beach, California, Mick and his team at Not Impossible Labs met to discuss Daniel's plight. This is exactly the kind of challenge they live for.

Mick was a successful film producer, animator, and special effects artist when he decided to reinvent himself. While he enjoyed his craft and was earning a great living, his heart led him in a new direction. He deeply felt the plight of those around the globe suffering with challenges that felt "impossible" to overcome. So in 2009, he launched Not Impossible Labs, which takes on seemingly impossible missions and then uses hacking principles to conquer them. Once a problem has been identified, they crowdsource solutions from inventors, technologists, and dreamers around the globe. They seek to develop innovative solutions that can ultimately be replicated and scaled, all for the sake of improving humanity.

According to the Not Impossible website, "The ability to obtain healthcare, literacy and technology shouldn't ever be limited by finances, geography or physical ability. Along with our community of passionate and talented engineers, makers, idea generators, and storytellers, we're making the impossible, Not Impossible."

In Daniel's case, Mick and the team got working on the problem of providing Daniel with affordable prosthetic arms so he could feed himself, contribute to his community, and regain his dignity. Using many principles and approaches we'll cover throughout the book, Not Impossible Labs was able to create a solution for Daniel using a 3-D-printed prosthetic arm. Their journey was not without obstacles, but ultimately, they not only helped a young boy across the globe, they also leveraged their invention to help thousands of others. These low-cost prosthetics are now being used in developing countries, directly impacting thousands. The efforts have been magnified further by Not Impossible's global reach and their ability to shine a light on important issues through masterful storytelling. This small organization, with a tiny team and limited resources has not only helped kids in war-torn regions, they've helped thousands of others around the world who were facing "impossible" situations of their own.

Mick's unorthodox practices embody hacking at its finest: a burning curiosity and willingness to confront conventional wisdom. Democratized ideation from a diverse and vast array of contributors, rather than relying on single bets from entrenched "experts." Conducting low-cost, controlled, high-volume experiments instead of launching a single, bet-the-farm initiative. Finding a hole in the problem and then exploiting it to its logical end. Believing that no barrier is impenetrable.

WHY AND WHAT?

Hackers hack for different reasons, from social validation to massive financial gain. Their motives vary widely, but what they share is an insatiable curiosity, a willingness to experiment with unconventional approaches in order to conquer their challenges, a desire to forgo traditional thinking in favor of fresh possibilities.

In this sense, hackers have been the source of progress for generations. Martin Luther King, Jr. hacked racial injustice and protesting. Galileo hacked the scientific norms of his day. Charlie Parker hacked traditional harmonic structures, becoming the father of modern jazz.

Lab researchers hack new drug therapies to eradicate disease. Nutritional scientists hack molecular structures to deliver food that tastes better, lasts longer, and delivers optimal health benefits. Entrepreneurs hack entire industries whose leaders are asleep at the wheel, in order to better serve customers and unlock incredible fortunes.

So what does it mean to hack?

I've studied dozens of definitions, but to me there's a simple answer:

Hacking [hak' ing] *verb.* The act of solving complex problems in unorthodox ways. Discovering fresh, unconventional approaches that replace prevailing wisdom.

Since the first media coverage of hacking, a passionate discussion around the difference between 'hacking' and 'cracking' has raged. The simplest definition comes from cybersecurity giant Symantec: "The general view is that while hackers build things, crackers break things." Hackers believe in deconstruction for the purpose of learning and innovation, whereas crackers engage in demolition – breaking something just to break it. A cracker will steal a company's data; a hacker will just send an email showing where the vulnerability is. The skills are often the same, the motives and outcomes are what vary. For this book, I'm using "hacker" because it's more general, and because "cracker" has many other associations. If something is being stolen, defaced, or used illicitly, it is probably a cracker, but my concern is the underlying mindsets and methods, not the motives. I hope my hacker friends will forgive my broader use of the term, for the purpose of clarity.

Well-known hacker, Eric S. Raymond maintains a digital copy of the Hacker Dictionary at www.catb.org/jargon/html. This dictionary is considered the hacker standard and is the place to go if you want more information about hackers vs. crackers, or other hacking terms.

You may wonder...how is hacking different than traditional innovation approaches? Isn't this just a new name for an old thing? As I'll show you through the mindsets, tactics, and incredible examples in this book, hacking is the new model for innovation. The new model for growth.

Consider MySpace. It was a true Internet darling in July 2005, when it was purchased by media giant News Corporation for $580 million. In June 2006, it surpassed Google as the most visited website in the United States and was unquestionably the dominant leader of social media. Now the folks at News Corporation were smart people with a deep understanding of traditional innovation and growth models. They had the finest degrees, limitless resources, and a proven CEO, Rupert Murdoch, at the helm. What could possibly go wrong?

In short? Mark Zuckerberg.

Zuckerberg, quite simply, is a hacker. In fact, he proudly embraces that title. Zuckerberg used hacking to obliterate the top social media site, despite a tremendous resource disadvantage. After several rounds of layoffs, MySpace was sold in 2011 for a mere $35 million. The once most-visited website plunged to a pitiful ranking of #1749 by 2016, and the company is now a shell of its former self. Meanwhile, Zuckerberg's Facebook is the #2 site today (just behind Google) and boasts a market cap of $323 billion as of this writing. Zuck is the 7th wealthiest person in the US with a personal net worth of over $40 billion.

When Facebook filed to go public in 2012, Zuckerberg penned a letter to prospective investors. The letter shared that the value of his company, both current and future, is based on their approach, which he labels "The Hacker Way":

> The Hacker Way is an approach to building that involves continuous improvement and iteration.... Hackers try to build the best services over the long term by quickly releasing and learning from smaller iterations rather than trying to get everything right all at once. To support this, we have built a testing framework that at any given time can try out thousands of versions of Facebook. We have the words "Done is better than perfect" painted on our walls to remind ourselves to always keep shipping.... There's a hacker mantra that you'll hear a lot around Facebook offices: "Code wins arguments."

His point is that hacking, and Facebook, is a meritocracy where titles and tenure are meaningless when it comes to decision-making. The best ideas win, not the person with the loudest voice or fanciest title.

"The Hacker Way" is such an important element of Facebook's success, they paid homage to it when building the company's corporate campus. The street name has been changed, making the address of this multi-billion global company 1 Hacker Way, Menlo Park, CA 94025.

BE FROGGER

Traditional innovation approaches are simply out of date. Which is a real problem for you, whether you're a manager at a giant multinational or run your own small business.

A confluence of forces has formed to create a potent cocktail of change. Friction-free global markets fueled by fully-transparent, real-time information have rendered previous competitive advantages impotent. By 2020, Millennials will represent 50% of the global workforce and a nearly equal portion of consumer buying power. Their expectations, needs, and internal drivers are very different than previous generations, which fuels the need for change in nearly every business. Shifting demographics, increasing speed, exponential complexity, emergent technologies, geo-political turmoil, and even shifting ideologies are creating a business landscape with an unprecedented rate of change.

Growing up in an era when video games hit the mainstream, I was always drawn to the game of *Frogger*. The player assumes the role of a motivated frog, trying to make his way across a river. Without the ability to swim, he must hop on a variety of things such as logs, turtles, and lily pads as they glide through the river rapids. The challenge is that nothing remains stationary. Each leap onto stable ground is temporary, since all the items are zooming down the river. Even the respite of a dry log is temporary; if the frog tries to stay on stable footing too long, he falls into the river and dies. To win, he must leap quickly from one short-lived success to another. As the game advances, safe harbors become less frequent and faster moving, leaving the poor frog in a constant state of unrest and instability.

Sound familiar?

To a great degree, we are living in a three-dimensional game of *Frogger*. Competitive wins, top tier financial performance, and brand supremacy are all temporary states, met with an ever-increasing stream of change. Yet the models we use to lead, innovate, and grow have not evolved to meet the challenges of the day. Traditionalist approaches are yielding diminishing returns as the playing field becomes more complex and difficult. While most business leaders succumb to their instincts of doubling down on what worked in the past, those embracing the new model – hacking – will enjoy a disproportionate share of the spoils.

A quick compare-and-contrast:

Traditionalist	Hacker Approach
Top-down	Bottom-up
Monolithic	Democratic
Few giant bets	Many small experiments
Protect old ideas	Create new ideas
Static	Constantly changing
Rules-centric	Idea-centric
Slow, clunky	Fast, agile
Lethargic	Burning urgency
Resource-heavy	Scrappy
Avoid risk	Embrace risk

The hacking approach will become your most powerful system to meet expanding obstacles, challenges, and opportunities. The approach is not relegated to tech startups or fringe markets, but can be applied to drive growth in any business setting – from a Fortune 500 biotech company, to the corner dry cleaner, and everywhere in between.

A core tenet of hacking is that it is a meritocratic approach. In other words, hacking doesn't require a fancy title or limitless resources. Zuckerberg toppled Murdoch by embracing hacking. Fittingly, David defeated Goliath through a hack. Facing a much larger and well-equipped foe, David identified and then exploited a small weakness to bring a seemingly impenetrable opponent to his knees. A traditional approach would be to summon more resources, attack only when enough conventional strength was amassed, and engage in classic combat. Yet David was able to hack his way to victory using an unorthodox approach. Hacking is imminently accessible no matter your age, race, rank, gender, education, background, or political views. Hacking is the great equalizer.

WHAT HACKING IS NOT

There's a lot of confusion as to what hacking is and isn't. For our purposes, hacking is all about solving complex problems in unorthodox ways. Using creativity to breakthrough your biggest barriers in order to achieve more. As such, it's important for us to define what hacking is not:

Hacking is NOT a quick fix, jury-rigged, haphazard, temporary solution. Hot-wiring a car or duct-taping a leaky pipe is a short-term patch, not a long-term hack.

Hacking is NOT evil by nature. It is a systematic approach to overcoming obstacles and discovering new possibilities. It is a neutral methodology that can be used for good or bad.

Hacking is NOT simply perpetrating cybercrimes. Yes, we primarily view hackers in this context, but they are simply using hacking approaches for deviant purposes. You can use the same powerful approaches to invent a new drug therapy, launch a breakaway product, or sell more life insurance. No computer code required.

Hacking is NOT inherently destructive. In fact, it can be quite the opposite. Elements of hacking philosophy are at the root of many societies' greatest advances throughout history, from art to science, politics to invention.

A HACK UNFOLDS IN REAL TIME

"Your move, BMW. The entirely new Audi A4." These words appeared on a large billboard in Los Angeles, along with a high-quality photo of a brand new Audi A4. Clearly, the ad was rhetorical in nature. The whole point of the ad was that there's no way BMW could possibly respond to this cool new car.

The problem for Audi: BMW is an innovative company. They are a company that knows how to leverage the strategies of hackers, how to respond to a threat with a non-traditional approach, how to adapt quickly. So within only one week, in the identical sight line of the Audi billboard, BMW fired back with their own ad. The ad featured a mean looking, jet black BMW 330i (the direct competitor to the Audi A4) with a giant one-word headline: "Checkmate."

This is the type of agility hackers use, and the exact approach needed to win in today's competitive business landscape. Think how the folks at Audi must have felt when their new ad completely backfired. But instead of retreating to lick their wounds, they decided to respond with a hack of their own. Two days later, on the very next billboard, Audi responded. Their ad featured a huge photo of the $145,000 Audi R8 supercar with its low profile, wide body, and gorgeous lines. The headline: "Your Pawn Is No Match For Our King."

This launched the billboard wars of LA. Both companies began volleying back and forth, trying to outdo one another. As a result, *both* companies won because they both knew how to adapt fast, how to embrace an unconventional approach, and how to unleash creativity to solve a threat. The fun continued for several weeks in a constant game of one-upmanship that included digital billboards, signs on actual cars driving the neighborhoods, and even a hot air balloon showing the BMW Indy racing car touting the headline, "Game Over. "

During this period, competitors were shut out of the conversation. Had Lexus or Mercedes embraced the hacking mindset, they could have jumped into the fray to vie for the hearts and minds of customers. Instead, they sat silent on the sidelines.

In the end, Audi was the one taking the victory lap. The last few billboards that ran weren't created by their ad agency, they were created by their customers. The hackers at Audi had the idea to open up the competition on social media and invite customers to submit billboard ideas to run in the LA market. Thousands of creative ideas flooded in via social media, many of which were made into giant signs including a headline saying, "Chess? I'd Rather Be Driving. "

Imagine engaging your customers so deeply that they fight with one another to write your ads for you. To me, the best part is the fluid nature by which this came to be. There was no strategic committee that met in a windowless room with demographic data, crafting a scheme to get customers to write ads. In fact, the creativity came after an initial idea launched and backfired. There was no top-down mandate from the executive team. Instead, the savvy folks at Audi used a reversal technique often deployed by hackers to win the match.

These types of innovative maneuvers may appear to require huge budgets or the innate creativity of Mozart. Truth is, there is a systematic approach to harness this type of breakthrough thinking. The hacking model you will learn in the pages ahead will give you a toolkit to unlock the same problem-solving wizardry that's being used to win big in the most challenging business battles.

THE NEW MODEL

Whether you're hacking your way out of a jam or hacking blue-sky opportunity for growth, the unorthodox approach from the clandestine world of hacking can fuel your success.

This book is organized into three parts:

Part I: Hacking Foundations lays the foundation and will acclimate you to this new system of innovation, growth, and leadership. Here, we'll become immersed in the mindset of hackers, explore the various types of hackers, dispel myths, and understand the core philosophies of these ingenious problem-solvers.

Part II: Hacking in Action is a journey into hacks of all shapes and sizes. We'll see how business leaders use hacking philosophies and techniques to drive sales, master operations, reimagine corporate culture, generate social change, and fuel growth. We'll examine the parallels of infamous cybercrime breaches and breathtaking entrepreneurial exploits. You'll relish real stories of underdogs who outsmart the competition, dreamers who hack for social good, and big corporations using hacking strategies to create billions of new market value. Throughout this section, I'll help you understand the specific strategies deployed, providing you a toolkit of your own. You'll not only hear the stories, but you'll learn the tools and techniques, which can be directly aimed at the biggest challenges and opportunities you face.

In **Part III: Masterclass**, we'll narrow our lens to hone in on practical application. You'll enjoy in-depth stories of how hacking mindsets and tactics can be broadly implemented for unbelievable results. We'll look at how you can bring together different mindsets and techniques to bring your desired results to life.

There's also a **Quick Reference Guide** to help you keep these mindsets and tactics fresh in your mind.

Through exercises, techniques, and proven strategies, you'll be armed for battle and ready to put this new model to work.

The stakes have never been higher. The challenges have never been greater. The speed and complexity have never been more overwhelming. Yet the opportunities have never been more profound. Get ready to open your heart and mind and conquer your toughest obstacles and adversaries, while unlocking bold new opportunities for success.

Let the games begin!

CHAPTER 2: THE 5 CORE MINDSETS

Kevin Bull was facing the challenge of his life. A successful stock trader and entrepreneur, Bull trained hard and finally made it as a walk-on to pursue his dream: to compete on national TV as an American Ninja Warrior. The other contestants were more athletic, more experienced, and better prepared. The odds were simply not in Bull's favor.

Instead of brute strength, Bull leveraged the hacker mindset to do the unthinkable. Cannonball Alley, the 8th obstacle in the 2014 Venice City Finals, was a formidable challenge, consisting of three dodgeball-sized balls, suspended by ropes over a large pool of water. Competitors had to cross over by grabbing one swinging cannonball and leaping to the next. The objective was to make it to the other side without falling in the water. Sixteen of the world's best athletes attempted the challenge before Bull, and all sixteen of them failed.

The challenge required enormous upper body strength, after having already completed seven obstacles. Each contestant failed to make it through this incredibly demanding task, and Bull, who lacked the raw power of those who failed before him, knew he needed a different approach. He summoned his inner hacker.

Hackers are innately curious, refusing to accept conventional approaches as the only routes to success. They believe that any barrier or obstacle can be tackled with unorthodox, creative approaches that balk established practices. In Kevin's case, he knew a completely different method would be his only chance of accomplishing this task that everyone had failed. Other competitors assumed the only way to conquer the dreaded Cannonball Alley was to increase upper body strength, but Kevin chose to do the complete opposite. After clearing the first two balls and moving to the third – the place where so many others had failed – Kevin stunned the crowd by flipping his body upside down and grabbing the last hanging cannonball with his *legs*. Just as his upper body strength had deteriorated under intense overuse, his fresh legs were able to grasp the target. Kevin locked his legs around the ball, used his upside-down body to swing in the direction of the finish line, and was able to leap in mid-air to land on his feet on the dry platform at which he aimed. Spectators leapt to their feet and screamed with both approval and astonishment, as this unlikely ninja became the first man to triumph over the course.

What mindset enabled Kevin Bull to both literally and figuratively flip traditional thinking upside down in order to win?

Understanding the mindset of hackers is the first step toward your own death-defying success. Kevin used a core hacking philosophy in order to win like cyberhackers used similar thinking to breach the "secure" systems of the FBI in 2015. Whether you're an entrepreneur trying to be the next Zuckerberg or you're working to end famine in Syrian refugee camps, a hacking mindset will enable you to view your biggest challenges in an entirely new light.

THE 5 CORE MINDSETS

Having studied all kinds of hackers – from the illicit exploits of cyber-criminals to the kindhearted researchers who hack in order to eradicate disease – there are some common shared philosophies. Unlike the specific techniques we'll cover throughout the book, which are used to solve particular problems, the hacker mindsets are the foundation to Innovation Hacking. This set of beliefs will serve as the underpinning for your own hacking exploits, and allow you to build a hacking culture in your own organization.

Hooded criminals, lab rats, innovators, entrepreneurs, and business executives alike have embraced these five core philosophies in order to hack through their most difficult challenges:

1. Every Barrier Can Be Penetrated
2. Compasses Over Maps
3. Nothing Is Static
4. Quantity Is a Force Multiplier
5. Competence Is the Only Credential That Matters

These five fundamental beliefs are the underpinnings of the hacking ethos, and your framework for creating change. Now, let's explore each of them in depth as we lay the foundation for your own hacking adventures.

EVERY BARRIER CAN BE PENETRATED

Maurice Maeterlinck famously said, "If the bee disappeared from Earth, man would only have four years left to live." Not necessarily a fan of stings, he was referring to the important role bees and other insects play in fertilization and cross-pollination. Unfortunately, our planet has seen an alarming decline in populations of bees, butterflies, and other important insects, which, in turn, is threatening global food supplies, as the human population expands like never before. A large problem indeed, and one that needs to be hacked.

Hackers first approach any problem by identifying the barrier that must be infiltrated, along with a desired outcome:

The Barrier: Declining population of bees

Desired Outcome: Reverse the trend to save humanity

You'll notice the barrier need not be a software security system and the desired outcome need not be committing a crime for the hacking mindset to be deployed. The key mindset at play is that *Every Barrier Can Be Penetrated*. Hackers universally embrace the belief that fortresses are meant to be breached, mountains are meant to be climbed. The fact that something has never been done or that the challenge seems daunting entices the hacker rather than deters her. In fact, the more difficult a barrier appears, the more enthused the hacker becomes to rupture it.

The Hackers: Harvard Microbiotics Lab

The Solution: RoboBees

Refusing to accept that only bees could be bees, researchers toiled to discover a different approach. While most people would try to solve a bee shortage by feeding, protecting, or breeding more actual bees, the Harvard hackers used an unconventional approach to solve the problem at hand. With the trend of unmanned aircraft (drones) growing in mainstream usage, they decided to build robot bees. So much for that old adage, "never send a robot to do a bee's job."

The RoboBee is not your grandfather's insect. They can lift off, hover to conserve energy, fly through dust, and swim. They fly faster than a real bee, yet weigh less. In addition to conducting pollination missions, this tiny invention can ultimately expand to serve other purposes. "The RoboBees can eventually be used for search and rescue, for example in areas where larger robots won't fit," says Harvard Microbiotics Laboratory researcher Elizabeth Helbling. "They would also return with the information faster, as you wouldn't have to wait for one robot to come back, but instead have a whole swarm of them covering a forest or similar." And Helbling and the researchers at Harvard aren't the only ones tackling big problems, problems that desperately need a hack.

Pablos Holman, a lifelong hacker, is an expert on hacking problems, large and small. He's also a vocal proponent of spreading hacking methodologies, and the hacking mindsets I'm sharing with you:

> Hackers are in the business of breaking things. I don't think it's particularly weird or audacious. Hacking is just a learning style or methodology. Rather than relying on the instructions, we'll just try everything. We'll take something apart, break it into a lot of little pieces, and figure out what we can build from it.

One of Holman's biggest hacks? Mosquitoes. Mosquitoes aren't only a nuisance during your holiday picnic, they carry deadly diseases such as Zika and malaria, which alone kills over 600,000 people per year. Bed nets, antimalarial drugs, and insecticides have helped, but according to the World Health Organization, the problem still ranks as the 17th most frequent cause of death, ahead of lung cancer, traffic accidents, and diabetes. Who better to attack one of our planet's most pressing issues than someone who has been labeled "The Madonna of Hackers"?

For the last 17 years, Holman has been a member of The Shmoo Group, self-labeled as "a notorious group of hackers and security professionals." He loves doing live demos where he instantly accesses audience members' "secure" credit card info and computers, revealing passwords and other data, or plugs into a hotel TV system to display the movie of his choosing, in any room on the property. With messy hair, tinted glasses, jet black clothes, and tattered gym shoes, Pablos looks like he came right from central casting for a hacker role. Not only does he look the part, he's the embodiment of the hacking mindset put to positive use. He's the ultimate Innovation Hacker.

Pablos deploys hacking mindsets to invent and create. He's teamed up with Microsoft co-founder Paul Allen's Intellectual Ventures to tackle some of the biggest problems facing humanity, like mosquitoes transmitting malaria.

Holman and his fellow hackers at Intellectual Ventures conducted a series of simulations to explore how malaria continues to spread throughout Africa. Each simulation exposed new opportunities to breach their barrier, to stop the spread and ultimately eradicate this fatal disease. As they continued to concentrate on the problem, unorthodox ideas started to emerge.

A core tenet of this first hacking philosophy – that **Every Barrier Can Be Penetrated** – is a profound attraction to curiosity and exploration. Hackers don't look at things as they are; instead, they constantly question every premise. Taking nothing for granted, they ask an endless stream of questions about each problem they face, every element of prevailing wisdom. With the intensity of an inquisitive child, they refuse to accept life as it is, favoring instead what it could be.

Accordingly, Pablos Holman and his team explored crazy options for stopping insect-borne disease. They looked at chemicals, screens, drugs. Yet none of these yielded their desired breakthrough results, and frankly none of them were "hacker cool." Hackers seek to explore new boundaries, to fuel change. So they landed on an idea only the hacker mindset could discover: they decided to shoot down the mosquitoes with lasers.

The team devised a system to track the wing patterns of mosquitoes and then fire a deadly laser beam to take them out mid-flight. It is much like the *Star Wars* defense system, but for mosquitoes instead of intergalactic nuclear missiles. The lasers can be mounted on fence posts around farms or in densely populated villages to create a photonic fence that eliminates the pests before they have the chance to spread disease. This advanced system can distinguish between mosquitoes and other insects, allowing helpful bees and butterflies to pass unharmed. It can even distinguish between male and female mosquitoes based on their wing beats, killing only the females, which are the ones that sting humans. To bring their invention to life, Pablos and his team didn't use combat-grade carbon fiber or billion-dollar computing power. Instead, they used common parts from ubiquitous consumer electronics, such as Blu-ray players and laptops.

Holman is now directing his energy toward hacking the way we eat. In a *Wired* interview, he said:

> I've been thinking about the way that people eat. The way that people eat in the US is wildly inefficient; there's lots of packaging and lots of waste. We don't have any data about what you ate yesterday or on any other day of your life. Personally, I think that'll happen soon. Imagine a 3D food printer with three buttons: 'what I ate yesterday,' 'what my friend ate,' and 'I'm feeling lucky.' Imagine it printing you a meal that's customized for you, injecting your pharmaceuticals and correlating to your diet to create something that's good for you. It could introduce an optimization that's missing from the system.

Pablos Holman embodies the hacker ethos – he believes every barrier can be conquered; his curiosity and sense of exploration define his being. He believes in defying traditional approaches, challenging "proven" assumptions. His disregard for current systems, coupled with a desire to break things for the sake of breaking them, makes him perfectly equipped to tackle problems in any field. Embrace hacker mindset #1 – **Every Barrier Can Be Penetrated** – and you'll be equally suited to topple the most insurmountable obstacles you face.

EVERY BARRIER CAN BE PENETRATED

BELIEFS: Walls exist to be broken

                      It's necessary to break things in order to seek new outcomes

                      Taking on tough challenges to prove you can beat them

                      Assuming nothing

                      There's always a better way

CHARACTERISTICS: Disdain for status quo

                      Disregard for current systems

                      Defiance

                      Thrill-seeking

COMPASSES OVER MAPS

This principle is based on a directional aim at a desired outcome rather than a focus on a specific route to the finish line. Hackers shun step-by-step directions and believe meaningful progress is achieved better and faster by a willingness to adapt quickly along the journey. Hundreds of course corrections or micro-innovations yield a better result than pre-programming a route in advance and mindlessly following directions.

A map, you may say, is certainly a handy tool to help you reach your destination. When the map is accurate, you can sit back and follow your course, no thinking required. Your brain can *really* take a vacation if you're using the GPS guidance from Google Maps or Waze. When the system tells you exactly how to navigate every twist and turn, you can focus elsewhere and simply comply. But what if the map is wrong? When conditions change, such as roadwork or an accident, your GPS system no longer maximizes efficiency. Or when new roads are built before the system is updated, you find yourself relying on an outdated set of instructions.

Think about how you and your team navigate the work in your own organization. Do people require detailed, step-by-step maps of exactly what to do at every moment? Management-by-operating-manuals worked fine back in the days when markets were local, customers were homogenous, product cycles occurred over decades, and complexity was minimal. Workers didn't need to think all that much on their own, as long as following the map would ensure their safe arrival.

But with today's furious speed and mind-numbing complexities, there's no such thing as a map to success. Naïve bosses who still hand out maps don't understand that the model no longer works. The cost to produce a map in the past may have been justified, since change was slow. But we now face a rapidly proliferating rate of change – imagine the difficulty of creating a street map if the roadways completely changed five times an hour. Not to mention, business victories now involve pioneering new ground, requiring the equivalent of off-roading through uncharted territory.

When teams or organizations turn off their brains and simply follow the corporate GPS, progress shrivels. Empowering employees to use a compass, by contrast, is a far more effective approach to leadership. Provide a clear vision of your destination point, and give your team the tools to navigate their own paths. Encourage them to make their own informed decisions in the face of ambiguity. Give them the target and resources and then let them use their ingenuity and judgment to find the best route.

This is exactly the kind of thinking that allowed Jessica O. Matthews to chart an unlikely and unprecedented course.

Her eyes were burning, her chest pricked from coughing, and she began to feel dizzy. Seventeen-year-old Jessica was attending a family wedding in Nigeria, but her mood was anything but festive. The trouble began when the power went down, a common occurrence in a region with an insufficient electrical grid. Locals are accustomed to losing electricity seven to nine times a day, forcing their routines awry, but they have routines for the blackouts, too. A diesel generator that was fired up to re-light the wedding was the culprit of Jessica's discomfort, as exhaust pollution made all the guests' lungs begin to burn. Her cousins reassured her not to worry, that she'd get used to the poisonous exhaust fumes.

At the point when the air was the cloudiest and thickest, and her oxygen most depleted, Jessica had her moment of clarity. "The saddest thing to me," said Matthews, "is that they had gotten used to the idea of dying." This poignant insight led to her mission: to improve humanity by energizing the world.

Jessica went on to earn a Harvard MBA, but instead of following her classmates to Wall Street for a six-figure gig, she decided to double down her commitment to energizing the world. In 2011, she launched a company called Uncharted Play. Her idea was to use kinetic energy to create clean electricity. She recalled her cousins – the same ones acclimated to choking on exhaust fumes – running with joy on the soccer field. "I thought, why can't you take a soccer ball that is already in motion and harness the energy that is being generated during play as an off-grid power source?"

Her passion for creating electricity in non-traditional ways led to her first invention, the Soccket ball. Essentially, she inserted a micro-generator inside a soccer ball that harnesses energy from play. The Soccket can produce three hours of light from each hour on the field.

This is the point where most of us would call it a day. She had created a great soccer ball company that had the added benefit of generating electricity. Jessica's Harvard training would tell her to pursue distribution channels, maximize profits, and refine production for scale.

But Jessica didn't think that way. She didn't think of her company as a soccer ball manufacturer, but instead she was building an organization committed to using movement to create energy. The next invention came quickly, an energy-producing jump rope that could be used indoors. The logical next step would be to expand her business into other energy-creating toys. The company's mission was to use play to create energy. Or was it?

Remember, she didn't set out to build a toy or fitness company. Her mission was to generate electricity through movement. The Soccket was just the first stop-off, not the destination on her journey. So her next move was to use her core technology called MORE (Motion-based Off-grid Renewable Energy) and expand into other concepts that could generate power. What about strollers or suitcases that could charge a mobile phone as they are rolled about? The product ideas started to flow. What about licensing their micro-generating systems to other manufacturers so they could be integrated into thousands of products around the world?

Deeply connected to her purpose, Jessica's company has taken off. *Inc.* named Uncharted Play one of the "Top 25 Most Audacious Companies in the World." *Fast Company* included them among the "World's Top 10 Most Innovative Companies," while *Popular Science* added them to the "10 Best Things" list. Uncharted Play has been profitable for the last three years, with profit margins doubling each year. At the time of this writing, Jessica is about to close "The largest Series A financing that any black woman has ever raised." After learning about, and subsequently playing with Jessica's first invention, President Barack Obama commented, "The Soccket turns one of the most popular games in Africa into a source of electricity and progress."

Capturing the attention of world leaders, building a remarkably successful company, and driving game-changing humanitarian impact was propelled by the core hacker mindset of **Compasses Over Maps**. Shifting terrain, unexpected roadblocks, and surprise attacks can be conquered only by travelers who can think and act *without* detailed instructions. Creativity over compliance. Empowerment over control. Thinking over following. Compasses over maps.

The leaders at software giant Intuit have a saying: "Fall in love with the problem, not the solution." Jessica's success was fueled by her relentless focus on the problem – overtaxed electrical grids and a need to produce clean energy with non-traditional methods. Had she fallen in love with the solution – a soccer ball that generates electricity – she would have never expanded her company or been able to leave a gigantic, non-carbon footprint on our planet.

Hackers are drawn to problems over solutions. In fact, the art of hacking involves seeking to uncover the most elegant solution by trying numerous approaches to overcome an obstacle. Even if an approach delivers a positive result, the relentless pursuit of a better way drives the hacker to continue her craft in search of an even better approach.

Inherent to core mindset #2 is a willingness to take on pursuits without a charted course. In the same way a football team takes the field with a general strategy, but may need to change plays on the fly, hackers look at their sport as unscripted play. Rather than a detailed master strategy followed by mindless execution, these innovators journey down an unmarked trail with creative confidence.

THE BIGGEST BANK HEIST IN HISTORY

A masked man walks into a bank, hands the teller a note demanding that unmarked bills be placed in a paper bag and handed over. Or else. For many of us, this is what comes to mind when we think of a bank robbery. It's been done the same since long before the days of Bonnie and Clyde.

Perhaps the most famous bank robber of all time, the notorious John Dillinger robbed 13 banks across five states in the Midwest, making away with over $300,000 in loot. His criminal feats were so compelling that his exploits have been glamorized in 14 star-studded motion pictures.

Compare that to the 2015 heist that most of us never heard about. Over 100 banks across 30 countries were taken for over $1 billion. Though robbers like Jesse James are more infamous, even his spoils pale in comparison to these perpetrators, who have never been identified or caught. Russian cybersecurity firm Kaspersky issued a report that documented these new robbers' exploits. Thought to be a gang of hackers from Russia and China, they leveraged hacker mindsets to perpetrate the biggest heist in history.

Studying the crimes, Kaspersky reverse-engineered their approach. It began not only with a clear motive (stealing money) and target (banks), but also with intense curiosity. Rather than following a traditional approach, the hackers relentlessly questioned conventional tactics. They dared to try completely new strategies.

One part of their scheme involved breaking into the source code of ATM machines, allowing them to be remotely controlled. From thousands of miles away, the gang instructed specific machines to literally spew cash at exact times. They enlisted 'money mules' to approach the ATM machines at a precise time and collect the cash without even pressing a single button. Another aspect of the plan included deducting small amounts from thousands of accounts and then routing these funds from one account to another, through a series of inter-connected servers, making the eventual flow of funds untraceable.

To accomplish this historic heist, the robbers first had to get inside the fortress. To do this, they sent thousands of emails to unsuspecting bank employees around the world. The emails lured bank employees to open an attachment. With a single click, secretive malware was installed on the banks' computer systems, providing the hackers unfettered access from the inside.

Rather than executing a quick grab-and-go, the patient hackers used their newfound access to study the inner-workings of each target bank. Their sense of exploration drove them to find new, better possibilities. They carefully studied each bank's security protocols, audit trails, reporting structures, and asset flows. Their underlying quest for more insight led them deeper into their victims' cyber-vaults, allowing them to reveal unprecedented access to near limitless funds.

Hacker mindset #2, **Compasses Over Maps**, enabled a crime of epic proportion and allowed these deviants to cover their tracks for a clean getaway. Rather than locking on a plan before launching their scheme, they learned and adapted along the way. They playfully taunted bank security professionals by rigging ATMs to spit out cash, and they harnessed curiosity to walk away unscathed, with over a billion dollars.

We should all feel uncomfortable here. There were real victims in this crime, and the criminals who committed these thefts should be brought to justice. I certainly don't condone their crimes and am not encouraging you to break the law. But if we put aside their malicious intent, this small group solved a very complex problem in a novel way. Their innovative hacks outsmarted their competition and enabled them to achieve, if not exceed, their desired outcome. Embracing the hacker mindset of **Compasses Over**

Maps can empower you to achieve your own outcomes with the same skill of these notorious criminals. But please direct your hack toward positive, legitimate ends.

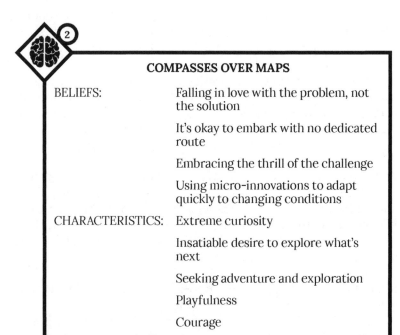

COMPASSES OVER MAPS

BELIEFS:

Falling in love with the problem, not the solution

It's okay to embark with no dedicated route

Embracing the thrill of the challenge

Using micro-innovations to adapt quickly to changing conditions

CHARACTERISTICS:

Extreme curiosity

Insatiable desire to explore what's next

Seeking adventure and exploration

Playfulness

Courage

NOTHING IS STATIC

After procrastinating for nearly a week, you finally get around to actually putting the clothes in the washing machine. You are pressed for time, but you're finally out of clean underwear. You grab the bottle of detergent, turn it upside down, and...nothing. After 15 seconds completely inverted, a small drop peeks out from the bottle and lands in the machine. Frustration mounts as you realize that you'll need to make a special trip to the store for more detergent, or, well, you're out of other options.

This frustration is the exact thing the folks at Amazon are on the lookout for.

What began as an online bookstore has expanded into the 9th most valuable company in the world, valued at over \$340 billion, with 230,000 team members intently focused on discovering what's next, rather than just executing what already is. Jeff Bezos, now the 8th wealthiest American, views the company as a living organism whose purpose is to constantly evolve and adapt to changing circumstances. Right from the start, he worked to build a company that was fluid in its offerings and approach. The only immovable principles: an obsession with serving customers better and a commitment to ongoing innovation.

So how does this help with you standing in front of your washer without detergent or clean underwear? Instead of whipping the empty jug across the room in defeat, you press the small button affixed to the front of your washing machine. The button connects to your home Wi-Fi network, logs into your Amazon account, looks up your last order of detergent to ensure you get your favorite brand, and immediately ships you a fresh bottle overnight, billing the purchase to your credit card. All with the single touch of a button, the Amazon Dash button.

This little invention is one of hundreds that keeps Amazon on the forefront of change and progress. As you may expect, you can get a Dash Button for just about anything. A Glad button placed inside a kitchen drawer can be pressed to re-order plastic sandwich bags. Low on shaving cream? Press the Gillette button you placed in your bathroom to have it rushed your way. Paper towel, bug killer, dish soap, and even condoms are available with the touch of a button. Amazon is making it dead simple to do business with them.

Fueling Amazon's incredible success is the fundamental hacker mindset that **Nothing Is Static**. Transforming from an online bookstore, to a full-scale online department store, to offering technology and web hosting services to other firms, and recently even venturing into space travel, the company is in a state of constant motion. Bezos reinforced this philosophy by saying, "A company shouldn't get addicted to being shiny, because shiny doesn't last." What dazzles a customer today will be soon be commonplace, so he pushes his team to reinvent early and often.

HACKING LANDMINES

There are over 110 million landmines planted beneath the earth's surface, killing 60,000 people per year and injuring many times more. This worldwide issue is a terrifying daily threat to people in the desert region around Kabul, Afghanistan.

Growing up just outside Kabul, Massoud Hassani witnessed some terrible tragedies as a result of these killing machines. As a young man, Massoud decided to make it his life's work to put at least a small dent in this giant problem. He had no money, specialized training, or fancy credentials. So he had to hack the problem.

First, he was convinced that **Every Barrier Can Be Penetrated**. He knew there had to be a better way, and refused to accept the notion that fatalities were just to be expected. Next, he entertained a deep sense of curiosity and exploration, a willingness to choose **Compasses Over Maps**. He asked countless questions about conventional mine-clearing methods, challenged prevailing wisdom, and pursued the problem over a given solution.

As Massoud immersed himself in the world of landmine safety, he was struck by how little progress had been made. The traditional approach – more or less the same since the 1960s – is expensive, dangerous, and not all that effective. Yet major defense contractors, nation-states, and academic researchers remained entrenched in the old, static approach.

Hassani's breakthrough innovation came from borrowing, a hacking tactic we'll cover later in the book. As a young boy, he would frequently look into the distance and watch tumbleweed blowing gently across the desert sand. This inspiration led him to create the Mine Kafon, "mine exploder" in his native language of Dari. The Kafon looks like a giant ripened dandelion waiting to blow into the wind from its stem. The device is approximately six feet in diameter and contains a central core, approximately 50 bamboo rods emanating from the center, and clay disks affixed to the end of each rod. The invention is light enough to be wind-propelled, like the tumbleweeds Hassani watched blowing across the desert in his youth. But the Kafon is also heavy enough to detonate the land mines planted beneath the earth's surface. Boom.

The UN estimates that for every 5,000 mines cleared, one clearing specialist is killed and two others are seriously injured. In contrast to these traditional approaches, the Mine Kafon is unmanned. This human toll is now eliminated. Further, the cost-per-landmine-cleared has been dramatically reduced. The Kafon is over 120 times less expensive than classic methods. The Mine Kafon is the most important advancement in mine-clearing technology in the last four decades, saving thousands of lives and millions of dollars. The design was so profound that it is now on permanent display at the Museum of Modern Art in New York City.

Having written about the Mine Kafon in my previous book, *The Road to Reinvention*, I've since had the privilege of getting to know Massoud Hassani. In preparation for a call in late 2015, I was expecting him to be basking in his glory. Here's a kid from rural Afghanistan, with no resources or help, who has gone on to make a massive impact on the world. Additionally, he started a company and is now building a terrific business providing Mine Kafons throughout the world. But instead of ruminating in a celebratory glow, Massoud was fully immersed in the next challenge.

"Detonation is an important problem," he told me. "But detection is an even bigger issue. There are often miles of open space with only one landmine lurking to cause harm. After the success of the Mine Kafon in detonation, I've shifted my efforts to find a more comprehensive solution. I've reinvented."

Today, Massoud is using low-flying drones and is able to cover large swaths of land very quickly. He attaches a robotic arm with a high-powered magnet, flying over open areas to search for mines. In real time, he's beaming back a video feed along with GPS coordinates, so that newly-detected land mines can be quickly located and conquered.

Massoud Hassani, a hacker of the highest order, achieved unparalleled success with his Mine Kafon. Understanding mindset #3, **Nothing Is Static**, he quickly used his initial success to tackle the next challenge. Essentially, he disrupted himself. He made the most important change in land mine clearing in over 40 years, and one year later he did it again. I expect that he will have done it again when I speak to him next. Rather than becoming complacent, Massoud continues to challenge himself to learn more, do more, hack more. Massoud Hassani continues to push the boundaries and will use each success as a stepping stone for the next.

LOW RIDER

A man from a tiny rural town in Germany identified his target: an opportunity to abscond with millions in profit. He carefully crafted his hack, a new technology that was sure to infiltrate his mark and best all previous attempts. Through rapid experimentation and unorthodox approaches, this hacker was poised to profit greatly, and send shockwaves throughout the world.

Who was this mysterious misfit? While the description could represent a modern day cybercriminal, our protagonist is none other than Ignaz Schwinn, the grandfather of leisure bicycles, as he founded his company in 1891.

The rise from obscurity to market dominance was driven by interwoven hacks. Schwinn studied the market conditions and was able to see demand taking off for two-wheelers. After a massive surge in demand to over a million units, a slowdown actually provided Schwinn with a clever opening. As other companies struggled through the downturn of 1905, Schwinn took the oppositional view and used it as an opportunity to profit from the weakness of his foes. Voraciously gobbling up limping competitors, he built a modern factory enabling him to mass-produce low-cost bikes. While this sounds obvious today, it was a bold and creative move in Schwinn's pre-World-War-I era.

Innovation continued for decades in all aspects of the business. In 1933, Schwinn Bicycles, now run by Ignaz's son Frank W. "F. W." Schwinn, introduced a radically new concept: a bike that looked like a motorcycle. The Aerocycle had chrome fenders, an imitation gas tank, a shiny headlight, and a push-button bell. Instead of milking the company's cash cow, F. W. and team pioneered into uncharted territory. The Aerocycle, also known as the "cruiser" or "paperboy," quickly became the industry standard, driving the company to new heights of growth and profitability. Schwinn revolutionized all aspects of the bike, driving major breakthroughs in tires, seating, handlebars, gears, brakes, and design. They were anything but static.

By the 1950s, Schwinn was the industry leader – they not only pioneered new products, they upended traditional distribution approaches. At the time, most bikes were sold to mass retailers and private labeled (a Sears Supreme or a Woolworth's Racer). Schwinn, taking an opposing approach, insisted their name and guarantee appear on all bikes. In exchange, they sold to a vast network of distributors, ultimately letting the retailers capture far more profit-per-bike than was possible with the entrenched model. Since retailers and distributors made more cash by selling Schwinn bikes than anything else, you can easily guess which ones they recommended most aggressively to customers. Schwinn was at the innovative forefront of bicycle racing, manufacturing, retail and distribution, branding, and product design. Ironically, it was this very success that led to their undoing.

A shift occurred in the subsequent decade, transforming the firm from a company of hackers to one of protectors. The company squandered their energy fighting to raise tariffs on foreign competition, taking their battle to the courtroom instead of the marketplace. In an effort to maximize profits, they squeezed their distribution network and pressured them to dump competitive products. This led to a decade-long battle with the Department of Justice, ending in a gut-wrenching decision by the U. S. Supreme Court finding Schwinn guilty of restraint of trade and unfair trade practices.

It's easy to think such a shift wouldn't happen to you, that you'd see it coming and never fall victim to such an obvious trap. But shifts of this nature happen in small increments. They are not launched as company-wide initiatives, complete with t-shirts and battle cries. Instead, they happen one shortsighted decision at a time. Little acts of neglect leading to big holes of eroded value over time. In the same way the frog that enters the warm water, which increases by only one degree in temperature at a time, doesn't realize what's happened until it's too late, Schwinn's decay went largely unnoticed until the cascading effect of hundreds of bad decisions ultimately led to ruin.

A glimpse of hope shined through with Schwinn's invention of the Stingray, a bicycle design representing a low-rider motorcycle with a low-slung banana seat and raised handlebars. But the innovation was easily copied and discount competitors walked away with the lion's share of profits. In the same way the company was built through a succession of innovative hacks, it fell through a string of bureaucratic blunders. Shifting from pioneer to protector, Schwinn largely missed out on or played copycat to new industry trends such as the 10-speed, BMX, and mountain bike crazes. With declining revenue and a void of innovation, the company shifted to cost-cutting mode to salvage near-term profits. Accordingly, they didn't modernize their manufacturing plants, and in an effort to extract every drop from their products, they ran into combative labor relations issues as they overworked and underpaid employees. Unable to compete, the once high-quality company outsourced all manufacturing to the lowest-cost source they could find in Asia.

The hits continued as Schwinn's decline accelerated into a free fall of despair. By the time the company filed for bankruptcy in 1992, the brand was a shell of its former self. The company's name was sold to the highest bidder, a financial firm that cared only about numbers and not a lick about bikes. Predictably, the company was bought and sold several more times over the next two decades, today being an asset of a holding company owned by another holding company.

Stories like this are far too common. Once-great leaders and organizations become intoxicated by their own successes. They fail to adapt, fail to hack, fail to innovate, and then simply fail. In the *Harvard Business Review*, Martin Reeves defines the 'Success Trap' as "Companies that over exploit their current business models yet and fail to explore future growth opportunities." From Blockbuster Video to Compaq, PanAm Airlines to Oldsmobile, the success trap has been the death knell of hundreds of previous market leaders. For most of us in the business world, this is common sense, even cliché. Common sense, unfortunately, is not always common practice. Leaders fail, and more often than we'd like to think.

Why don't more organizations embrace hacking as a long-term strategy? "Unfortunately, these firms are rare – most follow a path towards lower exploration and risk falling into the success trap," explained Reeves, Senior Partner at the Boston Consulting Group and author of *Your Strategy Needs Strategy*:

> *Why does this happen to large companies with a legacy of success? Paradoxically, doing so often seems like the right choice. Fine-tuning the established, successful model provides higher immediate rewards at low risk. Over a five-year period, one in three companies makes that mistake. This comes at the cost of lower growth, which jeopardizes the company's future. Fast forward a few years, and lower growth means fewer interactions with new, demanding customer groups and less inspiration to innovate. Eventually the company is likely to be out of touch with changing market requirements. At that point, it is often too late to course-correct. Once in the trap, it is difficult to escape: seven out of ten fail to leave it in the next five years and get back onto the path of higher exploration.*

Hacking mindset #3 – **Nothing Is Static** – is your primary weapon to fight this trend toward complacency. Hackers understand that the only constant must be our ability to learn, grow, and adapt. They understand that innovation is a continuous process, not a once-a-decade initiative. In these turbulent times, embracing this philosophy is no longer optional; it has become mission-critical to sustainable success.

NOTHING IS STATIC	
BELIEFS:	Knowledge and ability must never be stationary
	Adapting quickly is paramount.
	Speed wins
	Every system is in a constant state of flux
	Complacency is poisonous
	Yesterday's solution is today's trash
CHARACTERISTICS:	Crave new learning
	Embrace rapid change
	Find comfort in letting go of previous notions
	Forward-looking
	Commitment to continuous improvement

QUANTITY IS A FORCE MULTIPLIER

As the stock market crumbled in 2007, a loose gang of six Russian hackers were raking in profits. According to federal prosecutors from the U. S. Department of Justice, the hackers "used sophisticated hacking techniques to steal more than 160 million credit and debit card numbers, target more than 800,000 bank accounts, and made off with at least $300 million." Not only were the targets large in numbers, so were the breach points. The criminals obtained their rewards not through a single infiltration, but by penetrating dozens of retailers, banks, and payment processors. From 7-11, to Nasdaq, to Global Payment Systems, Inc., multiple entry points were exploited.

Unlike a typical heist involving a single devious strike, these attacks occurred over a seven-year period between 2005 and 2012. Due to the massive number of small, individual attacks (estimated in the millions) the crimes went largely unnoticed for years.

In contrast to a typical criminal structure, or commercial enterprise for that matter, the organization was loose and democratized. One hacker with code names including "Grig," "G," and Tempo was 26-year-old Aleksandr Kalinin of St. Petersberg. Another, 29-year-old Dimitriy Smilianets of Moscow, is now in U. S. custody. Each of the six worked both independently and collaboratively. Sharing ideas and teaming up, the group bore no formal allegiance to one another. The baton of leadership was passed freely among the men as they realized that the best ideas, always shifting, should establish the only form of organizational hierarchy. The gang came from diverse backgrounds, ideologies, and training, yet collaborated to perpetrate the largest hacking scheme ever prosecuted in the United States.

In this case, hacker mindset #4 was the weapon of choice: **Quantity Is a Force Multiplier**.

Ones and zeroes aren't the only numbers adored by hackers. In fact, there's a core belief that bigger is better in nearly every aspect of the hacking process. A bigger target means not only more loot, but also a lower probability of being detected. A large quantity of small attacks (or ideas) generally beats a single attack (or idea), even if the latter is significantly better – more input from more people with more diversity of thought.

Let's say you set out to open a new Italian restaurant. The traditional approach would involve carefully studying the market to select an ideal location. Next, you'd invest in kitchen equipment, décor, and permanent signage. A single chef would craft the menu of his or her choice, which would then be printed en masse and released with a sense of permanence. Marketing message crafted by you or your agency get printed in ads that will run for months. Big bets, decided upon in advance, with limited post-launch variation. If the veal parmesan isn't selling, you may switch to chicken but your concept is mostly locked and loaded.

The hacker, on the other hand, would approach the problem in a very different way.

First, she'd embrace mindset #1 – **Every Barrier Can Be Penetrated** – and set out to not only open a moderately successful restaurant, but to crack the code and do something unique. Next, through mindset #2 – **Compasses Over Maps** – she would likely take a step back to consider if Italian was even the right cuisine to serve. She'd connect with her broader target, which may be to open a successful food company, and not assume that Italian is the right choice even if it was her first instinct. Knowing **Nothing Is Static** (mindset #3), she would learn as much as she could to enhance her knowledge and shun conventional approaches.

With the first three mindsets in play, **Quantity Is a Force Multiplier** can also contribute. "How can I quickly test dozens of variables before locking down a solution?" she might ask. Perhaps she negotiates with other restaurants to add one special dish – that she would prepare and deliver for free – to their menu for 30 days. In this way, she could test dozens of recipes, price points, and ingredient combinations against different times of day, locations, and clientele. Or she may strike a deal with a local food truck where she takes over for a couple weeks, providing the owner a vacation along with all the near-term profits, so she can use the truck as a real-world test kitchen. The hacker would want to leverage rapid experimentation to the extreme, so she may offer an online delivery service, a mobile app, a recipe blog, a make-your-own-food kit, or a subscription service instead of the obvious solution of a single physical restaurant. She would deconstruct every aspect and even question the geography by running simultaneous experiments in other markets. Rather than just her own recipes, she'd establish a loose coalition to offer diverse ideas. Instead of traditional business partners, she may seek advice from dozens or hundreds of people far outside the food industry. She'd want the marketing perspective not only from a creative agency, she might seek ideas from professionals in the musical arts, software, or accounting industries.

Multiple tests, multiple ideas, from multiple sources. Unlike typical R&D, market research, and B-school planning sessions, her hacker approach would be comparatively fast, low-cost, and fluid. The goal of her hacker mindset is not to produce a 70-page business plan, but to uncover an untapped opportunity. Once that crack in the wall is identified, she'd follow with a similar barrage of "attacks" to fully exploit the opening. The hacker would rather use a changeable chalkboard than a printed menu, a pop-up restaurant over a permanent structure. Anything to support the mindset of large quantities of little experiments.

The end result may not even be an end result. Instead, think of a series of interconnected hacks that follow this structure:

1. Test many variables, identify a solution that shows potential

2. Further test the promising ideas, quickly discard the others, and move on to new ones

3. Once an idea shows merit, isolate and exploit it

4. Test, measure

5. Re-hack (refine, adapt)

6. Evaluate results and look for next hack

Our enterprising restaurateur is far more likely to win big while mitigating risk through the hacker approach. Quantity, in all its forms, drive quality – because she has conducted so many experiments, she can be confident that she is offering the best food, from the best ingredients, in the best location, at the best prices.

CAN YOU HEAR ME NOW?

Back at Not Impossible Labs, a new "impossible" challenge is being attacked. A jazz vocalist named Mandy Harvey was dealt an unimaginable setback at age 18. A rare disease attacked one of her primary tools – her ability to hear – putting her career and future in grave jeopardy. Within nine months, the disease took its toll; Mandy was completely deaf.

We can only imagine how Mandy must have felt. Hopeless, depressed, defeated. But somehow, she summoned the inner strength to continue her musical journey. Still possessing perfect pitch and timing, she decided to continue singing despite the fact she couldn't hear a single note. "Hope must never be lost," said Mandy. "In it we find strength. And it is our duty to show and give it to others. Hope keeps life moving because it pulls us out of any dark situation." With this powerful sense of purpose and determination, Mandy has been performing professionally for the last seven years as the only completely deaf jazz singer in the world.

Mandy gave her message of hope to all of us, but who is proving hope to her? The hackers at Not Impossible Labs set out to develop a way for Mandy to "hear" her music once again. To discover the hack, Not Impossible Labs went wide. Instead of working insulated within their organization, they put the challenge to the entire hacker community. They enlisted the ideas of scientists, research geeks, artists, and of course...software hackers.

Since a core hacking tenet is that many minds are better than singular genius, they wanted to cast a wide net for ideas from a diverse set of thinkers. The answer emerged not as a single lightning bolt of inspiration, but as a small concept that was built upon by many minds over time. As they explored the concept of hearing altogether, these creative hackers wondered if they could help Mandy "hear" in a completely different way. Since her auditory capacity could not be restored, what if they tapped into one of her other senses to allow her to embrace the music?

Their ingenious solution was put to the test in November 2015. Mandy was outfitted with a series of small motors, attached to various parts of her body (wrists, ankles, waist). The motors created small vibrations, triggered by computer sensors that did the hearing for Mandy. They vibrated in different ways for different periods of time depending on a number of factors in the music, including tempo, pitch, and volume. For the first time in seven years, Mandy played with her band and "heard" the music in a rich, multi-sensory experience. Tears ran down her face, along with the cheeks of the camera crew and the Not Impossible team, as she connected with her music at a level she'd not felt for nearly a decade.

Not Impossible Labs, like most good hackers, seeks input from a large number of diverse sources to uncover the most elegant solutions to complex problems. They leverage the power of numbers compared to the traditional approach of only seeking solutions from within. Small-thinking managers dismiss concepts with the not-invented-here mindset while sophisticated hackers solve the world's biggest challenges by proactively seeking external insights.

THE NETFLIX OF FITNESS

Yony Feng is exactly what you'd imagine when thinking of a whiz kid software engineer. After earning both his Bachelor's and Master's degrees in Computer Engineering from the Georgia Institute of Technology, he quickly moved to the heart of Silicon Valley. In high demand for his masterful computer skills, Yony served in senior positions for both Cisco and Skype as he continued to hone his craft. This top-notch engineer is curious, articulate, and whip-smart, with the insightful wisdom of a Zen monk.

With his highly coveted talents being courted by the top technology powerhouses of Silicon Valley, why the heck did he upend his family, relocate to New York, and take a gig at a fitness bike company? Well, Peloton ain't no ordinary fitness company. In fact, calling them a fitness company is kind of like calling Apple a phone company.

Part stationary bike manufacturer, part content producer, part tech company, Peloton is hacking home fitness. With Yony leading the charge as Chief Technology Officer, they are poised to become the "Netflix of Fitness": delighting customers, building a rocking company, and making society healthier.

"Going to a spinning class at the uber-trendy Soul Cycle or Flywheel Sports is a fantastic experience," Yony told me. "But these classes are expensive, rarely convenient, and not available in many parts of the world. Home fitness bikes may function well, but the shared experience is lost with traditional alternatives."

Yony and his team set out to replicate the energizing experience of a live class that interacts with both the instructor and fellow cyclers. Peloton offers a premium stationary bike for home use that has a gorgeous built-in screen. The bike and accompanying technology are connected to the cloud, allowing riders to participate in dozens of live classes each day. Riders are sweating along with the instructor in real time, while seeing how they stack up to fellow cyclists in an interactive leaderboard. Compare your performance across the world, or limit your competitive set by age, gender, or geography. If you don't see a live class that fits the bill, you can choose from over 4,000 pre-recorded rides. The high-definition content streams to your screen, while your bike updates itself automatically. Adjustments such as level, tension, and resistance change as you ride, all controlled by the software.

I spoke with a Peloton customer who exhibited cult-like fervor for his machine. "I get an incredible experience, just like at class," he beams. "But it costs less, saves me time, and I get to do my workouts on my own terms." This loyalty is echoed in the company's growth, which experienced a 5x boost in revenue from 2014 to 2015 and is forecasted to triple sales in 2016. Peloton has sold over 40,000 bikes to date, shipping to each of the 50 states and 22 countries. They've raised over $120 million of venture capital and are well positioned to be the breakaway leader in a whole new category of home fitness and content delivery.

To achieve such remarkable success, Yoni embraced mindset #4: **Quantity Is a Force Multiplier**. He explained that high-volume, rapid experimentation is their secret ingredient, which has led them to develop products that make customers fall in love.

"We conduct *tons* of experiments to improve the riding experience," Yony explains. "We carefully study how our suite of products, technology, and content make our customers feel. In order to have riders truly feel like they are in class, we are constantly fine-tuning the experience. We test dozens of seating options, handle bar styles, and pedal choices. We test sound, lighting, and music. We bring in riders to our New York Studio and experiment with tiny fluctuations, such as the angle of the screen, to improve the overall experience. "

Yony's inner-hacker has stepped into the spotlight. Rather than the traditional new product approach – launch big and launch final – Yony lives in an ongoing state of hacker flux. A massive number of experiments, testing and controlling even the smallest details and then refining along the way, has been the underpinning of Peloton's success. They hacked their way into a crowded and highly competitive market, and at this rate, will continue to hack their company to ever-expanding success.

	QUANTITY IS A FORCE MULTIPLIER
BELIEFS:	Many minds beat singular genius
	Quantity drives quality
	Big targets are easier to hit
	1000 paper cuts can create a deadly force
CHARACTERISTICS:	Rapid experimentation
	Democratization of ideas
	Crowd- and open-sourcing innovation
	Neural diversity
	Team-oriented

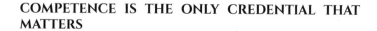

COMPETENCE IS THE ONLY CREDENTIAL THAT MATTERS

With heavy metal music blaring in the background, Gordon Freeman barely made away with his life. The violence of the authoritarian police state became unbearable, requiring Gordon to use every available technology to protect himself and ensure survival. The problems all date back to the accident at the Black Mesa Research Facility that Gordon led, where an experiment on an alien crystal sample went horribly wrong.

The Video Game: *Half-Life 2*

Game Developer: Valve, LLC

Estimated Game Revenue: Over $700 million

The adventures of Gordon Freeman have been the fancy of gamers since the original *Half-Life* shipped in 1998. The 2004 sequel described above won 39 "Game of the Year" awards and was named "Game of the Decade" at the 2012 Spike Video Game Awards. It is considered to be one of the greatest video games of all time.

Valve, LLC, the company behind *Half-Life*, *Counter-Strike*, and *Day of Defeat* is valued at over $2.5 billion. In addition to producing their own games, the company developed Steam – an online gaming distribution platform (think iTunes for video games). The company has zero debt, no outside investors, and has higher per-employee profit than Google, Microsoft, and Apple. Valve was able to build one of the most successful gaming studios of all time by embracing the principles of hacking.

We can easily conjure up images of the prototypical progressive company: people with funky titles, a foosball table in the break room, and a juice bar lurking somewhere. But Valve takes progressive to a whole new level. The company is the living embodiment of core hacking principle #5 – **Competence Is the Only Credential That Matters**.

Gabe Newell is technically the CEO, but he has no direct reports. In fact, no one works for anyone at Valve. There are no bosses, managers, or leaders. There are also no titles – everyone's job is simply to contribute as much value as possible. Much of their non-traditional, hacker philosophy becomes clear when reading their crowdsourced employee handbook, "A fearless adventure into knowing what to do when no one's telling you what to do."

Gabe founded Valve in the Seattle area in 1996, setting out to make great games and an even greater team environment. Coming from Microsoft's rigid policies and complex hierarchies, Gabe was determined to use a radically different approach. He wanted to create a culture that fostered greatness, creativity, and impact by removing any and all structures that could hamper innovation.

"When you're an entertainment company that's spent the last decade going out of its way to recruit the most intelligent, innovative, talented people on Earth, telling them to sit at a desk and do what they're told obliterates 99 percent of their value," Gabe declares. So Gabe created "Flatland," a completely flat organizational structure where nobody reports to anybody else (including Gabe, whose decisions are subject to the same scrutiny as everyone else's).

At work, team members pick their own projects to work on without a single directive. They choose to spend their completely unstructured time in whatever way they believe will create the most value. All teams and projects are temporary, as are all desks. Each workstation is on wheels, allowing teams to be formed, grown, or disbanded with ease.

Valve is a company without rules. There are no schedules, orders, or pre-set processes. If you want advice, ask a colleague. If you need help, lean over and ask your peers. People at Valve are very vocal, since they have a strong sense of ownership, but no one has to listen to anyone else. Decision making is completely decentralized, with the core belief that the wisdom of all is better than the judgment of one. As a result, the best ideas carry the day rather than the person with the fanciest title or loudest voice.

At times, a temporary team leader will emerge to help keep a project organized. But instead of ordering people around, the leader's key role is to serve others. Everything is fluid at Valve, even pay. Without leaders, you may wonder how performance reviews and pay increases are accomplished. The answer? They rely on the hacker principle that **Competence Is the Only Credential That Matters**. Performance reviews are conducted 100% by peers, providing practical guidance for improvement. Pay is based on stack ranking, in which four criteria determine which "stack" an employee falls into. Your pay is adjusted annually based on how peers rank you on: a) skill level/technical ability, b) productivity/output, c) group contribution, and d) product contribution. Neither tenure, nor title, nor age, nor education, nor looks, nor gender play any role in determining compensation. Your earning is solely driven by your contribution. Valve pays in the upper-range of competitors, but instead of rewarding internal political factors – like how much someone kisses up to the boss – the company exclusively rewards merit.

Traditional managers who read this may be horrified and quickly dismiss the lack of structure as far too risky. What if someone messes it all up? Gabe responds:

> So if every employee is autonomously making his or her own decisions, how is that not chaos? How does Valve make sure that the company is heading in the right direction? When everyone is sharing the steering wheel, it seems natural to fear that one of us is going to veer Valve's car off the road. Over time, we have learned that our collective ability to meet challenges, take advantage of opportunity, and respond to threats is far greater when the responsibility for doing so is distributed as widely as possible. Namely, to every individual at the company.

Valve isn't a disorganized mess, nor it is a fantasyland utopia. Productivity is sky-high compared to others in the sector, and they are growing at a dizzying pace, with record profits. They apply rigor to each decision, but instead of the "boss is always right" decision strategy, Valve uses data. They remove personal biases by debating the merits and brutal facts of each decision. Since no single person has authority to override another, the ideas and decisions with the most merit are the ones that triumph.

The system itself leads to better output by not relying on a limited number of leaders to make the tough calls. Without the layers of managerial control, you may assume they get less done. Yet Valve is worth 37% more per employee than Exxon Mobil and 78% more per employee than Amazon, two companies with highly regarded traditional structures. While counterintuitive, the hacking approach of distributed authority allows organizations to do more with less.

You may have never heard of Gabe Newell before, and may be surprised by his estimated $2.2 billion net worth. And that's just the way he likes it. His biggest accomplishment isn't hogging the spotlight and taking credit while barking orders. He's used a non-traditional, hacker approach to building the best culture in order to maximize impact and value. The success isn't about him; it's about a shared experience of creativity and innovation. And everyone benefits.

Valve represents the future of corporate culture, with meritocratic decision-making and advancement. It also demonstrates mindset #5 – **Competence Is the Only Credential That Matters** – with precision. From cybercriminals to biohackers, from software startups to multinational companies that choose to embrace the unorthodox, hackers of all types have a total disregard for authority. They believe respect and power must be earned, not issued. And that a person may have the best idea one day while having the worst idea the next. Merit is the only arbiter.

	COMPETENCE IS THE ONLY CREDENTIAL THAT MATTERS
BELIEFS:	It's what's right, not who's right
	Hierarchical advancement is outdated
	Data – not instinct or position – should drive decision-making
	Titles are meaningless
	Skills supersede politics
CHARACTERISTICS:	Scrappy
	Do more with less
	Reject authority
	Crave thought diversity

CHAPTER 3: OVERVIEW — 10 PRIMARY TACTICS

When painting on canvas, artists sometimes use a technique called *scrumbling*, which involves painting thin layers of opaque, light colors over dark colors to produce a certain broken color effect. Actors utilize an approach called *Stanislavski's method*, where they draw upon their own feelings and experiences to convey the 'truth' of the character they are portraying. The actor puts herself in the mindset of the character, finding things in common in order to give a more genuine portrayal of the character. In jazz improvisation, there's a specialized technique called *tri-tone substitution* where the performer superimposes one scale or chord on top of another in order to create musical tension.

Innovators in every artistic field leverage proven techniques to enhance their creativity. While the techniques themselves don't deliver a masterpiece, they aid the artist in his craft, and allow him to overcome challenges and advance his final work. There are proven frameworks used in architecture, laboratory discovery, electrical engineering, and, of course, hacking.

Hacking, like other creative disciplines, has a toolkit of specific techniques that, in the case of many cyberhackers, enables them to perpetrate unthinkable crimes. White hat hackers use the same hacking techniques as their black hat counterparts to scale businesses, discover new drug therapies, and solve complex societal problems.

In **Chapter 1**, we learned why I believe hacking is the most effective strategy in the modern business world. In **Chapter 2**, we went deep inside the mind of hackers, learning how core hacker mindsets are the foundation to unprecedented innovation.

Now, we are ready to shift from *why* to *how*.

With the primary objective of driving innovation and growth, we'll explore the 10 primary tactics of hackers. Throughout the next several chapters, we'll examine each to see how the same techniques used by villains can be extracted and applied for legitimate purposes. You'll see real-world examples of each technique, not only from the underworld of cybercriminals, but also from a variety of business industries, community leaders, and inventors using the same techniques to improve humanity. In addition to understanding the techniques, you'll learn how to do a *legit flip* – transferring the focus of each core tactic from evil to good in order to grow your business, enhance your career, and help your community.

The 10 primary tactics are summarized below to orient you to these powerful approaches. In Chapters 4-13, we'll unpack each technique by exploring dozens of examples to help you fully absorb and embrace this new model of innovation.

BRUTE FORCE

The Hack: Repetitive and high-volume attacks. A good way to think about the Brute Force approach is banging on a wall with a sledgehammer. Brute Force's close cousin is called a Denial of Service (DoS) attack, which involves shutting down or disabling a system, by overloading it with requests. Brute Force attacks involve guessing passwords or other pieces of information by simply trying one combination after another. This is the methodology I used as a teenager to score long distance calling card numbers. Each attack is not especially clever, but the high volume of attacks adds up to the desired breakthrough. Brute Force attacks in particular can lead to the discovery of a small opening that can subsequently be exploited, in the same way pulling one loose thread in a knit sweater can unravel the whole garment. Simply put, Brute Force involves quantity, not quality.

Legit Flip: Using Brute Force for legitimate purposes generally involves Rapid Experimentation – trying large quantities of various combinations to solve complex problems can lead to an elegant solution. If you run an e-commerce business selling baby products, for example, you may try hundreds of keyword combinations on Google to see which attracts the most lucrative customers. You may also test hundreds of variables on your site including colors, images, placement of buttons, wording on discounts, and feature of the day. Based on the data, you could determine which approaches drive the best results.

Brute Force is a powerful strategy early in the ideation process and also later when testing existing assumptions. Large quantities of ideas can ultimately drive higher quality than selecting easy, obvious answers that emerge when selecting from a smaller pool of options. Brute Force can be used to discover small windows of opportunity, which can later be expanded through other hacker techniques. It is also the right tool when raw persistence is needed, such as high volume sales calls or hundreds of clinical trials for a new drug therapy. Your goal is to use Brute Force to get smarter, not just to work harder. This approach is often a great starting point and is then followed by other tactics to eventually lead to your ideal hack.

SOCIAL ENGINEERING

The Hack: Social Engineering is hacking without any code. Social Engineering involves the manipulation of people to gather personal information. These methods often start with easily obtainable (e.g. public record) information, which can then be leveraged for greater access/damage. These attacks rely on creativity and improvisation to create plausible scenarios for gathering (or changing) the desired information.

Instead of writing code to break into a corporation, a hacker may befriend an employee and convince the unsuspecting target to provide access.

Often Social Engineering is combined with other techniques. For example, a hacker may use code to break into the email account of a middle school kid whose mother is a bank executive. An email reaches mom from the daughter's account with an innocent request, "Hi Mom. Check out this assignment I received in school." When Mom clicks the attachment, malicious software gets installed on her work computer, providing unfettered access to the hacker. While this hack eventually involved some computer code, it was Social Engineering that opened up the opportunity. The primary characteristic of the Social Engineering tactic is perpetrating breaches through human/social interaction. Ultimately, this hack is getting the shopkeeper to hand over the keys rather than breaking in by busting a lock on the rusty back door.

Legit Flip: In the same way the hacker infiltrates a company using the help of others, Social Engineering can be deployed in a legitimate way to drive desired business outcomes. A classic example is HoTMaiL's building of a massive user base with zero paid advertising. The clever entrepreneurs behind HoTMaiL wanted to get customers to do their advertising. In a brilliant display of the Social Engineering tactic, the company added a small phrase to the bottom of every HoTMaiL message: "PS: I love you. Get your free e-mail at HoTMaiL."

This small, harmless addition drove geometric customer growth. They started with just 3,000 new customer signups per day, which began to compound. In six months, they had one million users. Only five weeks after that, they had two million. By June of 1998, less than two years after the company was founded, HoTMaiL had nine million subscribers and was purchased by Microsoft for nearly $400 million. At the time, the company had zero revenue; the entire value of the company was its ability to attract large numbers of users for free. In other words, $400 million of value was created in less than two years through a single act of Social Engineering.

CROWDSOURCING

The Hack: If you want to open a locked door, conventional wisdom is to call a locksmith. One problem, one solver. Hackers, on the other hand, prefer to tap a wider set of minds in order to uncover the ideal solution. The most infamous hacker organization, Anonymous, will issue a challenge to its global network, knowing that a large number of ideas from a large number of sources generally beats a single stroke of genius. The technique involves seeking input from a sizable group of people, ideally with great diversity of thought, in order to crack through a desired barrier.

The leaders of cybersecurity at the Pentagon had an insight: to stop a hacker, you need to think like a hacker. Not wanting to rely solely on their own team of experts, the Department of Defense recently launched an initiative called "Hack The Pentagon." The program offers a "bug bounty" to participants who are able to uncover vulnerabilities in the Pentagon's cybersecurity systems. Over 500 people registered to put their hacking skills to the test in an effort to win the $150,000 reward. "I am always challenging our people to think outside the five-sided box that is the Pentagon," Secretary of Defense Ash Carter said in a statement. "Inviting responsible hackers to test our cybersecurity certainly meets that test. I am confident this innovative initiative will strengthen our digital defenses and ultimately enhance our national security." Carter embraced the technique of Crowdsourcing to help achieve his goal of impenetrable security, but the tactic can be deployed effectively to accomplish nearly any objective you may face.

Legit Flip: Sourcing ideas from the crowd has become an increasingly effective path toward innovation. Let's say you start a new business and need to design a logo. The traditional approach is to hire a graphic designer who will provide a few different options for your approval. Embracing the hacker technique of Crowdsourcing, in contrast, you would want to see many ideas from hundreds of designers. Enter 99 Designs. This website is a crowdsourcing marketplace that matches graphic designers with those in need of design. Here, you'd describe your company and the kind of things you're looking for in a logo. Next, you offer a bounty for the one you ultimately select, typically a few hundred dollars. Your request is then submitted to thousands of designers, eager to earn some cash for their skills. Within a couple days, hundreds of logo designs from all over the world are submitted for your review. If you see one or two that are getting close, you can ask the designer to make changes to color, shape, font, etc. Finally, once you are completely happy, the logo is yours and the winning designer keeps the bounty. Imagine the variety of design thinking from thousands of creative minds compared to retaining a single artist for the job. Crowdsourcing in action.

THE EXPLOIT

The Hack: In computer hacking, identifying exploits involves uncovering small holes or vulnerabilities and then exploiting those weaknesses to gain entry, break, or otherwise influence a system based on the hacker's objectives. Finding a tiny crack in the wall, the hacker doubles down to expand the opening – it is the compounded impact of exploiting a small weakness and blowing it open into a gateway of opportunity. If X action produces Y result, using the Exploit, doing 100X may produce 100,000Y. In other words, the opening expands geometrically as it is exploited.

Legit Flip: Rather than trying to tackle a massive challenge all at once, the Exploit tactic may involve starting with a tiny win and then leveraging it to the Nth degree. For example, if you are a sales person selling office supplies to corporations, winning a Fortune 500 account is the ultimate accomplishment. Rather than trying to capture the entire company's business all at once, you may start by selling one small order to one small department. Then you can grow your business to other departments from inside the fortress walls. Sales professionals call this a "land and expand" strategy, which is the exact approach a hacker embraces when using the Exploit tactic.

BORROWING

The Hack: They say imitation is the sincerest form of flattery. While hackers copy various types of software code that have worked for others, borrowing is a concept that transcends mere forgery. Borrowing involves taking an idea, concept, or approach from a completely different realm and applying it to the task at hand. A hacker may study how Jay Z manages to sell so many concert tickets and then Borrow the same approach when taking on a software challenge. The core concept is pattern-recognition: finding inspiration from a completely different aspect of life, studying its essence, and then applying it in a novel way. If you think about it, the entire premise of this book is Borrowing the mindsets and tactics of hackers and applying them to business innovation.

Legit Flip: Too often, we look for inspiration within our own industries, companies, or histories and then get frustrated when our ideas lack imagination. Instead, expand your view into completely different arenas to discover fresh possibilities. For example, the metal-cutting company Valenite studied the jaw patterns of predatory fish clamping down on their prey in order to find innovative ways to beat their competition. This tactic can also take the form of the Different Lens – brainstorming, or better yet, role playing, to solve problems. How would someone else solve your problem – a chemist, a textile artist, Neil deGrasse Tyson, Olivia Pope?

TOMs Shoes famously branded a model where business meets philanthropy. For every pair of shoes purchased, the company donates a second pair to someone in need in a developing country. The "buy one, give one" model was an instant success, rocketing the company to tremendous success. So when launching their e-commerce eyeglass company, the founders of Warby Parker borrowed the model and offered the same "buy one, give one" approach. This model has since been replicated by dozens of other companies who now offer "buy one, give one" dog food, baby clothes, cosmetics, books, and toothbrushes. The key is that a successful pattern was borrowed, not from a direct competitor but rather extracted for use from a source outside industry boundaries.

DECONSTRUCT

The Hack: As the name implies, the technique of Deconstructing involves disassembling something in order to fully understand how it works. This can be a sort of tinkering – taking apart physical machines or software systems and adding/removing components to improve their functionality. In the classic heist movie *Ocean's Eleven*, the sophisticated robbers extensively studied the security systems that protected their desired loot, in order to find vulnerabilities. They ordered similar equipment and Deconstructed it to see exactly how it operated so they could discover creative opportunities for infiltration. They practiced each step of their plot, understanding the basal elements of each obstacle, in order to perfect their plan of attack, far in advance of their heist.

After deconstructing a system or code, hackers will often employ Substitution – they put the system or code back together, replacing a line of legitimate code with their own (usually malicious) secret sauce. Addition, Subtraction, and Substitution are all possible components of the Deconstruction approach.

Legit Flip: Deconstruction doesn't only apply to code or even physical equipment. It can apply to process as well. In non-computer terms, this is taking something apart (product, system, company) and seeing how it works – its individual pieces and its collective whole – and then putting it back together, but differently. This could mean removing components, adding new ones, or changing the role/function of existing pieces.

This method is often used in product innovation. Coffee without the caffeine (Subtraction) created the multi-billion-dollar industry of decaf. Swapping a zipper for buttons (Substitution) enabled Levi's to produce millions of their button-fly jeans. Carmakers substitute cloth seats for leather to command an up-charge while watchmakers swap out a leather strap for a steel one in order to offer more consumer variety. Of course, new revenue streams appear when new items are added without removing something in their place. Adding lump crab to the top of a steak in an elegant restaurant (Addition) enhances both the meal and the restaurateur's bottom line. When facing an innovation challenge, isolate as many variable components as possible and then experiment with various Additions, Subtractions, and Substitutions.

AGILE BURSTS

The Hack: Frustrated with election fraud and corruption in the Philippines, hackers warned the Philippines' Commission on Elections (COMELEC) to clean up their act. Time was ticking as the May 2016 election approached, but there was no sign of improvement. The hackers fired a digital warning shot, breaking into the election website and defacing it. Still, with no satisfactory response, hackers breached the system again, stole election records, and posted personal information on over 55 million voters for the world to see. The leak of highly confidential data, including passport numbers, fingerprints, names, and addresses, was devastating and represents the largest breach of governmental records to date.

The hacking tactic deployed to create such a ruckus? An Agile Burst. These bursts are time-sensitive. The hackers didn't have the time to pursue a patient approach; instead, a hacking sprint led to their desired outcome. The premise is to attack a problem with short bursts of flat-out activity. These can be 48-hour Hackathons, 1-week sprints, or even a 2-hour burst. A fixed amount of time coupled with extreme focus and intensity is the technique that has led to many of the most notorious cybercrimes.

Legit Flip: Hackathons have become a common mechanism to quickly generate breakthrough ideas. A Hackathon held by Johns Hopkins University, specifically focused on the Zika virus, uncovered many powerful concepts including a mobile app that alerts citizens of mosquito migration. GroupMe, a group messaging software acquired by Microsoft, was born during a new product Hackathon. Launched in 2007, Startup Weekend is a 48-hour sprint to help generate ideas for new companies. Since the first landmark event, over 23,000 teams have been formed in 2,900 Startup Weekend Hackathons in 150 countries. Hundreds of successful companies are now in operation, launched by the hacking technique of an Agile Burst.

THE REVERSE

The Hack: To be hacked, you have to be connected to the

Internet, right? Wrong. Ang Cui, a Columbia University PhD student demonstrated that a hacker could turn your device hardware into its own transmitter. By installing malicious code, Cui showed that the internal components to tech devices can be turned into RF transmitters, making it even easier for hackers to access information. Cui totally Reversed assumptions about how hacking works – by refusing to rely on software, he demonstrated the dangerous potential of hardware in compromising valuable data. In presentations at major hacking and security conferences, Cui demonstrated how innocuous items like office phones or printers could transmit information to outside parties. The Reverse technique is just what it sounds like – doing the exact opposite of conventional wisdom. Here, the polar opposite is embraced in order to crack the code.

Legit Flip:

> *Dear [Name],*
> *We shall be shipping Gold to you.*
> *You will earn 10% of any gold you distributes.*

Another spam email hits your inbox. Your move: delete fast. Junk email is dangerous, you know it's a bogus offer, and you've got far more important things to do. And what idiot replies to spam email? Yet you've probably had that delicious urge to reply, just to see what might unfold. Well, so did UK comedian James Veitch. He promptly replied to the con artist, which ended up changing his life...for the better.

Veitch has since tracked and cataloged these exchanges, in turn rocketing his own career. His hilarious TED talk has been viewed over three million times and his book, *Dot Con*, is a breakaway success. Recently, he even teamed up with *Mashable* to create "Scamalot," a regular web series where he details his harassment of the harassers.

Veitch's stunt is more than great comedy – he embraced the hacker technique of *The Reverse*. Like Veitch did, take your instinctive move, flip it upside down, and see if you can uncover a better result.

THE MASHUP

The Hack: A line of code from one program is combined with software from another. In the same way certain chemicals fuse together to create an entirely new substance, hackers can use the Mashup technique to up the ante on devious schemes. If a particular approach isn't doing the trick, the hacker may combine one approach with a another to undercover a fresh, potentially more effective option. The creative approach of combining distinct ideas together to create an entirely new one has been the genesis of devastating security breaches, but also the source of inspiration for many major innovations.

Legit Flip: "You got your peanut butter in my chocolate," an actor protests. "No! You got your chocolate in my peanut butter," another actor angrily retorts. "Delicious!" they both proclaim in unison upon trying the newly formed Reese's Peanut Butter Cup. Since launching in 1928, the Reese's concept has been combined with many other things, forming a Mashup of a Mashup. It has been fused with a corn puff to make cereal. It's also frequently mixed with other toppings inside ice cream to create a Flurry. The company currently offers 19 Reese's products, from sandwich spread to snack mix, and has licensed its brand and recipe to dozens of other manufacturers. One Mashup leads to another, and another.

Combining two or more distinct items or ideas to form a new one has long been a profound source of innovation. A bed combines with a chair to form the La-Z-Boy recliner. The smash Broadway hit *Hamilton* fused American history with hip-hop and other musical genres to rake in 12 Tony Awards in a highly competitive industry. When you're facing an innovation challenge of your own, experiment not only with individual solutions, but also with Mashups of existing concepts to uncover novel solutions.

WORKING BACKWARD

The Hack: Hacking into hundreds of companies and stealing the proverbial crown jewels sounds irresistible to cybercriminals. For such a big ambition, the hacker is likely to reverse-engineer a solution rather than running straight at this tidal wave. In March 2016, hackers did just that. Knowing that access to the IT leaders of cyberdefense at their target corporations would allow them to achieve their lofty goal, the creative hackers Worked Backward. How could they secure that information in the most efficient manner?

Rather than breaching one company at a time, the hackers started with the desired end state and went in reverse. This thinking led them to a new target: Verizon. Since Verizon provides security services to 97% of Fortune

500 companies, a hack into Verizon's records would be the jackpot. Cybersecurity journalist Brian Krebs reported:

> *A prominent member of a closely guarded underground cyber-crime forum posted a new thread advertising the sale of a database containing the contact information on some 1.5 million customers of Verizon Enterprise. The entire database was priced at $100,000, or $10,000 for each set of 100,000 customer records. Buyers also were offered the option to purchase information about security vulnerabilities in Verizon's web site.*

By working backward from the ultimate score, hackers thought to attack Verizon. Knowing that other cybercriminals would want the data for themselves, they sold and profited from it, in addition to using it for their own master plan.

Legit Flip: Starting with the end in mind is not a new approach, but it can be a powerful source of innovation, nonetheless. Scientists at University of California, San Diego used this approach to invent a new monitoring device for diabetes. Instead of starting with existing monitoring equipment that involved taking blood and analyzing its contents, these researchers decided to Work Backward. Their desired end involved a system that didn't break the skin, didn't interfere with the patient's everyday life, was inexpensive, and provided accurate monitoring. Since they reverse-engineered the problem, their innovation went in a totally different direction than anything that had come before. Their solution: temporary tattoos that monitor blood glucose levels through changes in the skin and perspiration.

Early tests have yielded highly encouraging results. While the tattoos are currently only able to change color to alert patients to major fluctuations, development is under way that will connect the tattoo sensors to a patient's mobile device. This will provide accurate, numerical readouts of glucose levels in real time and will even be able to send alerts to family members or healthcare professionals, should the numbers reach extreme levels. It was through Working Backward that this exciting innovation materialized. The same method can generate equally compelling results for you when put into practice.

WHAT'S NEXT

Don't worry if you're having trouble seeing how these 10 hacking tactics apply to the challenges you're currently facing. Now that you have a high-level overview, we'll explore each tactic in depth. You'll see how each technique has been applied in real-world situations attacking business problems of all shapes and sizes, along with the subtleties of each approach. By seeing how each method has been deployed to drive massive growth and innovation, you'll be able to connect the dots and apply these maneuvers to your own obstacles. Before long, each will become second nature as you deploy these tactics to innovate, lead, and grow.

Part 2
HACKING IN ACTION

CHAPTER 4: BRUTE FORCE

In the Palermo region of Sicily, Italy, 80% of business owners pay a *pizzo*. No, that isn't a fresh take on specialty pizza, but rather the age-old practice of protection money. Shopkeepers and accountants alike budget *pizzo* in their operating costs, right along with electricity and payroll. In a region where organized crime has held a tight grip on local business for generations, company owners have the choice to pay up or suffer the consequences. Better to fork over some cash than have your business burnt to the ground or your employees beaten in the alley. Officials estimate that the Mafia extorts $265 million per day across the entire country of Italy.

While the tools of the trade have evolved from wooden bats to titanium laptops, the racket hasn't changed. **Brute Force** is a long-standing strategy of criminals looking to profit from their victims. If anything, conditions have improved dramatically for the criminals. They need not join a gang, have a much lower chance of getting caught, and it's unlikely they'll lose a tooth in a street fight. Hackers have adapted the technique, allowing them to perpetrate their crimes thousands of miles away from their targets, while sipping espresso from the comfort of their apartments.

According to *Information Security Magazine*, "Brute force is a trial and error method used by application programs to decode encrypted data such as passwords or Data Encryption Standard (DES) keys, through exhaustive effort (using brute force) rather than employing intellectual strategies." Using this technique, hackers overwhelm a target with a relentless barrage of attacks in order to destroy the barrier protecting what they desire.

A closely related strategy is the Denial of Service (DoS) attack, in which hackers flood a network with so much activity that it brings the system to its knees. To illustrate how frequently this technique is deployed, the security team at Wordfence took a look at a typical 16-hour period. Wordfence provides a security plug-in for WordPress sites, which represent a large chunk of the entire Internet. In this short window of time, there were over 6.6 million attacks on WordPress sites they monitor, spread across 37,000 targets. In this "normal" period, they experienced 116 attacks per second. Things really get messy when the hackers turn up the heat. In one 2015 attack, a target site was hit at the rate of 275,000 requests per second, which fried the server and shut down service.

Now imagine you are the target, and your entire business is inoperable because your network is shut down. Here's where the *pizzo* comes back in. You receive a ransom note, letting you know the attacks will subside only when you fork over a hefty fee, in the form of an anonymous bitcoin payment, of course. Typical ransoms range from $6,500-$62,500, and the **Brute Force** hackers generally get away with it.

There are some common variations on the theme: A Threat Attack involves demanding payment before an attack actually occurs ("pay up now or we'll bring you down"). Another common angle is to hack into a system through **Brute Force**, steal information, and then demand ransom payment or the stolen data will be released to the public, a competitor, or a governmental agency – a practice best described as DataNapping.

Brute Force (and DoS) attacks are among the most common tactics of cybercriminals. While they appear to be an archaic and inelegant approach, they are extremely effective in perpetrating some of the largest security breaches in history. In February, 2000, a 15-year-old hacker who went by the handle of "Mafiaboy" (his actual name is the far-less-menacing Michael Calce) used a DoS attack that brought down Yahoo!, the number one search engine at the time. In 1999, David L. Smith from New Jersey unleashed an attack that he called Melissa, which was named after a stripper he visited frequently. Here, his DoS attack replicated itself as it spread, forcing Microsoft, Intel, Lockheed Martin, and Lucent Technologies to shut down their email networks.

Unrefined yet extremely effective, the **Brute Force** tactic is a fan favorite of villainous hackers around the world.

LEGIT FLIP

With no intention of evil deeds, cybercrime, or patronizing strippers, how can you apply **Brute Force** to your arsenal of legitimate innovation? When we dissect the **Brute Force** tactic and examine its core building blocks, there are two powerful and transferable attributes to the lawful world of business:

1. Rapid Experimentation
2. Pivots

Brute Force is also built upon the **Nothing Is Static** mindset – the best **Brute Force** executions involve lots of iteration and continuous learning.

Let's explore each of the underlying principles of the **Brute Force** tactic so you can clearly see how these approaches will drive meaningful progress for you as an Innovation Hacker.

RAPID EXPERIMENTATION

Taking a look at Amancio Ortega, "hacker" would not be the first word that comes to mind. The 80-year-old businessman has a weathered face, a mostly-bald head, and peering eyes. Despite being the perfect image of a lawyer or banker, Ortega actually exhibits more hacker tendencies. As the founder and CEO of Zara, the world's largest apparel retailer, he has hacked his way from a working class upbringing to being the 2nd wealthiest person in the world, amassing over $74 billion of net worth. Growing up as the youngest of four children in a small town in Spain, he dropped out of school at the age of 14 to pursue manual labor like his father. So how does a poor high school dropout with no resources transform into the world's most successful retail and apparel magnate?

Core to Ortega's success is the hacker principle of **Brute Force**. Not an especially gifted designer himself, he developed a method he calls 'instant fashion,' pioneering the design, manufacturing, and distribution processes to dramatically speed up time-to-market. This allowed him to respond to new trends quickly, and use Rapid Experimentation to topple competitors.

In the conventional fashion retail model, clothing designers dream up a new idea that they hope will be widely accepted. Perhaps they validate it with a focus group, but before long the design is set. Next, millions of garments are produced in low cost countries and shipped to retail stores for sale. Sometimes the design is a hit, but more often, a large percentage of inventory sits on the shelves for months. The brand spends millions in advertising to create demand, but eventually as much as 35% of the goods are sent to discount stores to be sold for pennies on the dollar.

Zara takes a completely different approach. Investing in their own factories in central locations to produce **Brute Force** results, they can design and ship a new product in less than a week. Choosing to let data drive their decisions instead of hope, a new product idea starts with a micro production run. For example, a new red dress concept may hit the market with a production of only 4,200 – two for each of the company's 2,100 stores. Rather than placing a big bet on an unproven design, the company relies on experimentation.

Zara has a highly sophisticated feedback system, allowing store managers to instantly report back customer feedback on new products. Customers may say they like the dress, but the shade of red is too bright. Feedback on the length, zipper, and other factors are gathered and evaluated in real time back at headquarters, and adjustments are made in a matter of hours. The next week, after implementing design changes based on customer feedback, a new 4,200 red dresses ship to the network of stores. Only after a series of improvements are made and customer demand has been validated is the dress mass-produced. Where most clothing manufacturers produce only a few dozen new styles each year, Zara launched over 12,000 new items annually.

Through Rapid Experimentation, continuous trial-and-error, Zara is able to keep inventory levels low and price points high. In contrast to industry norms, the company has a strict policy against advertising. Instead, they invest in new stores and Rapid Experimentation. While competitors turn inventory only a couple of times a year, Zara is able to enjoy 14 times the throughput of average retailers. And while competitive brands frequently end up at the discount shops, you'll never see a Zara sweater at TJ Maxx. Through rapid experimentation and a continuous improvement loop, they eliminate that waste by adapting quickly to shifts in consumer taste.

While the stereotypical hacker may purchase his hoodie at Zara, Amancio Ortega is the one who has truly won by embracing the hacker mindset. Rapid Experimentation vaulted Zara to $12. 8 billion of revenue in 2015, with no end in sight.

I should point out that some of Zara's practices have been called into question, with the company being accused of stealing designs, unethical labor practices, and creating racially offensive products. Zara's inclusion here is not carte blanche endorsement of the company and leadership, nor is it in any way glorifying unethical approaches. Most hackers – and people in general – are neither all bad nor all good. It's easy to bucket people and organizations into binary categories, but the realities are far more complex. While I neither support nor agree with many of Zara's actions, it shouldn't undermine their brilliant use of Rapid Experimentation. This contrarian approach led to tremendous success for the company, and changed how companies thought about fashion and tested their products with customers. Let's embrace the important lessons from Zara – those that can be learned from both their positive practices and their unacceptable ones. Throughout the book, we'll learn from people and organizations that lack squeaky-clean histories. In an effort to uncover uncommonly useful approaches, we need to learn from both the saints and the sinners.

Rapid Experimentation not only drives innovation, it reduces risk. Too often, we place the weight of the world on our shoulders, believing we must dream up a transformative innovation and then bet the company on its success. Innovation Hackers take a more effective and less risky approach: instead of thinking of innovation as a single gigantic effort, the best leaders (hackers, innovators) are constantly running experiments. They dream up dozens of little ideas instead of feeling overwhelmed with the task of inventing one groundbreaking thing.

Continuous Rapid Experimentation can apply to all aspects of our business lives – from product, to process, to leadership. Test how a new cold-call script measures up against the status quo in a quick, three-day experiment in one market. If the data is encouraging, expand the test. If not, discard the idea and try something else. Instead of the nail-biting fear of universal change, a series of expandable yet controlled experiments is a far more effective approach. Run an experiment with a new interview process for hiring fresh talent. Try out a new customer service experiment and see what the results show. Running a high volume of controlled experiments is your best chance at driving growth while mitigating risk. Test, measure, refine. Rinse and repeat. In the words of author and painter Hermann Hesse, "In order to achieve what is possible, you have to try the impossible over and over again."

AMPLIFYING KNOWLEDGE

The best hackers are the ones who invest the time and energy to sharpen their skills. Understanding that **Nothing Is Static**, that security measures and technology are constantly evolving, they know they need to stay one step ahead of their targets. To that end, they deploy the same **Brute Force** approach to learning in order to discover new, innovative approaches to their craft. To a large degree, a hacker's success is determined by how quickly they learn.

Einstein's famous theory of relativity ($E=MC^2$) celebrated its 100th anniversary in 2016. This elegant formula helped us understand how the world works and has impacted scientists and philosophers alike. The business world has its own formulas for success. Hard work + dedication = results. Power = money + influence. Big > small. Fast > slow. Fancy degree + time = corner office.

The thing is, the world has changed. The old rules no longer carry the day as we cope with neck-and-neck competition, mind-numbing speed, and exponential complexity. Add in macro trends such as global markets, digitization, cloud computing, Millennial workforce shifts, mobile technology, and geo-political turmoil, and you're wrestling a whole new beast – one that can't be conquered with some long-expired formula.

Hackers use an entirely different formula for success, and one that we can borrow for legitimate purposes:

PROGRESS = SPEED (times) LEARNING (divided by) COST (P = SL/C)
In other words, the success of your business or career will not be based on what you already know, but on how fast and inexpensively you learn. The amount of success you'll enjoy is directly linked to the velocity with which you learn. While cash may have been the fuel of growth in the past, learning is the new energy supply. Fortunately, it's renewable, environmentally friendly, produces no waste, and is extremely low-priced.

When calculating cost, the investment in learning (books, conferences, training, etc.) is like a rounding error compared to the real costs of not learning fast enough: opportunities squandered, time wasted, employee turnover, competitive losses, customer attrition, and damaged morale. To keep the true cost of learning low, learn as fast as possible. If you're not actively prioritizing learning, you may be unknowingly falling behind. Near-term competitive advantages come and go, but the learning organization wins in the long run.

To increase learning speed, it gets back to the **Brute Force** approach. Hackers don't waste time overanalyzing which scheme may crack the code. Instead, they throw hundreds of them at a problem all at once and then measure which works the best. Applying this approach to learning involves volume and force. If you commit to read for an hour every day, you'll likely discover more answers than trying to select one perfect book for the year. When refining your craft becomes a daily habit, mastery ensues. Push yourself and your team to learn more and learn fast, and your ability to innovate will skyrocket. Set learning objectives in the same way you set performance targets. Recap and share lessons learned. Experiment, measure, refine, learn.

BAGEL BASKETS

Back in 1999, Drew Greenblatt was looking to buy a company that would produce stable, consistent income. He ended up buying Marlin Steel, a small manufacturing company that had just one product: wire baskets for bagels. Since it was such a small market, the company had few competitors and was able to drive consistent, year-over-year profits selling their specialty baskets to Einstein Brothers, Bruegger's, and the hundreds of independent bagel shops throughout North America. At the time, the company had 18 employees and generated around $800,000 in revenue. What could possibly go wrong?

The honeymoon didn't last. Within a few years, Chinese manufacturers started making and selling the same steel baskets at a price point 50% lower than Drew was charging, less than the cost of his raw materials. To make matters worse, anti-carb diets shifted consumer demand for bagels from fad to forgotten. Sales were plummeting, profits had evaporated into losses, and Marlin Steel was on the brink of extinction.

They say when opportunity knocks, you should listen. Greeblatt's knock came in the form of a telephone ring, and thankfully he was the one who took the call. "It was an engineer from Boeing," Drew says. "He didn't think I was in the bagel-basket business. He just needed custom wire baskets."

The engineer called Marlin Steel since the company advertised themselves as a provider of metal baskets. He was in need of just twenty baskets, which would be used to transport airplane parts throughout their factory. Unlike bagel baskets, which rarely required rush delivery or manufacturing exactness, this buyer needed precision baskets within one sixty-fourth of an inch of his specifications and he needed them fast. "I told him, 'I'll have to charge you $24 a basket,'" Greenblatt said. "He said, 'Yeah, yeah, whatever. No problem. When are you going to ship them?'"

Drew didn't mind the precision or rush. What really captured his imagination was the buyer's total disregard for price. "I'm trying to sell a basket for $12, the bagel shops are saying, 'I'm not paying more than $6.' I'm ready to jump off a bridge, and here's a guy who just shrugs at the outrageous sum of $24. I was like, Wow. He's price insensitive." Drew's inner-hacker came out to play as this insight led to a transformational Pivot.

With no allegiance to the past, hackers unceremoniously drop things that aren't working in favor of a new approach. The willingness to let go and shift toward an entirely different strategy is known to both hackers and business leaders as a Pivot. Drew Greenblatt used the Boeing request as an opportunity to pursue an entirely new customer segment: manufacturers who needed specialty metal baskets. He dumped the bagel business and Pivoted the company into a new direction, one where he could compete, grow, and profit.

It wasn't an easy transition. His first shipments were cobbled together, crudely rigged to get the products out the door. But with his business about to collapse, he needed a life raft and this appeared to be it. While Pivoting from a single-item supplier to a custom basket maker was tough, it was worth it to pursue a much bigger market. At the time, there were only 3,100 bagel shops in the U. S., but there were 333,000 factories. Greenblatt set out to reinvent every aspect of his business, from production standards to design, to logistics. His baskets now needed to have mission-critical reliability to hold everything from microchips to turbine blades. He needed to retool his sales approach as well, now pursuing manufacturing giants such as Toyota, Caterpillar, Merck, and GE.

Despite the challenges, Greenblatt's Pivot paid off. Marlin Steel now has $10 million in revenue, and the team is gunning for $50 million within five years. They've invested $3.5 million in robotics to modernize manufacturing and have carved out a profitable niche in a competitive field. Had Drew Greenblatt failed to Pivot, and only viewed his company as a bagel basket producer, he'd likely have lost it all.

Successful Pivots happen more often than you may think, and have been the turning point for some of the most well-known companies:

Company	Pivot
Berkshire Hathaway	Textiles to an investment conglomerate
IBM	Punch cards to computers to IT services
Pixar	Animation tools to animated films
Suzuki	Looms to vehicles
EMC	Furniture to enterprise data storage
Instagram	Check-in app to photo sharing platform
Nokia	Paper mill to phones to network services

These Pivots are game-changing transformations, but your Pivots don't have to be as dramatic. When looking to spur innovation, don't ignore opportunities for micro-Pivots: a slight shift in internal processes, a fresh approach to customer loyalty, a divergent method for recruiting. Innovation Hackers use a **Brute Force** approach, turning the barrage of attacks *inward* on their products, processes, and services in hunt of a better solution. When stuck in a particularly pesky challenge, explore how you can Pivot your way to new heights.

HACK STARTERS

Here, and in each of the subsequent chapters on hacking techniques, I offer a few questions and challenges to spur creative exploration for you and your team. Think of them as conversation starters to summon your imagination and begin your innovation hacking process:

1. Think of a key challenge you're facing in any aspect of your business. If you had to attack the problem with 100 rapid experiments, what would the first five be?

2. Denial of Service attacks are used by hackers to bring down networks. What types of legitimate DoS attacks could you launch on a competitor (examples: flooding the market with marketing messages; launching multiple new products at once; or holding an innovative career fair lunch across the street from your competitor's headquarters, and luring people away during their breaks).

3. What is your current corporate learning strategy, and how could a Brute Force approach up your game to a whole new level?

4. What are three ways you could increase the force and velocity of internal training to amplify results?

5. List three areas of your business that feel stuck. Brainstorm at least 10 ideas of how you could Pivot each to uncover new possibilities.

6. If you lost your job tomorrow and had to Pivot your career in a different direction, what would you do? Once you arrive at a few ideas, how could you inject them into your current role to unlock more creativity and innovation?

Chapter 5: Social Engineering

 Considered one of the most skilled hackers of all time, Kevin Mitnick is a legend. Beginning his craft at age 13, he went on to perpetrate hundreds of cybercrimes. After landing in prison for a year, he negotiated a supervised release and then fled. For 2.5 years, Mitnick was a fugitive, staying one step ahead of the authorities and continuing his cybercrime spree with gusto. He was named the FBI's Most Wanted Hacker.

When he was finally caught, Mitnick spent five years in prison including eight months in solitary confinement. His time in the "shu" (segregated housing unit) wasn't due to poor prison behavior, but instead due to his reputation for exceptional hacking abilities. The prosecutor at the time convinced a judge that Mitnick's skills were so extraordinary, he could dial into North American Aerospace Defense Command (NORAD) through a prison payphone and whistle the launch codes to a nuclear missile, thereby launching a nuclear attack – a claim that has never been proven or refuted. Since his release, Mitnick has been the subject of several movies and books and now runs a cybersecurity consulting firm.

The primary weapon of the most infamous hacker in the world? **Social Engineering**.

Despite his solid technical skills, Mitnick's true genius was in his ability to manipulate others to do the heavy lifting for him. According to Kevin, "It is much easier to trick someone into giving a password than to spend the effort to crack into the system." In one of his first exploits, he called into Nokia from his own mobile phone and pretended to be a senior executive at the company. By studying the organizational chart and learning some detailed facts about the company, he was able to persuade someone in the IT department of his falsified identity. Mitnick claimed that he lost his copy of Nokia's top mobile phone's source code and needed it sent right away or he would be in big trouble. With this ruse, he was able to trick his mark into action. The loyal and unsuspecting employee complied, and within 15 minutes, Mitnick had the most important and confidential intellectual property of a multinational conglomerate.

According to Mitnick, "Social engineering is using deception, manipulation and influence to convince a human who has access to a computer system to do something, like click on an attachment in an e-mail." In other words, using innovative approaches to enlist others to behave in a way that benefits the initiator.

To a degree, Kevin and his hacker counterparts drew inspiration from the history books. One of the first and most illustrious **Social Engineering** hacks was the original Trojan horse. Famously, during the Trojan War, the Greeks needed to find a way to infiltrate their opponent's stronghold. The giant wooden horse was left outside the castle gates and the Greeks pretended to sail away. Thinking they had won, the Trojans wheeled their prize inside the fortress only to be surprised by Greek solders hiding inside the giant trap. In tribute to one of the first documented **Social Engineering** hacks, modern day cybercriminals aptly refer to one of their own malicious software programs as a "Trojan Horse."

To better understand how hackers use human manipulation to overcome their obstacles, you'll want to learn the five primary **Social Engineering** techniques of cybercriminals:

1. Phishing – False emails, calls, or websites seeking to extract sensitive information from the victim. Your bank calls with a fraud alert, asking you to verify your name and password to shut down and protect the account. If you receive an email announcing you've won the lotto and you just need to provide your bank account info in order to receive your winnings, you're likely staring at a Phishing attempt.

2. Quid-Pro-Quo – Here, you're offered a trade of some kind that is generally too good to be true. "Get a $1,000 reward for completing a customer survey." Or "Listen to this new song and we'll send you a free t-shirt." Once you agree to the exchange, you've been infiltrated.

3. Tailgating – "Could you please hold the door for me?" the smiling person behind you asks as you enter your office building. "Thanks so much. I left my security badge in the car." Here, the Tailgating method is used to gain illicit access by simply following someone with legitimate credentials. This not only happens in physical settings, but it can also occur in the digital realm.

4. Pretexting – This approach generally involves an impersonation. Posing as a superior, IT consultant, security guard, or some other authority figure, the hacker gains her access by manipulating the victim into thinking she should have legitimate access. This is the approach Kevin Mitnick used with Nokia.

5. Baiting – Dangling something of value as a lure to get a person to respond or click. For example, "Download a free music video" or "Click to receive the 2016 salary survey." Once a victim takes the bait, their computer becomes infected with malicious software.

Gary Darnell dialed up the manager of a Wal-Mart in a small Canadian town on an urgent matter. There was a multi-million-dollar government contract in play, and Darnell, a senior executive from Wal-Mart headquarters in Bentonville, Arkansas, had to select a few pilot sites. The small-town Wal-Mart was being considered, Darnell said, as one of the first sites, which could mean significant revenue, recognition, and new responsibilities for the store.

Darnell went on for nearly 10 minutes with details of the contract, internal Wal-Mart policy, and a juicy description of what this contract could mean to the local store. To select the location for this pilot, Darnell needed to learn more, he said. Next, the eager store manager shared nearly every detail of his operation. Who the local suppliers and contractors were, the type of computer systems installed down to the make, model, and serial number, and what time various employees take breaks.

After an encouraging and rigorous discussion, Darnell directed the manager to a specific website to complete the "online application" for final consideration. When the unsuspecting store manager visited the site and it appeared to be blocked, Darnell sounded frustrated, apologized, and said he would instruct IT to override the issue. He warmly told the manger to expect a callback in a few hours.

As the call ended, Gary Darnell stepped out of the soundproof room to a standing ovation. His real name is Shane MacDougall and he had just demonstrated **Social Engineering** to a live audience at a security conference in Las Vegas. In less than 20 minutes, MacDougall had complete control of the store's computer system, passwords, employee records, bank account, and confidential information that could be used against Wal-Mart. Luckily, in this case it was only a simulation and no crimes were actually committed. The demonstration was performed to show how easily well-intentioned people can be scammed, and how effective a simple **Social Engineering** tactic can be.

LEGIT FLIP

As you know by now, the goal of this book is not to teach you to commit fraud. Hopefully, by learning the techniques of **Social Engineering** you're now even a little safer from being scammed. But the real question is: how can you use a modified version of **Social Engineering** in your company, career, and community to drive positive results in a legal, appropriate way?

The key flip is turning a maneuver that is based on deception and manipulation into something you'd be proud to share with your mom. Instead of hoaxing someone to perform a task that they'll later regret, the legit version has a happy ending. A positive flavor of **Social Engineering** must have these three factors:

a) truthful, nothing misleading

b) a structure that is transparent rather than manipulative

c) most importantly, the end result should be a win-win

Yes, you will derive benefit but rather than gaining at someone else's expense, a positive outcome for all parties is the desired end.

Social Engineering, in fact, has been a tactic of great innovators throughout history. Rather than absorbing the full burden themselves, creative leaders enlist the help of others to expand their impact. In a responsible way, the challenge involves gaining leverage by recruiting others to help your cause. For business purposes, we can group those you're seeking to influence into two categories: internal (team members, employees, bosses, boards, investors, etc.) and external (customers, the media, competitors, governmental agencies, prospects, voters, potential employees, etc.).

THE REBEL

Ricardo Semler has been called a lot of things – a rule-breaker, a crazy lunatic, a wild and out-of-control leader – but for this renegade, who has built one of the most unorthodox and successful corporate cultures in the world, names and titles mean nothing. Defying tradition at every step of the way, Semler has used the hacking approach of **Social Engineering** to build a 3,000-person company of innovators that has delivered 40% annual growth rate in each year of the last decade.

A man of many accomplishments, Semler earned his Harvard MBA at age 20 and has twice been named Brazil's "Leader of the Year." His triumphs came as the result of shunning conventional wisdom, rather than complying. When he took over the family business at age 24, he instantly fired 60% of the existing managers, eliminated all secretarial positions, and set out to completely reimagine a modern team structure. At the core of his philosophy is the belief that most organizations are built on "corporate oppression," treating team members like adolescents that require constant supervision. Not only is it cruel, it undermines the talents and potential of the workforce.

Semler wanted to redefine corporate culture, building an environment that encouraged people to stretch beyond their self-imposed limits. Being a big believer in human potential, he bet that fewer rules and policies would translate into better performance. Since taking over the company in 1980, he has built one of the most unusual, and productive, organizations in the world.

"If it's okay for an employee to check email on Sunday night, why isn't it okay for them to go to the movies on a Tuesday afternoon?" Semler challenges. Based in São Paulo, Brazil, Semler's Semco Partners has grown to become one of the most successful companies in South America. The nontraditional culture is designed to bring out the absolute best in people, to harness their creativity and performance. To do this, Semler has broken just about every rule. There are no titles, org charts, or assigned desks. No time clocks, uniforms, or searches to protect against theft.

Employees at Semco set their own hours and even their own pay. Abuse is rooted out by teammates, since there is full transparency on all financial matters and everyone knows what everyone else is making. Major decisions are made on the front lines, not in some executive boardroom. Leaders are chosen, not appointed – peer reviews dictate whether a person is promoted or removed from a specific post. Semler subscribes to the hacker mindset of meritocracy, believing that **Competence Is the Only Credential That Matters**. Fresh ideas – even the wild ones – are celebrated at all levels, which eliminates the fear that weighs down most corporate cultures.

As traditionalist leaders install rules and policies for nearly every possibility, Semler works hard to remove any sign of structure or bureaucracy.

Results alone, not tenure, rank, gender, or age, are the measuring stick, and the trust-based environment brings out the best in people. All 3,000 people have some level of ownership in the company, and enjoy profit-sharing when performance is good, but also take a hit if they don't deliver results. With the mandate to "relentlessly relinquish control to make room for discovery," ideas from employees who might be overlooked in most organizations helped the company expand from manufacturing into real estate, banking, and even web services. Over a 10-year period of recession in Brazil, Semco's revenue expanded 600%. And over the last 20 years, employee turnover is an insanely low 1-2%.

According to Ricardo Semler, "Growth and profit are a product of how people work together." His belief that employees should be challenged and invigorated instead of controlled has shifted the creative responsibilities from a select group of executives to the entire global workforce. By exhilarating and rewarding others, Semco has been able to significantly outperform the competition and reach the highest levels of success. Semler's radical form of corporate democracy is an example of responsible **Social Engineering** in action: all stakeholders are better off as a result.

ICE BUCKETS AND FROZEN PACKAGES

Pete Frates, a Boston College student who was diagnosed with the degenerative condition amyotrophic lateral sclerosis (ALS, or Lou Gehrig's disease), was feeling hopeless and depressed. In an effort to raise money and awareness around the disease, and to provide a sense of purpose instead of letting the diagnosis defeat him, he launched an "Ice Bucket Challenge." He recorded himself dumping a bucket of ice water on his head, and then sent the video off to friends with a challenge: within 24 hours, dump a bucket of ice water on your own head and then share the video to raise awareness, or donate $100 to ALS-related causes for a less frigid alternative.

The video spread and gained momentum, but on June 30, 2014, it exploded. TV personalities on the Golf Channel televised themselves taking the challenge, and Pete's home video became an unstoppable movement. Two weeks later, Matt Lauer did the Ice Bucket Challenge live on *The Today Show*. Before long, the challenge was accepted by Justin Bieber, LeBron James, and Kim Kardashian. By August 13, there were more than 1.2 million Ice Bucket videos on Facebook and nearly 10 million more on YouTube. In addition to building unprecedented awareness, more than 739,000 new donors contributed nearly $150 million to the cause. It has now become a yearly tradition, and is heralded as one of the most successful fundraising campaigns in history.

A formal email request soliciting funds for important medical research would have likely generated abysmal results. In contrast, **Social Engineering** made the Ice Bucket Challenge an unprecedented fundraising success. The factors that contributed to the challenge's virality included a fun experience coupled with the social implications to each recipient if they complied or rejected the campaign. With international buzz and celebrities participating, it made it difficult to say no. On the other hand, participation was highly rewarded via social media and through peer interactions. Each instance created many more, and the effort grew upon itself. Millions of people participated or learned about the challenge, and ultimately took action. Pete Frates did not create meaningful results alone, but by leveraging the power of others to accomplish far more than one could tackle alone. The best part? In 2016, ALS researchers announced that they had made a breakthrough in the fight against ALS as a direct result of the funding brought in by the Ice Bucket Challenge. Frates' **Social Engineering** has changed the future for people living with this debilitating condition.

The leaders at global shipping company DHL were facing a chilling problem of their own. While they had the best delivery times and reliability in many parts of the world, it was becoming increasingly difficult and expensive to communicate their competitive advantages. They couldn't afford a traditional high-priced ad campaign, so instead they tapped into the power of **Social Engineering**.

Rather than blowing millions for a flashy TV ad, DHL took an unorthodox approach. In a busy European city, DHL shipped oversized packages to highly visible locations using their competitors such as TNT and UPS. Unfortunately for the competitors' unsuspecting carriers, DHL covered each package in thermoactive foil. The foil was cooled down below the freezing point, turning the package jet black. So the competitors picked up a large, black package without any reason for alarm. But when temperatures rose, the specialized packaging turned bright yellow, with bold red lettering that read, "DHL IS FASTER." Before long, competitors were toting around bright packages in DHL's corporate colors that alerted the public who was the best choice for shipping. Drivers of competitors had to play along since they were doing their job and their company was paid to deliver the packages. Curious passersby were stunned as uniformed delivery personal effectively carried around large ads for their competitors. Giggles and sneers ensued, all of which was caught on film by DHL's hidden cameras.

While DHL caught the fancy of a few hundred people in a crowded city in Europe, it wasn't really about the live audience. A video compilation of the stunt was released online, and has since been shared repeatedly due to their clever approach. Over 40 million people around the world have now seen the video. Over 40 million people now chuckle when they see a DHL logo, and remember that "DHL IS FASTER." Lacking the resources of a traditional ad campaign, DHL leveraged **Social Engineering** to get others to spread the word.

Viral marketing has been around for ages and word-of-mouth is the most effective sales approach for many organizations. To tap into this artery of opportunity, you must craft a win-win environment that rewards the person doing the sharing with social credibility. In the DHL example, you gain an increased social standing by sharing the clever video with your friends. If the reward is there for the sender, the message will amplify.

BUYING LIFE WITH AN EMBRACE

All of us can remember sitting in at least one class and thinking (if not saying aloud), "When am I ever going to use this in the real world?" Sometimes we're right and that calculus formula is just not a game-changer for us, sometimes it takes years before we realize that there was actually a reason we learned that thing after all. For Jane Chen during her MBA program at Stanford, it wasn't long at all before she knew exactly how to use what she was learning in her "Design for Extreme Affordability" course.

During the course, students were given the assignment to design something that could serve as a neonatal incubator. The catch was that the cost for their design had to come in at less than $200, or 1% of the cost for a traditional, medical-grade incubator, which was about $20,000. Chen and her team members – Rahul Panicker, Linus Liang, Razmig Hovaghimian, and Naganand Murty – started by taking apart the problem. Like Mick Ebeling and the Not Impossible team, Chen and her classmates intentionally avoided looking into existing solutions, and focused on the problem instead.

Infant and maternal mortality is one of the largest problems facing the world today. Though women in developed countries are not immune to these dangers, by far, women and children in developing countries are disproportionately at risk. According to the World Health Organization, in 2015, 4.5 million babies died within their first year of life. Approximately one million of those die on the day of their birth. The worst part of these numbers is that babies are dying from things that are preventable. The leading causes of death among these children are complications relating to being born prematurely or at a low birth weight, particularly, hypothermia.

Babies born pre-term or at a very low birth weights lack the body fat to regulate their body temperatures, and this simple problem is enough to end life for many of them. Not only are traditional incubators cost-prohibitive, but they require constant electricity and training that is not feasible, particularly in rural areas. The nearest incubator is often hours away, and the journey too costly for mothers to afford. This is the problem Jane Chen and her team were trying to solve. And 40% of premature births worldwide occur in India, so that was the natural place for them to start. They traveled to India to get hands-on experience in impoverished areas where technology like this is needed most.

By immersing themselves in India, the team fell in love with the problem – these incredible mothers who would do anything to save their babies, and this tremendous need they had for tools and education to help underweight infants, while using minimal resources. Using **Brute Force** via Rapid Experimentation, they worked through many different possible materials, shapes, and details, until they refined their product into a viable solution. The result looks nothing like an incubator at all, but like a little cocoon, which they called 'Embrace.'By the time they left their program, they had a revolutionary, life-saving technology and $125,000 in seed money to back the product. That sounds like a happy ending, but it's actually where things started to get dicey.

Jane was so excited about Embrace – this little cocoon was seamless and waterproof on the inside, which made it easy to disinfect and reuse, and it had a removable packet of phase-changing material in the back. This wax-like substance can be heated with boiling water and maintain human-body temperature consistently for up to 8 hours before needing to be changed or re-heated. The best part? The total cost for one Embrace is only $25. The Embrace team had a product that fulfilled a real need, they had an unbelievably reasonable price point, and they had some capital, so what could go wrong?

The team learned quickly that distribution can be a real problem. In the places that need Embrace the most, they had to rely upon local and national governments to pay for the devices and training. Unfortunately, this funding proved to be sporadic and unreliable. And in order to provide training, conduct clinical trials, and improve these distribution problems, they were going to need a much bigger and steadier source of income. Jane and her team weren't going to give up on helping babies and mothers, so Jane got the idea to **Social Engineer** the results that they needed.

Chen thought that if parents in America could buy something for their own babies while supporting parents in impoverished areas of the world, not only would it help her team achieve their mission of saving as many babies as possible, but it would spread the word about the problem and get more people involved. So Embrace stayed a non-profit organization and Chen started a new company called Little Lotus. Embrace owns the intellectual property to the technology and continues to spread the devices, and training about caring for premature infants, to areas in need. Little Lotus, a for-profit social enterprise, licenses the Embrace technology and sells it to hospitals and governments, as well as selling infant swaddlers and sleeping bags. The Little Lotus products are inspired by NASA fabric, which helps babies regulate their body temperatures, improving the length and quality of their sleep – a win-win for parents and babies. Then they use the 1:1 model, made popular by TOMs Shoes, so the proceeds from each Little Lotus product go to the distribution of an Embrace and the related training in the developing world.

Jane understood the mindset that **Quantity Is a Force Multiplier**, so instead of doing all the work herself, she found a way to leverage the resources of many people to advance her product and solve this problem. This legit flip of the **Social Engineering** model meets all the criteria – there is nothing dishonest about Chen's plan, Little Lotus is totally transparent and their website is covered with explanations of their world-changing mission. Finally, it is a win-win for everyone: parents in developed countries get quality products to help their little ones get more sleep, while being able to invest in the health and welfare of families around the world. And it's working – to date, the lives of over 200,000 babies have been saved through the Embrace technology, and American parents rave about their Little Lotus products. Win-win, indeed.

While writing this book, the Embrace/Little Lotus example took on special meaning as my wife gave birth to our twins, unexpectedly born 14 weeks premature and weighing only 2.4 pounds each. We were so fortunate that they had access to advanced medical care, and in fact, my twins spent nine weeks in those expensive incubators which quite literally saved their lives. Holding my tiny babies made me understand how fragile life is and how important it is for us to use our Innovation Hacking skills for good. Avi and Tallia, to whom this book is dedicated, continue to make great progress and have a bright future ahead. Personally, I can't wait to swaddle them in their Little Lotus garb knowing that is both helping them and helping humanity.

Hackers are proudly lazy. They believe in working smarter, not harder – they want to achieve the maximum impact with the least amount of work. For legitimate business purposes, **Social Engineering** is a powerful approach to deliver maximum benefit with minimal investment. By creating a structure that encourages others to contribute, you will be able to enjoy far bigger results than working alone.

 HACK STARTERS

1. Instead of motivating team members with simple rewards or punishments, what are some intangible, social rewards that could be deployed to drive the desired behavior?

2. What obstacles or rules could you eliminate to create the needed room for fresh thinking within your team?

3. What is the most important message you need to send to the world right now (marketing, investor relationships, media, etc.)? What are some ways you could use **Social Engineering** instead of traditional approaches? Brainstorm how non-traditional motivators such as social standing, desire to share human experience, or the competitive spirit can be harnessed in a responsible way to encourage others to spread the word on your behalf.

CHAPTER 6: CROWDSOURCING

 "We start with the recognition of the absurd," Mick Ebeling told me. "It is absurd that a man couldn't speak to his wife for 15 years. It's absurd that a child with cerebral palsy can't walk. It's absurd that over one billion people in the developing world don't have access to clean drinking water." After acknowledging the absurd, Mick and his team get angry. They harness an unquenchable desire to correct the absurdity. From there, Not Impossible internalizes the problem and makes it their own: "If you *can* do something and you don't, that's borderline criminal."

When Mick first set out to cure some of the world's most vexing problems, he knew he and a small team couldn't do it alone. There are already many well-funded research labs taking on many of the same challenges in a traditional way. With solid equipment, lab-jacket-donning scientists, and detailed action plans, the teams toil away in isolation. Deciding that big problems needed a wider and more diverse set of answers, Mick built Not Impossible Labs on the foundation of **Crowdsourcing**.

The essence of **Crowdsourcing** is to seek a wide array of input and ideas from as many people as possible. The core tenet is that the combined power of many minds is better than the comparatively paltry output of one. With diversity of thought, culture, and experience, a group of dozens, hundreds, or thousands of people pecking away at a problem uncovers more compelling results.

Describing himself as an "impatient optimist," Ebeling and his team get deeply frustrated when things aren't progressing fast enough. If he's working to help a boy without hands feed himself, every minute that goes by without a solution is infuriating. Fueled by this sense of urgency, the Not Impossible team attacks some of humanity's greatest challenges by releasing the problems to the world, instead of trying to solve them alone. **Crowdsourcing** is not for the faint of heart, however; it requires a serious ego check. Ebeling explained to me that he actually seeks to *not* be the expert: "Surround yourself with people that make you feel stupid. When you're the dumbest guy on the team, you know you're going to end up with a killer solution."

But what does this look like in action? How does an organization like Not Impossible Labs go from the ideal of **Crowdsourcing** to real, workable solutions for huge challenges? Mick says the next step is to consider solutions in an unconventional way: "Once we fully grasp the problem, we then look at the project like a puzzle. What needs to be done to remove the absurdity?" How much do you need to know about the solution to do this? Less than you might think.

In addition to the core hacking mindsets, at Not Impossible they have a mindset of their own that fuels their innovation – Ebeling calls it their "beautiful, limitless naïveté." That might seem counterintuitive – most of us assume we need to be experts to solve a problem. And while you should be an expert before doing something like brain surgery, according to Mick, too much background knowledge can actually hinder your problem-solving efforts. "We succeed because we don't have a fucking clue. The less we know about a particular solution, the better we are at attacking it at the onset. We refuse to let experience become a distraction."

When deciding on solutions, instead of referencing previous attempts, Mick takes the opposite approach by asking, "What's the non-standard way? How can we take a detour from the obvious, previously accepted path? We prefer to disregard conventional approaches and protocols."

They've certainly disregarded convention so far – from devices that use eye movement to draw or help a man say "I love you" to his wife for the first time in 15 years. And now, taking on perhaps the most grandly absurd challenge yet, the team is setting out to "hack water." To take on such a meaningful and difficult task, they are **Crowdsourcing** a worldwide network of scientists, software engineers, artists, statisticians, architects, musicians, and philosophers. They are tapping into a robust community of hackers in many fields, who love to use their skills for something good. As ideas collide from a construction worker and an academic, mixed in with insight from a food chemist and a civil planner, completely new solutions emerge. Innovation is at the intersection of a diverse set of thoughts from a wide group of contributors. As large problems go unsolved with insular approaches, Not Impossible Labs is forging new ground by leveraging the power of the crowd.

Still not sure you've got what it takes to be an Innovation Hacker? I've already shown you that hacking doesn't need to have anything to do with computers, but Ebeling actually takes this a step further. Mick believes hacking is part of us, a primal human quality: "We are all hackers; we, as a species, are innately born to problem solve. Sometimes you don't have the right tool, so you have to invent a new way forward."

But just because we're born to hack doesn't mean we can't get in our own ways sometimes. One of the biggest ways we sabotage ourselves is our love for systems. Ebeling warns that this impulse can be detrimental: "Protocols are incredibly dangerous and tend to suppress innovation and productivity by overcomplicating the process." So what does Mick recommend to move past existing tools and channel our inherent hackers? "Stop baking!" Don't worry, that doesn't mean you have to give up chocolate chip cookies, just applying that step-by-step mindset to problem solving. "When you bake a cake, you're simply following the instructions. That's not how you get disruptive, innovation solutions. Instead, we need to invent new recipes." With the power of **Crowdsourcing**, you can create those new recipes.

If your goal is to invent a new recipe for an award-winning bowl of chili, don't just enlist a small group of chili cooks. Go wide. Learn from vegetarians and woodworkers, environmental engineers and chemists, tweens and senior citizens. Talk to people that have never tasted chili. If you're looking to truly innovate, tap into the power of the crowd.

LEGIT FLIP

Eradicating disease and helping blind people gain sight may feel overwhelming if you're just trying to hit next quarter's numbers. Whether you're hacking humanity like the Not Impossible team, perpetrating cyberespionage from a windowless room, or pursuing a more manageable endeavor, like reshaping your product offerings to beat the competition, there is magic and inspiration in the crowd.

RAND, WHO?

When you need a solid map to get from one place to another, surely you turn to the most obvious and trusted source: Rand McNally.

Rand, Who? From 1856 until the end of the 20th century, Rand McNally was the leader in maps. The company had the best cartographers in the world, and distributed everything from railroad maps and U. S. river maps to city guides and road atlases. They had retail travel stores in 29 major cities and were the first company to embrace a numbering system for U. S. highways. The company was synonymous with maps and geography, and was the go-to source for academics, consumers, and businesses alike.

Despite their massive team of over 4,000 people across four business groups, ultimately they couldn't match the brainpower of the crowd. When interactive maps such as MapQuest hit the scene, Rand McNally was still able to hold their ground. In fact, they were a leader in embracing technology, creating one of the first digital maps back in 1982. They were able to keep up with tech, but it was the crowd that left them in the dust.

Born over 100 years later in a small town in Israel, a new mapping company took a different approach. Instead of the broadcast model of designing and selling maps from trained experts to the general public, Waze inverted the model. Their approach was to offer a free mapping platform in which consumers themselves became the source of value. As customers used the free mobile app, which offered basic functions such as road maps and driving directions, the insight from users became the inherent value. The map service becomes more powerful through the crowd of its users – the more people interact, the more value they create.

Users report information in an easy-to-use interface, which provides other users important insight. People update the map in real time, which offers things that Rand McNally could never provide – car accidents, traffic jams, speed and police traps all pop up as an alert to the user, who can then select alternative routes. Waze also identifies the lowest cost fueling options to a user along her route. Anonymous data, such as traffic speed and location, is gathered and sent back to the platform allowing it to self-improve on a continuous basis.

The contrast in utility for a map user is stark. Rand McNally's maps are crafted and printed, designed internally, and then distributed to users. Waze, on the other hand, leverages the power of the crowd to update their mapping solution continuously. The world-class cartographers at Rand McNally are no match for the now 60 million people using and updating Waze in real time.

The glaring contrast is also evident in each company's business performance. Rand McNally suffered through years of setbacks and layoffs. As the revenue dwindled, so did the workforce, which shrank from a peak of nearly 5,000 people down to just 200 today. The company was bought and sold, each time for a significant reduction in price, and succumbed to Chapter 11 bankruptcy. Waze, on the other hand, rose quickly against giant competitors such as Apple Maps, MapQuest, Facebook, and Google Maps. The company was purchased by Google in 2013, just seven years after its humble beginnings, for $1.1 billion.

Business models based on **Crowdsourcing** abound. Wikipedia upended Encyclopedia Britannica, WorldBook, and Microsoft's Encarta by leveraging millions of people to author their content. UTest is a platform of over 35,000 professionals that offers software testing services for companies looking to take their quality to the next level. The value of Yelp, TripAdvisor, and Angie's List is derived from the collective wisdom of millions of people contributing opinions and insights, which in turn provides a more robust alternative to traditional review services such as Zagat's, Fodor's Travel Guides, and the Yellow Pages, respectively.

DO US A FLAVOR

Your entire business need not be a community platform to benefit from the crowd. Take a traditional CPG company like Frito Lay's namesake brand, Lay's Potato Chips. Not in a position to crowdsource production, distribution, or real-time data, they were able to leverage the power of **Crowdsourcing** through a clever campaign called "Do us a Flavor."

Launched in 2012, the company announced a contest for new chip flavors. Thousands of ideas were submitted from loyal chip fans for the chance to win a big prize and bragging rights if their chip recipe became a hit. The campaign was such a success that the company now continues to build on the concept each year. The 2013 winner, Cheesy-Garlic-Bread-flavored chips, contributed to an 8% sales increase in the three months after its release.

By 2015, things were really rolling. That year's challenge was to suggest flavors based on US cities. Suggestions came from every corner of the U. S. , including the Philly cheesesteak, Buffalo's chicken wings, and Chicago's deep-dish pizza. The winner would receive $1 million or 1% of the flavor's net sales for the first year, whichever amount was higher. Tens of thousands of ideas flooded into Lay's, which not only became a source of innovation but also a powerful mechanism for consumer engagement. The contest raised awareness, captured media attention, and helped the brand stand out in a crowded category.

Finalists Greektown Gyro, West Coast Truffle Fries, and New York Reuben were eventually toppled in an online consumer vote, crowning Southern Biscuits and Gravy as the 2015 winner. The **Crowdsourcing** efforts spurred brand lift and ultimately profits. Continuing to build on momentum, the 2016 **Crowdsourcing** contest expanded to cover the globe. As of this writing, finalists include Chinese Szechuan Chicken, Greek Tzatziki, Indian Tikka Masala, and Brazilian Picanha. The ideas of the crowd, combined with providing an engaged sense of ownership to their customers, continues to drive delicious growth and profits for Lay's.

This hacking technique has already hit mainstream business. From electronics to air travel, you can see the **Crowdsourcing** technique at work. Samsung, a company previously known for its "walled-garden" mindset recently debuted the Open Innovation Center in Palo Alto. The center entices entrepreneurs and innovators to collaborate with Samsung by offering capital, support, working space, and other rewards. Air New Zealand also took a **Crowdsourcing** approach for the launch of its new 777-300 aircraft. By tapping their customers from around the world, Air New Zealand got ideas for cocktails, eye masks, seating configurations, food offerings, and even boarding processes. The influx of creativity allowed them to spice up their new plane, engage with customers, and set the bar for the airlines – like Emirates and Cathay Pacific – that quickly followed suit.

PICKAXES AND SHOVELS

During the California gold rush in the mid-1800s, most wide-eyed miners ended up broke. Those who profited the most during the rush weren't those in search of gold, but the ones who furnished the supplies. Motivated miners willing to risk it all for the promise of gold needed pickaxes, shovels, tents, provisions, and other tools of the trade. Far more than the dreamers themselves, the merchants who enabled that dream were the ones who made away with gold.

Similarly, many businesses are now providing the modern-day equivalent of tools and supplies to facilitate the **Crowdsourcing** trend. Transcriptic, a company based in the heart of Silicon Valley, offers biotech researchers the opportunity to "access a fully automated cell and molecular biology laboratory, all from the comfort of your web browser." The company allows people from all over the world to submit ideas and experiments through a simple web interface, and then the experiments are conducted inside an advanced laboratory environment. This provides an even playing field for people that would not ordinarily have access to millions of dollars of equipment and resources. Hackers at heart, Transcriptic democratizes science by allowing people around the globe the opportunity to pursue their scientific curiosity without the traditional barriers of time, lab space, equipment, materials, or staff.

The Emerald Cloud Lab, a competitive biotech lab just a few miles from Transcriptic, also enables biohackers from around the world to conduct experiments without traditional barriers. A 19-year old in Bulgaria can conduct a MALDI Mass Spectroscopy experiment, while a 72-year-old in Mumbai can use the lab for an Enzyme-Linked Immunosorbent Assay test. The Emerald Cloud Lab is actually a new division of an existing company, Emerald Therapeutics. Capitalizing on the **Crowdsourcing** trend, they decided to open up their existing laboratory to the masses, enabling deeper innovation. Concurrently, a new business line came to life, selling pickaxes and shovels to scientific innovators around the globe.

As you look to leverage the hacker approach of **Crowdsourcing**, explore the many ways it can deliver value for your organization. It may be a fresh business model, marketing contests, providing infrastructure to others in an effort to support the global shift toward the crowd, or it may be an expertly-designed piece of artwork.

Hacking as a business philosophy isn't something I cooked up as a trendy hook to make money, it's a set of principles that I see in the world and actively use in my own life. And whether you feel the physical weight of the printed book in your hands right now or you're swiping through the pages on a mobile device, you're seeing some of that hacking in action.

While we were putting the finishing touches on the text, it came time to pick a cover. For a few weeks, I'd gone back and forth with the folks at the publisher to discuss some thematic ideas. The publisher had a team of designers come up with a few covers for me to pick from. There was definitely one I liked better than the rest, but none of them were hitting it out of the park. So I opened the discussion up to my team to get their take.

To my surprise, they didn't like the one that I thought was in the lead. And they weren't totally sold on any of the options either. So I gathered their feedback and went back to the publisher. A few weeks later, I got another round of designs. Again, I opened it up to the team to get their feedback, and again, everyone was underwhelmed. Then the answer was so obvious, I couldn't believe I hadn't thought of it sooner. We needed to **Crowdsource** the cover. Even though I had already **Crowdsourced** ideas with my team, that was thinking way too small.

Ironically, before the cover debacle, I mentioned the site 99 Designs in **Chapter 3**, as an example of **Crowdsourcing**. So when it came time to **Crowdsource** a cover, they were the natural choice. The amazing folks at FastPencil, my progressive publisher, fully supported this unorthodox approach, even though it balked tradition. I put together a summary of the book and opened the floodgates. The contest ran for about a week and I got nearly 150 complete designs. Ultimately, the awesome cover in front of you came from a designer in Kosovo who goes by the name Arbëresh®. I could've settled on the first design I liked, without realizing the rest of my team didn't like it. I could've gone another few rounds with the publisher tweaking designs that we were never really sold on. Instead, I used the power of **Crowdsourcing** to bring in fresh ideas, save us all time, and, hopefully, wow my readers.

Embracing the hacker mindset that **Quantity Is a Force Multiplier**, tapping into a wide set of ideas from a diverse pool of contributors is a powerful mechanism to stoke the flames of business innovation. Since innovation often occurs at the combustion point of opposing views, the more divergent ideas you can bring to a challenge, the better your results will likely be. We must move far beyond the traditional hoarding of ideas and the "not invented here" mentality in order to meet today's challenges. It's the power of the crowd, not the power of one that holds real potential.

HACK STARTERS

1. Identify an innovation problem of your own and think how you can geometrically expand the source of ideas by leveraging the crowd. Could you create a contest? Could you tap into an existing crowd platform to secure a large and diverse set of ideas?

2. Looking at your current problem-solving strategies, give an honest assessment of where you stand on the closed-to-crowd continuum. If you're not yet comfortable seeking input from millions, how could you expand your group by 20%, 50%, or 80% to solicit a broader perspective?

3. In your business, have you built systems or infrastructure that you could sell to the crowd (your own version of pickaxes and shovels)? If you have a large sales team, perhaps you could allow others to access it to sell their goods and services to your customers while you take a piece of the action. Do you have a facility, equipment, or technology that sits dormant at times and could be re-sold to others in the crowd?

CHAPTER 7: THE EXPLOIT

 All it took was a tiny hole in the fortress of security surrounding the United States Transportation Command (TRANSCOM) and they were in. Hackers working for the Chinese government identified a small opening by tricking a U. S. government contractor, and then used that opening to execute more than 20 breaches in the next 12 months. The break-ins resulted in compromised emails, documents, computer code, and user passwords. Stolen flight details, credentials, and passwords for encrypted emails put American lives at risk, considering TRANSCOM is involved in mobilizing and deploying U. S. troops and equipment worldwide.

The deviants didn't drive up to the TRANSCOM headquarters and storm the building, nor did they pull a grab-and-go all at once. Instead, they leveraged the **Exploit**, the hacking technique of finding a small opening and subsequently expanding it geometrically. It's that single loose string in a sweater that unravels the whole garment when pulled.

The Chinese hackers used a technique called Spear Phishing to find their single entry point. The tactic usually begins with an email from what appears to be a trusted source or a person of authority. NSA expert and visiting West Point instructor, Aaron J. Ferguson, refers to this as the "Colonel Effect." In an experiment to illustrate the power of this technique, he sent out an email to 500 cadets from the fictitious Colonel Robert Melville of West Point. The email instructed the cadets to click on a link to verify grades, so it appeared to be a legitimate and relevant request from a trusted source. In turn, over 80% of the recipients clicked the link, which is all the hacker needs to begin her exploit. One click and she's in.

Unlike a full frontal attack, in which the target has high visibility and immediately responds (the attack on Pearl Harbor, for example), an **Exploit** can be far more sinister. Since the initial breach is small, attacks can be executed over and over, right under the target's nose, going unnoticed until it's too late. In the same way a single cancer cell begins unseen and then replicates quickly, **Exploits** are a dangerous and highly effective tool of hackers.

THE HACKERS OF THE HACKERS GOT HACKED, BY THE HACKERS THEY HACK

Russian-based Kaspersky Lab is one of the top cybersecurity companies in the world. They protect over 400 million people and 270,000 businesses around the globe from cyberattacks through their software, technology, and services. They are on the forefront of stopping online threats – which makes the breach of their own systems all the more ironic.

Attackers penetrated Kaspersky's own networks in an effort to siphon intelligence about the crimes they were investigating. As *Wired* reported, "A case of the watchers watching the watchers who are watching them." The hackers also wanted to better understand the inner workings of Kaspersky's software so they could discover new ways to avoid detection.

The hackers didn't swarm Kaspersky in broad daylight. Instead, they started with one teeny breach. A single employee in one of the company's Asia-Pacific offices was targeted using the Spear Phishing approach. Once a miniscule opening was found, the deviants exploited their win. The first infected computer (known as "patient zero") quickly spread the malignant software to others in the network, replicating itself and growing exponentially. Through a single opening, the illicit software spread and grew, eventually becoming one of the largest, most complex and sophisticated bundles of code the company had ever seen. The software was written to cover its own tracks, tricking internal security systems and checkpoints into believing that everything was fine. The silent killer spread, allowing the hackers unprecedented access to sensitive information. Highly confidential information about large corporations in Belgium and a power plant in India were nothing compared to the grand prize: the ability to spy on Iran's nuclear talks with the UN Security Council. As their **Exploit** grew in scope, the hackers were able to hijack audio from "secure" teleconferences, access travel itineraries of dignitaries, and gain complete access to some of the most sensitive information in the world.

A small, undetected opening that initially appears innocuous can ultimately lead to profound results.

LEGIT FLIP

You're trying to grow your business and accelerate your career, not topple political regimes or discover nuclear launch codes (I hope). In your efforts to drive innovation, growth, and transformation, the **Exploit** can be a powerful approach for your legitimate business objectives.

THE SWEET SOUNDS OF INNOVATION

Amar was downright fed up. As a graduate student at MIT in the late 1950s, he was light on cash. Scrimping and saving, the audiophile had finally been able to purchase a top-of-the-line stereo system, hoping to enjoy some high-quality tunes with his friends. But after months of sacrifice to afford the stereo, he was deeply disappointed with the sound quality. What he hoped would sound like a concert hall, more closely resembled a loudspeaker in a subway station.

This led Amar to conduct extensive research into audio systems and the way the human ear experiences sound. The prevailing wisdom at the time was that sound quality was a function of power and speaker size, but Amar wasn't convinced. He came to the conclusion that the principal weakness was the manner in which sound transferred from a speaker to the human ear, as it bounced off walls and other objects in a room. It wasn't just the sound itself, but rather the way the sound waves travelled and the role the listener played in that transfer. This was his solitary opening – a single fresh approach that balked tradition. He designed just one product, the 2201 model, which was a completely different type of speaker. It used a connected group of 22 small speakers pointed in different directions to simulate the impact and quality of a much larger system. This sole invention put Dr. Amar G. Bose on the map. Next came the **Exploit**.

A novel approach to a speaker in 1964 wasn't exactly historical, and if Bose had stopped there, his name wouldn't be synonymous with high quality audio. Rather than sitting back and enjoying the spoils from his one innovation, Bose used the hacking technique of the **Exploit** to make history. Building off of his first product, he further refined the concept to launch the Bose 901 in 1968. This model became a commercial hit and is still manufactured today, nearly 50 years later. The company expanded in the following decade and became the standard by which others were measured in high quality audio.

The **Exploit** continued as Bose released the industry's first custom-engineered automotive sound system in 1983 for several General Motors vehicles. A host of other products followed that leveraged the same opening Dr. Bose discovered when founding the company: Bose noise cancelling headphones are the standard for pilots and air travelers worldwide; the wireless Bose Mini, a small Bluetooth speaker that delivers concert-quality audio is one of the most highly coveted accessories for smart phones of all types. Bose has a leadership position in home theater audio, commercial sound systems, musical amplification, PA systems, and even computer speakers. Bose systems have been used at the Olympics in Canada and France, and are the sound systems at the Sistine Chapel in Rome and the Great Mosque in Mecca. With over 11,000 employees and $3.4 billion in revenue, the Bose Corporation continues to exploit an innovation that was born from the frustration of a grad student.

HILLARY HOOCH AND TRUMP TONIC

Avery's Beverages – a company founded in a red Connecticut barn over 100 years ago – was struggling. When Sherman Avery started making handcrafted soda back in 1904, he wasn't facing the crushing competitive pressure of industry giants like Coca-Cola and Pepsi. The root beer and ginger ale he made didn't need a celebrity endorsement or a Super Bowl halftime sponsorship; customers loved it based on the simplicity of good old-fashioned cane sugar and natural flavoring.

But over the years, the fierce marketplace of carbonated beverages became too much for this small-town producer. To make ends meet, the company started offering bottled water and by their centennial anniversary, 5-gallon bottled water deliveries were the lion's share of revenue. Sure, they were scraping by, but the business was as flat as a week-old bottle of uncapped cola. Things were so bad, that the company was strongly considering dropping the soda business altogether and just focusing on water.

For fun, in 2008, Avery Beverages tried a little experiment in conjunction with the presidential election cycle – they produced a small batch of Barack O'Berry and John McCream sodas. The whimsical new offerings immediately sold out. Instead of chalking it up to good luck and buckling back down in the 5-gallon water business, the leaders at Avery saw this as their opening to hack. While their quality had always been good, getting their message to stand out above the overwhelming competitive noise had been nearly impossible until now. They realized that fun, themed flavors and names could help garner publicity, customer attention, and sales. Linda's Smackdown Soda and Dick's Blue Menthol were sold during the 2010 Connecticut senate race between Republican Linda McMahon and Democrat Dick Blumenthal. Upon the news that Osama Bin Laden had been killed in 2011, the company quickly launched So Long Osama, a blood orange soda.

The **Exploit** continued with the launch of their Totally Gross Sodas. "Dedicated to the ten-year-old in all of us," flavors include Dog Drool, Bug Barf, Zombie Brain-Juice, and Monster Mucus. These "SODAsgusting®" flavors became an instant hit among kids, college students, and curious adults. Swamp Juice, the first flavor in the series, "looks like bog water, but tastes like Skittles," according to Avery's operations manager Will Dunn.

Sales and excitement grew with the 2012 launch of Crème De Mitt, as Mitt Romney challenged Obama for the presidency. When the New England Patriots made headlines for "Deflategate," Avery responded by launching Deflated Ball Brew. Today, the company is always on the lookout for topical and newsworthy ideas to inspire new flavors and names.

With the controversial 2016 Presidential election, Avery enjoyed a 35% boost in revenue by launching fresh flavors dedicated to the candidates – Hillary Hooch, with the exact flavors listed as "classified," and Trump Tonic, a grape soda with extra acidity boasting the tagline, "Make America Grape Again." Both flavors have been flying off the shelves and fueling Avery's growth and success. They discovered a small opening – themed beverages – and then leveraged the hacking technique of **Exploiting** to continuously expand their initial gain.

Too often, innovation efforts are conceived of as the corporate equivalent of a military shock-and-awe assault. Innovation Hackers, on the other hand, embrace the mindset of **Compasses Over Maps**, fostering curiosity and exploration. They are constantly on the prowl for little openings, threads that can be pulled and pulled. They prefer dozens or hundreds of small tests to massive and risky bets, and only double down when they've been successful in one of these endeavors. As you seek to tackle your own innovation challenges in any aspect of your business, run as many experiments as possible, find your opening, and then exploit the hell out of it.

HACK STARTERS

1. What little experiments have you tried that have shown early promise? How could you use the **Exploit** technique to further progress and expand their impact?

2. Isolate one functional area of your business such as sales, production, marketing, HR, or technology, and brainstorm five micro-experiments that could yield fresh results. Run the prototypes and measure the outcomes with the precision of a scientist. When you identify the one that performs best, brainstorm another five micro-experiments that could further expand your top-performing idea. Measure those, select the best performer at this new stage, and repeat the process: find a small window of promise, brainstorm five ideas to layer on top of it, measure, select the top performer, and try another five subsequent experiments to further the **Exploit**. Continue repeating the process until the value from the initial spark has been fully realized.

3. Comparing yourself to your direct competitors, what is one small area of advantage or differentiation that you enjoy? If you doubled down on it, how could you exploit the little advantage into something much bigger? What are three ways you could pry open that small gain into a competitive advantage that defines you?

Chapter 8: Borrowing

 Back in the day, the gangs in Milwaukee were known by their numbers. The 1-9s could be distinguished from the 2-7s since the numbers corresponded to the street names of the territory they controlled. While typical crimes such as petty theft and drug sales were carried out by the normal street gangs, it was the 414s that made history.

The infamous "gang," which included Gerald Wondra, Neal Patrick, and Tim Winslow, looked nothing like what you'd imagine. Pocket protectors, high-powered calculators, and large eyeglasses distinguished the 414s from the typical colored bandanas, gold chains, and baggy jeans. In fact, these three were nothing like you'd expect. These high schoolers were enamored with computers instead of handguns, and their meek physical appearance couldn't intimidate a chipmunk.

In the summer of 1983, the 414s formed out of a computer club, with only benign intentions. They didn't want to rough anyone up or create any harm; they were just curious kids looking to push the boundaries of what they could accomplish with their primitive computers. In the same way I programmed my Atari 800 in the early '80s to try various calling card codes, the 414s (named for the Milwaukee area code) directed their computers to randomly dial numbers looking for other computers to engage. Once they identified a computer randomly, the remote system would often identify itself. Scrolling across their green screen displays, the name of the organization and the type of operating system would appear. At the time, cybersecurity was a non-existent field, making it incredibly easy to breach systems across the country.

For the 414s, they would stumble on a system that piqued their curiosity, such as a bank or hospital, and then they challenged themselves to crack through the simple passwords. Remarkably, the generic system passwords that shipped with software were available by reviewing software manuals in the library. More surprising, many administrators never bothered to change the default setting. So if a system identified itself as GW-BASIC, the 414s could discover and then try out the default password that shipped with the software. Easily breakable passwords such as "SystemSystem" or "Administrator" actually worked, giving the young hackers unbridled access.

This rudimentary approach allowed them to break into the Sloan Kettering Cancer Center in New York, gaining access to patient records, life support systems, and billing info. They hacked into a multinational bank and got through to the servers that controlled large-scale money transfers. They accessed their local electric company, gaining the ability to shut down the power grid. With unfettered access, they could have committed large-scale crimes and done unimaginable damage. But these were kids looking for fun, not hardened criminals. Instead of causing real harm, they would instruct a printer at the New York hospital to start spitting out hundreds of sheets of paper, just for laughs. Or they'd play pranks on one another inside these secure systems, leaving clues or playing hide-and-seek. The violations were barely noticed, until they took it too far.

Inspired by the movie *War Games*, in which Matthew Broderick's character – a high school misfit – cleverly hacked into NORAD (North American Aerospace Defense Command), the 414s viewed it as a challenge. Believing in the hacker mindset that **Every Barrier Can Be Penetrated**, they set out to use their smarts to hack the U. S. government's nuclear program. With no intention of actually launching an attack, their goal was simply bragging rights, proving their intelligence. It was the same motivation of trying to solve a complicated jigsaw puzzle, but on a much more dangerous scale.

Law enforcement officials were stunned not to find a sophisticated ring of Russian spies as the FBI raided the homes of each adolescent boy. When his younger sister answered the door and shouted upstairs, "Neal...the FBI is here to see you," the teenager knew it had gone too far. Neal, Gerald, and Tim, suburban kids from decent homes, had been caught hacking into the Los Alamos National Laboratory, one of only two sites in the U. S. where nuclear weapon research and testing was conducted.

Their approach was a **Borrowed** idea, in this case, borrowed from a movie. Borrowed ideas are not only a technique of hackers, but have been an important source of innovation throughout history. The basic premise begins with observation in a situation outside your specific challenge. You may gain inspiration from the arts, nature, other industries, or related problems. After a pattern or concept is recognized, it is then **Borrowed** and applied to the task at hand. Henry Ford's groundbreaking automotive assembly line was actually a concept borrowed from the meat packing industry. With Uber's success in on-demand ground transportation, a whole host of companies have emerged trying to become the Uber of healthcare, tailoring, accounting, and cold pressed juice. **Borrowing** ideas or inspiration from outside your industry or sphere of influence and then applying it to your present-day situation can become a favorite technique when looking to drive innovation.

The 414s were arrested, but at that time there were no cybersecurity laws on the books under which to prosecute. Since they didn't do any damage, they couldn't be prosecuted for crimes under the penal codes of the day. Ultimately, they each received a $500 fine and two years of probation, with the stipulation that they couldn't use a modem. The story of a couple suburban teens actually hacking into the highly guarded nuclear lab at Los Alamos quickly became a media sensation as Neal Patrick (the youngest member of the 414s) appeared on *The Today Show*, CBS *News*, and *Crossfire* in addition to landing on the cover of *Newsweek*. Patrick testified in front of Congress at age 17, which eventually led to the passing of six cybercrime laws that are still on the books today. All due to the clever deployment of a **Borrowed** idea.

Borrowing can work in many directions. You may be stuck on how to motivate your customer service agents and then discover a fresh approach by learning how zookeepers manage herds of rhinos. The manufacturing problem that's perplexed the engineers for months may be conquered by **Borrowing** ideas from the way Indy 500 pit crews conduct tire changes in record time. **Borrowed** ideas may even help you decide what to pursue next.

Hackers in the Houston area were looking for new ways to use their skills for illicit profit. Many of the examples we've covered so far involve a cybercriminal hacking into another computer via the Internet and instructing it to do something bad (transfer money, provide confidential info, etc.). In this case, the Texan hackers borrowed a different crime and then applied it to their skillset. Having seen on TV and movies the sloppy way cars are stolen – crudely cutting wires or jamming a screwdriver into the ignition – these hackers envisioned a less clumsy technique as an alternative. **Borrowing** their target (cars) and applying it back to their craft (hacking), they developed a much more elegant approach. Armed with only a laptop, they figured out a way to plug their portable computers into Jeep and Dodge vehicles that were left unlocked, and then start the ignition and drive away. In less than 14 seconds. This **Borrowed** hack allowed them to get away with the theft of over 30 vehicles before getting caught on camera and ultimately arrested for their crimes.

LEGIT FLIP

One of the greatest artists in history, Leonardo da Vinci, was also one of history's greatest inventors and its earliest hackers. From *The Last Supper* to the *Mona Lisa*, da Vinci clearly had a gift for capturing both reality and imagination. Another of da Vinci's gifts was creating detailed plans for inventions, which at the time, had to seem nothing short of batshit crazy. In the 1400s, when many people were scared that bathing would give them diseases, da Vinci was drawing out plans for armored chariots and a 33-barrel machine gun. Some of da Vinci's most outlandish creations featured **Borrowing** heavily. Today, one of his better known concepts was a flying machine; this machine incorporated structural elements from birds and bats to create the wings. Another design? A humanesque robot, which of course drew heavily from human anatomy to enable its movements. Sadly, most of da Vinci's inventions were never even attempted. But, you don't have to be bogged down by the unethical motives of criminal hackers or the unfortunate bathing habits of 15th century Italy, you can use **Borrowing** at will to make bring your innovation to life.

SPRAY PAINT, TATTOOS, AND OCTOPI

If the last 25 years were the era of IT transformation, it's been suggested that the next 25 will be healthcare's day in the sun. With major advances in biotech, stem cell research, nanotechnology, advanced drug therapy research, and wearable devices, the way we live and how treat the sick is poised for massive transformation. And the source of many breakthroughs already underway is the **Borrowing** tactic.

Dr. Jörg Gerlach, a German physician and researcher, focused his life's work on skin cell treatments, transplants, and devices. He spent years helping patients recover from a variety of traumas, often due to severe burns. Serious burns are one of the most painful injuries humans endure – they often take months to heal and are treated by complex skin grafts, which are prone to infection. The grafts often involve human cadaver skin, which is not only painful but also a bit creepy. Serious burns may never heal completely, often resulting in unsightly scars and years of complications.

Looking to advance his field and provide much-needed relief to patients, Dr. Gerlach employed the hacker technique of **Borrowing**. Instead of looking for new ideas within the existing treatment options, Gerlach tapped into a most unlikely source of inspiration: spray paint. Observing how graffiti artists use spray cans to evenly dispense paint when tagging buildings in urban settings, Dr. Gerlach borrowed the concept and applied it to treating burns. His invention, the SkinGun, closely resembles an electronic spray gun, and uses a mixture of saline solution and self-donated stem cells from a burn victim. The mist is evenly applied to a burn, allowing fresh layers of skin to regrow quickly. The process eliminates infection, reduces pain, and decreases the healing time of a serious burn from six or more agonizing months down to a couple of days. Plus, the end result is a far better outcome, often completely avoiding any scarring.

In a video produced by *National Geographic*, Dr. Gerlach demonstrates the power of the SkinGun. Matthew Uran suffered horrible burns after a mishap at a Fourth of July bonfire. According to medical journalist Sabrina Bachai, "The side of his body was completely burned, and his arm looked like a piece of charred meat, like someone had left a hot dog on the flame too long." Instead of taking months of painful healing, the SkinGun was used and Matthew's body had completely healed within 48 hours.

Too often, we double-down on existing practices when looking to advance our efforts. But as creativity expert Edward de Bono famously said, "You can't look in a new direction by looking harder in the same direction." Dr. Gerlach discovered a new and better idea by looking outside his field of study. By observing a different concept in spray paint and then borrowing it for his own pursuits, he was able to create incredible impact for patients. In addition, in 2013 he was able to sell the SkinGun technology and related processes to RenovaCare, Inc., a company committed to worldwide distribution of this important medical device. Dr. Gerlach did well *and* did good, by borrowing an idea from an unlikely and totally unrelated arena.

Like Dr. Gerlach, Amay Bandodkar spends a lot of time with skin. Instead of regrowth, Amay along with a team of nanoengineers at the University of California, San Diego, is focused on using skin as a sensor to provide important medical information to both patients and healthcare professionals. Frustrated with current methods to check glucose levels in diabetic patients, graduate student Bandodkar knew there had to be a better way. Currently, most people with diabetes use small pinpricks to draw blood and then test the blood droplet with an expensive machine to monitor and control their levels. This process often has to be repeated multiple times per day. Due to the discomfort, inconvenience, and costs, many patients forgo regular testing, resulting in serious medical complications and even fatality in extreme cases.

Bandodkar tapped into **Borrowing** to invent a far better approach. With the support of Professor Joseph Wang's lab at the Nanoengineering Department and the Center for Wearable Sensors, Bandodkar built a prototype from a concept that may seem antithetical to healthcare: tattoos. What if they could build a wearable, temporary tattoo that could measure glucose levels through the fluid in between skin cells? Named by *Mashable* as one of "26 Incredible Innovations That Improved the World in 2015," early prototypes have delivered encouraging results. The disposable tattoos are painless, easy to use for patients, and cost only a few cents per day, far less than traditional glucose testing systems. As development continues, the team hopes to integrate the tattoos with mobile devices, providing accurate, numerical readouts in real time. The system will also be able to monitor levels and send alerts to the patient, family members, or healthcare professionals if levels exceed specified thresholds.

Across the pond, researchers in the Department of Informatics Centre for Robotics Research (CoRe) at King's College, London, were looking into their own **Borrowed** solution. The team was focused on complex surgical procedures and the devices used to conduct them. Specifically, they were concerned with the limitations of modern macroscopic and robot-assisted surgical systems, which had difficulty maneuvering in confined spaces. The devices tended to be too stiff – potentially damaging internal organs or being unable to reach certain areas during a surgery – or they were too floppy, lacking the rigidity needed to conduct the procedures.

Rather than looking within their own field, the research team pursued the concept of Biomimicry: human-made processes, devices, substances, or systems that imitate nature. Their inspiration came from examining animal movements, including the elephant trunk and octopus arm. The team marveled in the ability of an octopus' arm to quickly transform from stiff to floppy – at times, regions of the same arm could take on different levels of rigidity. This borrowed idea allowed the team to invent the STIFF-FLOP (STIFFness controllable Flexible and Learnable manipulator for surgical OPerations). They essentially created a robotic version of an octopus' arm that can execute more precise, less risky surgical maneuvers.

Biomimicry is a fancy term for an old hacking technique – borrowing ideas, patterns, or concepts from the wild, like da Vinci did for his many imaginings. As the trend increases in popularity, unlikely agents have joined forces to advance innovation. The San Diego Zoo launched a Center for Bioinspiration, helping corporate clients discover inspiration in nature. Academic institutions such as the University of Akron and Arizona State University now offer Biomimicry programs for students and fee-based research for corporations.

Anthony Brennan, a professor of materials science and engineering at the University of Florida, was trying to figure out how to prevent barnacles from sticking to ship hulls. Instead of studying shipbuilding techniques or boat-coating materials, Brennan looked to nature. He observed that whales notoriously pick up large quantities of barnacles, but similarly sized sharks attract none. Further exploration of sharks led to the insight that microscopic textures on sharkskin ward off both barnacles and bacteria. This insight led to the formation of his company, Sharklet Technologies, that recreates shark textures for a variety of surfaces. Today, business is booming as he's protecting medical devices, office desks, iPhone cases, and hospital countertops. "People are surprised that we found such an elegant, environmentally friendly solution from such a fierce predator," said CEO Mark Spiecker in an interview with *Inc.*

A BLAZIN' BORROW

When I go to Subway for lunch, I'm a "turkey, no cheese, all the veggies except onions and olives, with a little bit of light mayo" kind of guy. While at Chipotle, I'm more of a "yes, I know the guac costs extra" sort of person. The beauty of both of these places is the intersection of inexpensive, fast, and customized. Some patrons choose to start with a menu staple and doctor it up, while others elect to start from scratch and build something of their own design. This intersection has taken the food industry by storm, spreading beyond the sandwich or burrito and into salads, with SweetGreen and Chopt (plus my hometown Detroit's own 7Greens). Mongolian barbeque locations have popped up to take your stir fry bowl to the next level; even frozen yogurt is now done your way with chains such as Orange Leaf and Menchies expanding rapidly.

But when Rick and Elise Wetzel (Wetzel's Pretzels founders) looked for a similar concept in the world of pizza, they struck out. Pizza places were either fast and rigid (the Little Caesar's $5.00 hot-and-ready pizza with no customization) or personalized and slow (order ahead or sit down restaurants). The "in between" was readily available ground for the taking. In a big-chain culinary world of fast customization, the Wetzels salivated at the opportunity.

Ultimately, they decided to start their own chain to fill this void, using the **Borrowing** tactic. Like Henry Ford, the Wetzels continued the tradition of borrowing an assembly line process from others, like Subway and Chipotle. Their **Borrowing** brainchild was named Blaze Pizza. Blaze allows you to customize your pizza, with choices ranging from cheese to proteins, from vegetables to sauces. As you work your way down the assembly line, staff assist at each step; when you get to the end of the line, your custom-built pizza is cooked in a stone-hearth oven in record time.

The trick to adopting assembly-line customization to pizza was to break the barrier of speed. The crew needed to apply NASCAR-fast speed to an item that typically needs to 12-40 minutes of baking time. The breakthrough – thin crust pizzas baked in a special-built, extremely hot oven (900+ degrees, 60,000 BTUs) – brings a masterpiece to life in only *three minutes.*

The founders of Blaze broke through the roadblock via their unwillingness to accept traditional constraints (not being able to cook pizza fast enough) and embraced the hacker mindset that **Every Barrier Can Be Penetrated**. They displayed a **Compasses Over Maps** approach by setting out to crack the challenge without a specific route in mind. After the Wetzels recognized a market gap, they needed tremendous courage – and belief that **Competence Is the Only Credential That Matters** – to take on the behemoths of the pizza industry. They weren't dissuaded by their small standing among the pizza giants, but rather driven to transform an industry based on their better offering. They discovered a vulnerability of the big guys that could be exploited with a fresh, bold approach.

The **Borrow** continued. Looking at trends that were capturing consumers, the Blaze team observed several dining crazes that could be borrowed. Craft beer, exotic lemonades, and cane sugar sodas? Check. Environmentally sustainable packaging and sourcing? Got it. Healthy, locally-sourced ingredients, made-from-scratch dough, artisanal craftsmanship? Borrowed. To a great degree, the entire business was a **Borrow**, from the white hot category of pizza, to the assembly line production, to the customized experience, and everything in between. While the ideas have been borrowed, their success has been handcrafted. Blaze Pizza is now recognized as the leading fast-casual pizza chain and has attracted investment from celebrities including LeBron James, Maria Shriver, and movie producer John Davis. In August 2016, just four years after their founding, the company opened their 150th store, making them the fastest restaurant ever to achieve that milestone.

BEYONCÉ, MAD MEN, AND YODA

We've explored the notion of borrowing ideas for products, services, and processes from other industries, nature, and the arts. Building on that foundation, **Borrowed** thinking can be another powerful weapon in your innovation arsenal.

One version of **Borrowed** thinking is a technique I call the Different Lens. To begin, brainstorm a list of people, industries, or perspectives. Examples may include: an archaeologist, a 4-year-old, someone living 200 years in the future, Elon Musk, a Navy SEAL, a zoologist, Brad Pitt, Picasso, a professional bowling champion. The more diverse and strange, the better. Next, take a stack of index cards and write one name or role from your list on the back of each. You're now armed for a Different Lens brainstorm session. First, clearly articulate the real-world challenge you're facing. Perhaps it is developing a new product to combat a competitive launch. Maybe you're looking for a way to improve closing rates throughout your sales force, attract and retain Millennial workers, or reduce error-rates in your manufacturing plant. Once the challenge has been identified, turn over one card. If the card reads "architect," the group brainstorms how an architect would approach their real-world challenge. Once the ideas start to dwindle, flip over the next card and look at the problem through the next lens. Instead of thinking about how your competition is solving this problem, think about how Beyoncé would slay it. Before long, you and your team will see the problem in a whole new light, and by borrowing the thinking from others, you'll gain a fresh perspective that will lead to the innovative solutions you seek. And the Different Lens is just the beginning of what's possible with **Borrowed** thinking.

The company I founded in 1999 and later sold in 2012 was called ePrize. Part technology firm and part marketing agency, we built and managed digital promotions for some of the largest brands in the world such as Coca-Cola, Nike, P&G, and Microsoft. At one point, we had the opportunity to win a very large piece of business from a major Consumer Packaged Goods advertiser. To snag the account, we were pitching ideas head-to-head against several other creative agencies that represented some of the best thinking in marketing. The client would decide who got the account based on the quality and creativity of ideas submitted by each contender.

So there we were, brainstorming away in a windowless room. Unfortunately, our ideas were rather lackluster. After hours of toiling, we were simply rehashing old concepts and making very little progress. I could feel the account slipping away from us. We needed originality; this was certainly not the time to **Borrow**. Or was it? Instead of borrowing our actual concepts, we decided to borrow our thinking. Realizing that we needed a mindset shift, we embarked upon my favorite brainstorming technique: RoleStorming.

The problem with most brainstorm sessions is that only the safe ideas are shared. Fear creeps into the room, and we end up talking ourselves out of our most creative thoughts. The thinking goes something like this: "I have a wild idea. But what will my boss say? What if I look like an idiot? What if they like my idea, but it fails? What does that mean to my career? Too risky...I better keep my mouth shut."

To conquer this fear and liberate big ideas, RoleStorming is the perfect antidote. Instead of brainstorming as *yourself*, you brainstorm *in character*. To use the Different Lens method, you brainstorm what a person might say; in Rolestorming, you become that person – you think, move, speak like them – and you solve the problem as them. Imagine RoleStorming as Steve Jobs. No one will laugh at Steve for coming up with a big idea. In fact, they may laugh at Steve for coming up with a small one. So you (Steve Jobs) are free to share your wildest ideas with no fear of retribution. To RoleStorm, just pick someone other than yourself and pretend you are that person during the idea generation process. In other words, borrow the perspective and psyche of someone else and invite them to your meeting.

You could pretend to be JFK, Oprah, or Thomas Edison. You could play the role of Gandhi, Adele, Winston Churchill, or Steph Curry. Bring Angela Merkel, Frederick Douglass, or Wayne Gretzky to your meeting. Get Jay Z, Lisa Ling, or even da Vinci himself to help you land the deal (though you may have to brush up on your Italian). The trick is to fully embrace how they may solve your actual problem and leave your own self, ego, and fear behind. For the best results, everyone needs to have a role, then all egos and negativity are left at the door, and you have a powerhouse meeting opportunity. You certainly won't have trouble with meeting attendance.

Back at my shop, our breakthrough came when we RoleStormed as the characters from the hit TV show *Mad Men*. What better inspiration than immersion in a racy ad agency in the 1960s, during the golden era of Madison Avenue marketing? One of us pretended to be the handsome and creative Don Draper. Another took on the role of the often drunk Roger Sterling. As our team embraced different roles, we borrowed the thinking of the *Mad Men* characters and it broke our creativity loose. Borrowing their mindsets, we quickly generated fresh ideas and ended our deadlock of stale, mediocre thinking. The ideas generated from this RoleStorming session, along with some *Mad-Men*-inspired props used during the pitch, were the key to winning the multimillion-dollar account. While the ideas were original, they were born of **Borrowing**.

Years later, while working with a group of executives, I met the most formal man I'd ever seen. Dark suit, pressed white shirt, conservative tie; this guy was stiff as a board. My responsibility for the workshop was to facilitate creativity, but how was I going to get this human statue to let loose? I decided to conduct a RoleStorming exercise, and before I knew it, Mr. Formal was playing the role of Yoda. I had never seen a personal transformation like this before – within a few minutes, his jacket was off, tie was undone, and he was leaping around the room like a schoolboy. Most importantly, the white boards were filled with new ideas. I didn't teach him to be creative; he had that inside him all along. We all do. The barrier was the role that he played in his company and in his culture; a role that forbid such playful experimentation. By changing that role and having him borrow the mindset of Yoda, this formal exec was able to bring fresh thinking to the forefront. When using the **Borrowing** technique, the combinations – and the possibilities – are endless.

HACK STARTERS

1. Identify an important challenge you're facing and then explore how you can **Borrow** ideas from outside your field to uncover innovative solutions. First, simply observe patterns and approaches, and then look for concepts that can be borrowed and brought to life. Cycle through the various sources we've covered:

    a. The arts (music, painting, movies, literature, sculpture, etc.)

    b. Nature (Biomimicry)

    c. Completely unrelated industries (if you're a landscape architect, what could you borrow from the world of fashion, sports, biotech, or software engineering?)

    d. Related industries but not direct competitors (how Blaze Pizza borrowed the custom assembly line from Subway)

    e. Trends (observing trends in customer behavior, population shifts, media consumption, etc.; see what patterns can be borrowed from changes or trends in the marketplace)

    f. Other geographies, countries, or timeframes (how would someone in Beijing solve our challenge compared to someone in Belize? How would this opportunity be tackled 20 years ago or 50 years from now?)

2. Try **Borrowed** thinking to attack a problem or opportunity you're facing. Take the Different Lens or RoleStorming exercises for a test run in an effort to bring completely different approaches to your most pressing issues.

Chapter 9: Deconstruct

By the time I turned 10 years old, I was hooked. My vice wasn't cigarettes or girly magazines like many of my friends – I was obsessed with BMX bikes. I had posters on my walls, subscribed to all the dirt bike magazines, and loved everything about these tricked-out two-wheelers. I didn't just want to marvel in the colorful designs. As an enthusiast, I wanted to understand how they worked, how they were built, and how they performed best. And not content to be just a spectator, I wanted to participate.

Not the best rider on the block, I focused my energies on the bikes themselves. One day, after receiving a brand new Mongoose brand BMX bike for a holiday gift, my parents were horrified when they returned home and saw that I had completely disassembled my new prized possession. I didn't just pop off the seat and handlebars; I took apart the crank, ball-bearings, brakes, chain, and gear system. Unless something was welded together, I **Deconstructed** it. I could only truly understand the inner workings of my fascination by examining the way each part interacted with the next.

Once the bike was disassembled down to its core, individual elements, I could then tinker with variations. What if I Substituted a Shimano crank instead of the one supplied by Mongoose? What if I tried out different ball bearing configurations, a different mixture of grease to reduce friction, or those new lightning pedals from Diamondback? After months of tinkering and experimentation, I handcrafted an original. A unique concoction of various brands and parts, my bike was a sight to behold. While I never won a BMX race, I felt the same thrill of victory in the assembly of my custom wheels. I had improved upon what came before, through a potent combination of **Deconstruction** followed by Substitution.

Today, if I were to walk into a bike shop, I'd likely pull out my credit card, which contains a security chip. These chips are designed to prevent fraud and are heralded as being far superior to a traditional card with a magnetic strip.

In contrast to the way the strip works – transferring the same security code from the card with every use – the new chip-based cards use a different, random number for each transaction. The one-time codes are generated, validated, and then deleted after 60 seconds so that a working code can't be copied and reused by hackers looking to cash in.

As we've learned, hackers believe that **Any Barrier Can Be Penetrated.** So when the new chip-based credit cards appeared on the scene, it was an immediate opportunity to break through this new "unbreakable" standard. To accomplish this, a group of hackers began their mission by disassembling the new security protocol. What appeared impenetrable from the outside, had to have some vulnerability once examined in greater detail. The hackers **Deconstructed** the card, the code, the readers, and the cash registers. They took apart every aspect of the payment system at each step of the transaction process. When you **Deconstruct** something down to its fundamental elements, you can spot fresh opportunities for creativity and innovation. Here, the hackers sought one little thread that could be pulled, one piece of the puzzle that was loose enough to breach.

The opportunity came to light when examining that 60-second window where a randomized code was valid. If a hacker could break into a cash register or computer terminal during that period, they'd have one full minute to steal freely. If they could rig a cash register to wirelessly beam the valid code to a nearby device, their fraud could be perpetrated before the codes expired. A smartphone in close proximity could be standing by, ready to immediately make a mobile purchase. Or a nearby ATM machine could be waiting to receive valid codes and then process a cash withdrawal, confusing the data it receives with the presence of a physical card.

In a demonstration to show the vulnerability of the new chip system, Senior Security Research Manager Tod Beardsley of the cybersecurity firm Rapid 7, did just that – he rigged a cash register and a nearby ATM machine. As unsuspecting customers inserted their new snazzy credit cards into the reader, the ATM machine next door started spitting out $100 bills. By the time the demonstration was over, the floor was completely covered with dozens of fresh C-notes. No actual fraud was committed as the exercise was for demonstration only, but you can be sure that actual hackers are deploying similar techniques right now to scam unsuspecting victims out of their hard-earned cash. By first **Deconstructing** the target into its individual components (here, the credit card chip's payment authentication process) and then substituting variables (instead of transferring the valid code only to the merchant, duplicating it and sending the valid code to another source concurrently), the hack transpired.

The **Deconstruction** approach is a powerful tactic, especially when you think you're close. When you already have the tools, systems, or ideas that you need, but they're not quite right or not performing at their best, starting with **Deconstruction** allows you to honestly assess all of the pieces at your disposal. Then, working through possible solutions using Addition, Subtraction, and Substitution, you can harness the raw potential of your original idea in a new, unimagined way.

LEGIT FLIP

The term "hacker ethic" was coined by journalist Steven Levy in his 1984 book, *Hackers: Heroes of the Computer Revolution*. Speaking to the approach of **Deconstruction,** Levy writes, "Hackers believe that essential lessons can be learned about the systems – about the world – from taking things apart, seeing how they work, and using this knowledge to create new and more interesting things." **Deconstruction** is a process of creative discovery, a methodology for innovation and growth. And when used for legitimate purposes, a powerful engine of prosperity.

FUCI

It turns out, I'm not the only one with a bike obsession. "I just believe, and dream, that bikes can be so much more," said Robert Egger, creative director of bike-maker Specialized. "The bicycle for me personally, is the epitome of man and machine coming together. When they become one, it's unbelievable," Egger continued. "There's nothing else like it."

Starting with a passion for what could be and a healthy dose of hacker philosophy, Robert Egger set out to upend the status quo. "My belief is that there's no perfect design. The bicycle, although it's been around a long time, has much room for improvement. We can add so many great things...to make it much more than just a bicycle."

As in most industries, a governing body exists that defines the rules of what can and can't be done. In bicycle racing, it is called the Union Cycliste Internationale, or UCI. There are strict limitations and rules that govern acceptable practices for bike design, and the UCI has the ultimate say as to which bikes will be allowed in competitive races such as the Tour de France. Since hackers have a deep disdain for authority and believe rules are meant to be broken, Robert couldn't help but wonder what he could design if he tossed the rulebook in the trash. The result? The FUCI Bike. Yep, the name stands for "F*** the UCI."

In the same way I tinkered with my BMX bike back over 35 years ago, Robert Egger and his team deconstructed their beloved product down to the individual components, setting out to completely shatter acceptable practices. They examined every aspect of the bike's design and construction, from materials used to the very basics of bicycle manufacturing. They also deconstructed the UCI rulebook, taking apart each regulation and challenging themselves to defy them. If a rule was printed, the team sought to break it by taking a contrarian approach. But it wasn't just about thumbing their noses at the UCI, it was about imaging what a bike could be, what cyclists wanted their bikes to be.

According to Egger, "I hope that the FUCI bike is a small inclination towards what the bike industry can be. It's a concept for the future." To begin, the team looked at the most fundamental rule: that both wheels needed to be the same size. In true hacker form, the team decided on a design in which the back wheel – almost three feet in diameter – is significantly bigger than the front. The increased size leads to better performance in hilly conditions.

The rule-balking FUCI has headlights and brake lights, elements that are forbidden by the governing body, but clearly enhance safety for nighttime riding. These lights, along with a small motor that gives riders an extra boost when needed, are powered by another forbidden element: a lithium battery in the kickstand. Naturally, the bike has smartphone integration allowing real-time data about rides and routes, and doubling as a security feature, disabling the bike if the proper phone is not connected. The FUCI also has a small trunk for storing valuables, small tools, or spare parts.

According to UCI rules, "Any device, added or blended into the structure which has the effect of decreasing resistance to air penetration such as a protective screen" is strictly forbidden. Taunted by the rules, Egger and his team built a sleek windshield into the FUCI, which protects against flying bugs and road debris and also increases the aerodynamic nature of the bike.

While the bike is forbidden from use by the rule-happy governing body, it is a hit among consumers and enthusiasts. Beyond commercial success, it illustrates the power of bold, defiant thinking in action. It demonstrates what's possible by deconstructing existing orthodoxy, challenging assumptions, and then rebuilding in a fresh manner.

Had Schwinn embraced the same hacker approach on a continuous basis, the FUCI may have been invented by the old standard-bearer instead of Specialized, the new pioneer. In fact, Specialized has been hacking since the company was founded in 1974 by Mike Sinyard. Starting with a new take on bike tires – the Standard Touring Tire – the company followed with a string of disruptive innovations including the Stumpjumper, the first major production mountain bike in the world, now displayed at the Smithsonian Institution in Washington, DC. For Specialized to avoid the fate that ended up crippling Schwinn, they'll want to embrace Robert Egger's hacking philosophy as a core tenet to their culture. For you to enjoy sustainable success of your own, you'll want to do the same.

PROGRAMMING VS. PTSD

When Jerome Hardaway discharged from the Air Force, he had worked in special forces and on multiple deployments. From his specialized training, to his tours of combat, and his literal and figurative battle wounds, Hardaway returned to the civilian world much more skilled and knowledgeable than he had left it. Unfortunately, his return coincided with a recession. Transitioning veterans are given little enough assistance in finding their way back into civilian life, but a recession presented additional challenges in establishing the basic necessities, like employment and housing.

To get back on his feet, Jerome picked up a childhood interest – coding. While building his coding skills, Jerome began showing signs of PTSD and combat stress. He sought help from Veterans Administration (VA) resources in his local Memphis, but in order to receive assistance, vets already have to be in pretty dire straits. Hardaway describes it as needing to be at "rock bottom" before you can get help. Jerome was eventually able to find the treatment he needed, and voluntarily committed to a 6-month in-patient program.

Shortly after ending his program, Jerome was deeply moved when a young Army veteran, Justin Davis, was killed by police. Distraught after leaving the VA and believed to be suicidal, Davis was sitting in his car with a gun. Police engaged him and he was killed. There was much debate in the surrounding days about how the police handled Davis's situation, and larger issues about veterans with PTSD battling the transition to civilian life, and the lack of support available to them.

After Davis's death, Jerome learned that the VA and VA-sponsored organizations were not going to help with burial costs, and Davis's family was struggling to meet that burden. He leapt into action to help the family of this man he had never met, and raised around $10,000 to cover Davis's funeral. For Hardaway, the death of Justin Davis not only stressed the immediate need for transitional help, but reminded him of the barriers between veterans and the little help that does exist.

Within a few weeks, Hardaway's solution, FRAGO, was born. FRAGO is military jargon for plans changing on the fly – it means the mission has stayed the same, but the plans to achieve that mission have altered. In hacker terms, **Compasses Over Maps**: the destination is the same, but we're making a mid-course route correction.

FRAGO, now called #VetsWhoCode, was formed after **Deconstructing** the existing problem. According to Jerome's research, of the problems veterans face related to combat stress – homelessness, suicide, unemployment, etc. – 85% of those can be resolved by providing transitional assistance during the first 24-48 months. So, if these problems could be solved for most veterans via transitional assistance, that's what Hardaway would do: provide more widely-available help during those critical months of re-entry.

Jerome then **Deconstructed** "transitional assistance" and identified two areas that best set vets up for success: hard job skills, and the softer social skills to succeed in civilian workplaces. Next, Hardaway turned to Substitution. Instead of the menial, unskilled work usually offered to veterans, he thought he'd try offering programs based on his own interest, coding. He quickly realized that programming was a viable and lucrative career option for vets.

The #VetsWhoCode program offers veterans skills to be competitive in programming careers, and help finding great positions once they complete the courses. Their program is completely online, provides mentorship, job training and placement, and it's free. In just two years, they have already trained 75 vets in 12 states, with a 100% job placement rate. In addition to helping those veterans and their families avoid becoming PTSD statistics, these placements have infused $3.2 million back into the economy. They're garnering support from big names like Slack and Google, were featured at the White House Demo Day, and the #VetsWhoCode story has been covered by the likes of *The Huffington Post*, *Blacks in Technology*, and *General Assembly*.

Hardaway started with the mindset that **Every Barrier Can Be Penetrated** – refusing to accept PTSD as a fact of life for veterans, the bureaucracy of government-sponsored programs that impede vets from getting help, or the inequalities that have kept so many black founders out of tech fields. Next, Hardaway's FRAGO/**Compasses Over Maps** mindset helped him to rethink new routes to achieve his desired goals. Then, with the consistent application of the **Deconstruction** tactic, he took apart the problem, the existing solutions, and he put together a new solution to achieve this critical mission.

Though #VetsWhoCode is a non-profit organization, they are already making real differences in the economy – they are helping to retrain valuable members of society and helping businesses get the skilled tech employees they so desperately need. As Jerome puts it, he's just trying to give veterans a "fair chance at the American dream."

SARDINES TO THE RESCUE

What do fish oil, graffiti, and the World's Fair have in common?

If I ask you to think about graffiti, you might imagine kids with criminal tendencies marking underpasses with gang signs under the cover of night. Or you may envision urban artists, like Banksy, creatively reimagining their blighted landscapes. Whatever image you're conjuring up, it's probably not a 52 year-old Scottish-born merchant marine "tagging" old water tanks and trains with colorful paint for publicity.

In the late 1960s, when graffiti is credited as beginning in earnest, it took on its own look, and relied on spray paint as the medium. But over 30 years before the famed artist Cornbread began painting Philadelphia walls to get the attention of a girl, and almost 20 years before Ed and Bonnie Seymour invented spray paint, Robert Fergusson was painting colorful patterns on rusted equipment across Chicago in the years leading up to the 1933 World's Fair.

A hacker at heart, Fergusson was embarking on a guerilla marketing campaign to drum up attention for his new paint. Knowing that the whole world was looking at Chicago as it prepared for the fair, Fergusson moved to the Windy City and began his citywide painting spree. His campaign was a classic **Exploit** – using a small "in" to leverage as much as he could from it.

Fergusson had spent most of his life at sea, from whaling boats in his youth to merchant marine vessels during World War I. Fergusson was fascinated with the coating used to cover ships' decks – a mix of fish oil and flake graphite – that protected the steel decks from rust. Unfortunately, all that fish oil smelled awful and took ages to dry.

Since his boyhood, Fergusson had been trying to find an alternative deck coating. While working at a ship maintenance facility in New Orleans after the War, he began tinkering with different concoctions by **Deconstructing** the formula. He systematically isolated each ingredient and then tried Substituting them with alternatives. He tried different substances in place of the graphite, but none helped improve the product. Through ongoing substitution experiments, he travelled the world looking for the just the right ingredients, visiting commercial fisheries from San Diego to Alaska. Only after countless experiments was he able to land on the keeper: processed oil from the Pilchard sardine. The substitution produced the desired results – it didn't smell like rotting fish carcasses and it dried quickly.

Fergusson's hacking paid off. His company, Rust-Oleum, which was founded in 1921, gained mass acceptance in the 1930s and remains a household name. Nearly 100 years later, that spirit of Substitution remains. The company has dozens of products and sub-brands that were derived from Substituting other ingredients – such as epoxies, latex, and alkyds – for sardine oil. The corporate tagline that's still used today – "Rust Never Sleeps" – was borrowed by Neil Young for the title of his 1979 album. Today, Rust-Oleum has over 1,000 employees and over $1 billion in annual revenue. Now that's a lot of sardines.

FROM BUREAUCRACY TO BEAUTY

Which organization delivers the *absolute worst* customer experience? The runner ups from scouring dozens of customer shame surveys include cable companies, discount airlines, mobile phone carriers, taxicab companies, and home repair experts. But the top of nearly every list is reserved for a special kind of agony: the good ole Department of Motor Vehicles (aka, "the DMV").

The mere mention of the DMV makes us squirm in our chairs. We can all relate to that soul-crushing experience – waiting endlessly in a cold, uncomfortable environment, akin to being sent to time out as a guilty child. By the time you finish with your rude and apathetic associate, you feel exhausted and demoralized. That's how Chad Price felt too, but he set out to make a change.

The North Carolina Department of Motor Vehicles decided to privatize their service centers. With the hacker mindset that **Every Barrier Can Be Penetrated**, Chad committed to flip the whole thing upside down and completely reimagine the DMV experience. To do this, Chad put the **Deconstruct** tactic to use.

After winning the contract for Holly Springs, a suburb of Raleigh, Chad first wanted to take the whole process apart. He visited DMV branches throughout the state and observed the painful customer experience. He talked to citizens and elected officials, DMV workers and paper-pushing bureaucrats. He needed to understand all the moving pieces and how they were connected so he could Substitute out the agony with some delight. He studied the traffic flows, paperwork, and physical locations. He personally observed and documented each step of the customer process, looking for ways to disrupt it.

Today, the first thing you do is a double-take when you enter Chad's DMV in Holly Springs, North Carolina. You need to check to see if you're actually in the right place, since the environment looks nothing like what you've seen before. You notice the delicious gourmet cupcakes that are waiting for you on the counter, fresh baked daily. Perhaps you choose to enjoy a fresh smoothie, cold-pressed juice, or one of the dozens of exotic coffee flavors they offer. There are fresh cut flowers, area rugs, and a lovely children's play area to entertain the little ones while parents conduct their business. Warm color tones, friendly smiles, comfy seating, free Wi-Fi, helpful associates with welcoming smiles...wait, is this *really* a DMV?

The experience isn't only pleasant, it's also efficient. You can use a mobile app to check in before your arrival, and later receive a text when your number is coming up. Walk-ins speed through the check-in process on an iPad and are alerted with updates during their wait. Locals love the place so much, they've been known to come in for coffee and cupcakes just to hang out and read a book, even if they have no pressing business at the DMV.

I recently caught up with Chad to learn more about his hacker approach. "At every step of the way, the bureaucratic establishment told me all the reasons a transformation couldn't be done," said Chad. "They dismissed my idea that a DMV could be a terrific experience, and that I could make money at the same time."

His detractors had a point. The private DMV earns fees per transaction, and the market is limited by geography, after all. This captive audience has no choice but to visit, and the population won't change if the DMV experience is terrific or lousy. But a hacker at heart, Chad was motivated by the mindset that **Every Barrier Can Be Penetrated**: "First, I wanted to prove it could be done because everyone told me it couldn't. But I also felt we could make a business out of it."

Chad charges customers for the cupcakes, juices, and coffee, which helps offset the added costs of their beautiful facility and highly-paid, friendly workers. That part was obvious to me, but here's where he blew my mind: "Since our service is so friendly and efficient, I have customers that drive up to 100 miles to visit our location. They drive right past several other DMVs to get here, knowing that their round trip time will still be less and they'll have a great experience, too." Here, Chad refused to accept his market size as fixed and bet that a radically better experience would actually expand his customer base. Today, he's doing nearly twice the volume of any other DMV in the state, and as you can imagine, is one of the top ranked facilities in the country for customer experience. He's making top dollar and serving his community in a profoundly better way.

Using hacker mindsets and techniques, even the dreaded DMV came to life with a little imagination and creativity. Chad Price flipped DMV to mean "Department of Maximum Value," for both himself and his customers. It's easy to feel stuck doing things the way they've always been done, but the Holly Springs DMV shows that the only real boundary is our own imagination. Take a look at your most established notions and practices, and apply this same sense of creative wonder. You may just be blown away by the results as your customers line up and take a number for a hefty serving of originality.

Regardless of the challenges you face – from internal process to external products, from HR policies to environmental impact initiatives – the potent approach of **Deconstruction** followed by Addition, Subtraction, or Substitution can yield stunningly innovative solutions. Take apart existing structures into their core building blocks and then tinker with alternative inputs to explore new possibilities. It has worked beautifully for cybercriminals, bike manufacturers, paint companies, non-profit warriors, and innovative consultants alike. And it will work for you.

HACK STARTERS

1. Identify a pressing challenge, threat, or opportunity. On a white board, break it down into its individual components. Examine the construction, structure, rules, and core beliefs. By examining the inner workings, what ideas come to mind that could be changed to uncover new possibilities.

2. Once you've **Deconstructed**, what controlled experiments could you conduct in which you swap out various elements for alternatives? How could you Substitute one ingredient for something fresh, in other to bring an entirely new formula to life?

CHAPTER 10: AGILE BURSTS

 "I don't need time, what I need is a deadline," legendary jazz composer and bandleader Duke Ellington famously said. As one of the most innovative people in history, Ellington's counterintuitive message is clear: time-constrained environments can actually foster creativity rather than restrict it.

Hackers foster the notion of time-constrained creative bursts by embracing the Agile software development method. The term came to prominence in 2001, in conjunction with the publication of *The Manifesto for Agile Software Development*, which was drafted by 17 software developers who were trying to elevate their craft. A core element, and the one that was most revolutionary at the time, is the notion of working in short sprints rather than one large timeline. Prior to the agile movement, a group of developers would all work on a large project for months, building up to a single launch date. In the new model, short sprints are established that involve quick bursts of effort followed by numerous, smaller launches. Ranging from 48 hours to two weeks, developers work fast to ship code that must be tested, evaluated, and adapted many times along the way to a final launch.

Software engineers found that short, focused bursts under the umbrella of a ticking clock delivered more creative output and fostered better overall quality, as they could course-correct early on if things went wrong. The bursts also helped recalibrate resource needs along the way, delivering a more efficient project in the end. Having to quickly ship working lines of code forced the developers to get scrappy and find creative workarounds to obstacles and challenges.

Some of the most creative cyberattacks in history have also come under the pressure of a deadline. Facing the ever-increasing threat of Iran's developing nuclear program, the U. S. and its allies needed to deploy all available resources to prevent Iran's ambitions. By 2010, Iran had publicly stated that is was committed to "wiping Israel off the map." With the spread of Iranian-sponsored terrorist cells, allowing the country to develop nuclear weapons capabilities posed an existential threat not only to Israel, but also to democratic nations throughout the world.

As diplomatic efforts and sanctions sputtered, the United States and Israel secretly collaborated to fight back through hacking. A joint operation of hackers was established to slow down Iran's nuclear ambitions by whatever means necessary. The covert team has never been openly confirmed by either country, but anonymous U. S. officials speaking to the *Washington Post* claimed the effort was created "to sabotage Iran's nuclear program with what would seem like a long serious of unfortunate accidents."

Whoever they were working for, time was not on the side of this team of anti-proliferation hackers. Every day that passed was a moment closer to a fully functional Iranian nuclear program. Breaking the task into a series of sprints, the team used short bursts of creativity to attack their extremely important and time-sensitive mission. Within 60 days, the team launched what later became known as the Stuxnet Worm. The original program was less than one megabyte, making it easy to transfer behind enemy lines. Once inside, the sneaky software targeted the Siemens SCADA control systems that commanded Iran's uranium centrifuges. The clever hack secretly caused over 5,000 of the 8,800 centrifuges to spin incorrectly, stop randomly, and resume erratically. All the while, the system reported that everything was running smoothly. This undetected malfunctioning drove the Iranian scientists mad, making them doubt their own work. Not knowing they were being deceived, the staff toiled unproductively for months. Before finally being discovered, the Stuxnet Worm wasted thousands of hours and millions of dollars in uranium resources. Most importantly, it delayed the advancement of Iran's quest for nuclear power, allowing more time for diplomatic measures to take hold.

Overlaying the element of time into the creative process adds a new dimension that can be harnessed and expanded upon. Time restrictions can be applied to the ideation process, further development, or even the solutions that are created. In the Stuxnet example, time was constrained during the creative process. The forced deadline focused the team's creative efforts and yielded an elegant solution, because it had to. Instead of seeing it as a constraint, time became a crucial element to their plan, which led to the small, self-growing code they developed and were able to quickly sneak into Iranian networks. They considered time to be a key part of their overall strategy. Rather than destruction of Iran's network, which would be immediately noticed and repaired, the hackers sought maximum impact through a solution that caused damage slowly while going undetected.

Time was also a factor in another attack, one that CNN dubbed "the biggest hack in history."

The Target: Saudi Aramco, one of the world's largest oil companies

The Hackers: The "Cutting Sword of Justice"

The Impact: Over $1.0 billion of lost profits and additional expenses

The group claiming responsibility cited Aramco's support of the Al Saud royal family's authoritarian regime: "This is a warning to the tyrants of this country and other countries that support such criminal disasters with injustice and oppression."

Using a time-based approach, the group used the Islamic holy month of Ramadan to perpetrate their attack, because most Saudi Aramco employees were off work. The temporary worker who clicked on the fateful malicious email hadn't been fully trained in cybersecurity and intrusion prevention. The short-staffed team didn't notice the computer systems acting weird; they were just trying to get through their backlog of work. The hackers specifically targeted the holy month, designing their malicious software to spread quickly during a time the infection would likely go unnoticed. By the time most people returned to work and realized what had happened, the damage was done.

Realizing how deeply infected the system was and how fast the virus was spreading, corporate executives had no choice but to take the entire computer system down. This meant wiping every hard drive, yanking every cable from every wall. The highly automated company was brought to its knees by having to go back to a paper-based business. For months, the company was without phones, Internet, email, spreadsheets, word-processing, automated order-flow, and computerized distribution routes. The problems became so bad at one point, Saudi Aramco had to give away tanker trucks of free oil to keep the supply flowing and their customers satisfied. Forced to purchase over 50,000 hard drives at once, the company had to pay higher prices and tariffs. The full company network wasn't back online until five months after the initial breach, causing untold aggravation and costing the company an estimated $1.1 billion in losses.

Had the attack occurred during a normal time period, the impact could have been significantly reduced. But the clever hackers, who have never been identified or charged, used the element of time to boost their results by attacking precisely when their target was most vulnerable.

LEGIT FLIP

Innovation Hackers – from startups to corporate giants – leverage the method of **Agile Bursts** primarily through Hackathons. With a fixed, short window of time, teams are focused on a desired outcome and then throw everything they have at the problem in a flat-out sprint. Hackathons have been used to invent new companies, cure disease, reimagine organizational structures, and craft new solutions for customer engagement. Some Hackathons are internal, focusing on specific or company-based problems, while others are independently-hosted gatherings to create new ideas, companies, and products from scratch. Adam Savage, industrial and special effects designer of *MythBusters* fame, said it best: "Deadlines refine the mind. They remove variables like exotic materials and processes that take too long. The closer the deadline, the more likely you'll start thinking waaay outside the box." The intensity and focus, along with a ticking clock, can truly lead to breakthrough creativity.

SORRY SEEMS TO BE THE HARDEST WORD

My friend Gerri's husband died suddenly. In addition to processing this devastating loss, she also had to tackle the paperwork that comes with losing a spouse. Bank accounts, credit cards, loans, insurance, utility bills, and countless other things need to be quickly addressed – names removed, accounts transferred, death certificates submitted. This dizzying amount of work is what she was dealing with in the days after her husband died, handling as much as possible before she returned to work.

One of the calls Gerri made was to her phone/cable/internet provider – a major national mass media company. The customer service rep she spoke with was in a foreign call center, assigned to calls that involved changing account information. Gerri explained the situation, in a matter-of-fact robotic tone that she had adopted to keep it together when having repeat "my husband died" countless times throughout the day. The woman on the other end said, "I will need to speak with your husband before I can make any changes because his name is the primary on the account. "Gerri re-explained that her husband was dead, and she needed to know how to submit the death certificate so she could be made the primary on the account.

They went in circles. Then, in a rote voice, the customer service rep said, "I understand what you are saying, madam, but I need to speak with your husband before I can do anything on this account. Kindly have him call and we will make the requested changes." Clearly, the rep did not understand what she was saying. Gerri tried phrasing the problem differently: "My husband is no longer living. He is deceased. He had a heart attack Monday and is not alive. I have a legal death certificate and need to submit this to remove him from the account."

"Can I please speak with your husband, madam? If I can only obtain his permission, then I can make you a primary accountholder on the account. Or you could have him call back at another time and provide us with this permission."

"MY HUSBAND IS DEAD!" Gerri yelled, in tears, before slamming down the phone.

Eventually, she had to call back, escalating the call until they could get to a manager who understood the situation. The whole process took hours and multiple calls, but eventually, Gerri was made the primary accountholder on her own cable account. Problem solved.

But was it? The administrative issue Gerri called about had been fixed, but the issue of her experience on the call certainly wasn't.

What if a day or two later, while relaying this ridiculous ordeal to the friends who'd stopped by, Gerri had received flowers from the cable company, with a handwritten note – "Gerri, we are so sorry to hear about the death of your husband. We would also like to sincerely apologize that our service fell so far short, especially during such a difficult time. Our deepest apologies and condolences."

Wow. How different would that story – which was going to be told and retold anyway – be after that kind of response?

It's a nice idea, but when was the last time your cable company even genuinely said the words "we're sorry," let alone sent you flowers? According to Martin McGloin, that is exactly the problem with customer service today. Martin is the CEO and co-founder of a startup that's putting old-school touches on modern customer service. The history of his company – Sorry as a Service (SaaS) – is as unexpected as the apologies that they're sending on behalf of some of Europe's biggest companies.

This hip, Hackathon-born company has legitimate startup roots, but those roots don't go anywhere near Silicon Valley. Sorry as a Service started at Garage48 in Estonia. Despite the buzz around other European and American startup locations, the Baltics have a thriving startup culture of their own – one that gained worldwide visibility, first with Skype and then with European peer-to-peer money transfer giant, TransferWise, both of which started in Estonia. And Garage48 is one of the most well-known recurring Hackathons in the Baltics.

Whether you're coming from the Baltics or Brooklyn, Sorry as a Service is to Hackathons what unicorns are to startups – a dream, that, though possible, is incredibly rare. Major Hackathons occur many times a year throughout the world, and the dreamers pour in. Some, like McGloin, have nascent ideas they're hoping to develop rapidly, while others put their skills behind what they hope will be the next big thing. Hackathons are great for networking, putting ideas to a sink-or-swim test, recruiting talent, and fueling that startup spirit. But the unspoken truth of a Hackathon is that it is *very* unlikely that a viable company will come out of it. And everyone knows this going in, as did Martin McGloin, Sabine Pole, Indrek Põldvee, and Siim Talvik when they went to Garage48.

McGloin's background involved not only software development but experience in acquisition and scalable marketing. Inspired by Mr. Larsen – a bank manager from his childhood who understood the extra-mile model of customer service – and a conflict with his mobile provider, he came to Garage48 with an inkling of an idea. His idea was to help companies address customer churn – not by bringing in new customers, but by repairing damaged relationships with existing customers. Basically, helping companies learn how to say they're sorry.

McGloin, Pole, Põldvee, and Talvik joined forces at Garage48. These four strangers had very different backgrounds, such that this Hackathon and an international flight were about the only two places they might end up in the same space together. But Hackathons are known for bringing together pretty diverse groups of people; they saw the diversity of their team, and decided to use it consciously, to their advantage. Capitalizing on their different backgrounds and experiences, they did the impossible – took an idea from the ether to a viable company, in 48 hours. And they won the Hackathon. Fast forward a few months later and they had quit their day jobs, rented office space, and were off to a major startup accelerator, TechStars London.

The mindset that **Every Barrier Can Be Penetrated**, could be a summary of McGloin's own definition of hacking, which he says is "just a creative way of solving problems; recognizing your limitations and not being limited by them." So it's no surprise that SaaS's entire approach to customer service is a hack. Reaching new customers is hard enough, and with the sometimes astronomical cost of traditional and social media advertising, it can range from expensive to impossible through these traditional channels. McGloin learned that for many companies, the best (and most cost-effective) way to bring in customers is turning existing but dissatisfied customers into delighted customers. Happy customers tell their friends and families, allowing you to use both **Social Engineering** and **Exploit** tactics with your delighted existing customers to geometrically build your customer base.

But if it's so simple, why are so many companies failing miserably? According to McGloin, they're focusing on the wrong aspect of the customer's experience. Companies train their reps to respond to complaints rationally, not emotionally; but for the customer, that bad experience is an emotional, not rational, one. The result of this method is putting a trivial price tag on someone's emotional experience. McGloin says that he sees SaaS as "an opportunity to empower customer service agents to not think about a complaint as something that needs to be rationally responded to, but instead think, how do you build an emotional relationship?"

To test their approach – the physical, personal vs. the monetary, impersonal – SaaS used **Brute Force** via Rapid Experimentation to test different options. Working with TransferWise to gather data, they did a pretty low-budget experiment. They gave dice to the customer service reps and when dealing with complaints, the reps would roll the dice. When they rolled 1-3, they'd give the customer a gift card, 4-6, they'd send a hand-piped, personalized chocolate plaque. Both outcomes had the same dollar value. The results: a 35% increase in customer retention and an increase in their customer lifetime value, totaling an ROI *over three times* the initial cost of the sorry.

Yes, they're giving customers warm fuzzies, intangible emotional responses, but those responses are coming back to companies in very tangible ways. And not just in terms of their ROIs. One major SaaS partner in the UK received a handwritten note from a customer in Germany. After the company failed to deliver with a client, they sent her a handwritten note and chocolates. She replied in kind with a handwritten note:

> *I had a bad experience when my transaction took a long time. Then I got a great chocolate from David, and I was pleased. It made me laugh. However, my husband now thinks that I have a lover in Great Britain. He can't believe that somebody from your company would send me a chocolate to say sorry. So creative a way to apologize.*

This customer's letter shows not only the impact that the SaaS delivery had on her, but also the state of customer service – it was easier for her husband to believe she had a secret lover in another part of the world than to believe that a company sent a little chocolate to say sorry.

So how can a company learn to say sorry, in unique, personalized ways, *and* at scale? Sorry as a Service (SaaS) cheekily provides Software as a Service (the more well-known SaaS) – the model that has worked for big companies like Salesforce.com, Box, NetSuite, and Adobe. Instead of an old-fashioned box of software, your monthly fee buys cloud-based access to the software, updates, and support. Sorry as a Service integrates into major CRM systems and even custom platforms. They allow customer service reps to send out personalized sorries – the hundreds of possibilities include flowers, cookies, and chocolate – from right within their existing workflows. SaaS works with local sorry providers to make sure that the sorries are unique, personalized, and meet quality expectations.

While they're helping their customers hack old-school customer service in a digital world, SaaS is also hacking behind the scenes. Unsurprisingly, as the wunderkind of a Hackathon, SaaS uses **Agile Bursts** to drive their continued growth. Every Monday morning, their team checks in remotely from their four international locations. The first order of business is to assess last week's goals. Then, they work together to plan the week, focusing on the most crucial elements for that week's success. To strengthen their diasporic workforce, they utilize a variety of online tools to strategize for the week. Then it's go time – each week is like a Hackathon and they have to report their results by Monday. At 4:00 each afternoon, the whole team checks in again for a few minutes just to touch base and address any pressing issues before hacking on. And they regularly use **Brute Force** via Rapid Experimentation to test and validate potential new ideas.

SaaS team members are called "hackstars" because hacking is so much a part of their vocabulary and how they do their work. McGloin says of their unorthodox job titles, "It's a recognition of the fact that job titles are fluid. We don't want a title to restrict and end up limiting what you're do-ing." Embracing the hacker mindset that **Competence Is the Only Creden-tial That Matters**, McGloin explained to me that "the most important thing is our success, not that you religiously protect your job title."

Today, SaaS has delivered sorries to their users' customers in every country in the European Union. They're partnered with some of the biggest names on the continent, with their client list expanding daily. And they've done it by staying in touch with their Hackathon beginnings. Who knew sorry could be so much fun?

Hackathons – **Agile Bursts** of creative problem solving – are powerful in that they focus a team on ideation and delivering something (a prototype, presentation, experiment, etc.) in a very short window of time. These pa-rameters force the negativity out of the room, shifting the thinking from what can't be done to what can be, what *must* be. Concerns around long-term execution, regulatory burdens, and corporate bureaucracy vanish, replaced by imagination and creative verve.

HACKATHON BEST PRACTICES:

1. Allocate a specific timeslot, generally 24-48 hours

2. Assemble a maximally diverse team

3. Take aim at a particular problem or challenge

4. Keep it immersive – have food brought in, take breaks together, avoid people coming in and out, as much as possible

5. Establish a specific deliverable up front (could be a working prototype, a physical model, a business case, a hypothesis, etc.)

6. Offer rewards (actual and/or recognition-based)

7. Capture the moment with video or form an assigned note-taker

8. Conduct a series of follow-ups to ensure the ideas actually move forward and to recap key learnings.

ROCK OUT, HACK ON

David Kalt and I have a few things in common. We're both around the same age and both come from Detroit. We are both tech entrepreneurs and both are passionate about playing guitar. Unfortunately for me, that's where the comparisons end.

David co-founded OptionsXpress in 1999 and later sold the online options trading platform to Charles Schwab for over $1 billion. After the sale, he wanted to do something related to his love of music so he purchased the world-famous musical instrument shop, the Chicago Music Exchange. He quickly became frustrated at the slow and clumsy process for buying and selling musical instruments. With a background as a tech entrepreneur, he decided to shift the focus from local music shop to online musical marketplace. Changing the name to Reverb.com, he set out to become the "eBay for music gear."

Despite significant competition from the actual eBay, Reverb took off by providing a more specialized marketplace with deep industry expertise, low commission rates, and extraordinary service. By 2015, it had become the world's largest site for buying and selling music gear. Revenue passed $120 million and the company landed $25 million in new capital from A-list investors.

Despite great success, David was concerned. Faced with doubling the employee headcount – again – he worried that his team would get too far away from their musical customers. It was critical to him that the team remain obsessed not only with customer experience, but also their industry expertise. To tackle the problem, he turned to a hack.

Kalt established an **Agile Burst**: a five-week contest where employees from all roles in the company were challenged to buy and sell as many guitar pedals as they could on the Reverb platform. Graphic designers, software engineers, and accounting specialists each created an account and got a first-hand look at the customer experience. The contest not only got the team closer to the customer, it uncovered bugs in the system that were immediately corrected. It also generated a vast array of fresh ideas for improvement to the buying and selling processes. Instead of issuing a mandate such as "get closer to our customers," David used a time-based challenge to foster creative thinking and generate fresh perspective. By promoting employee engagement through Hackathon-style initiatives, David and Reverb.com will undoubtedly continue to rock on.

ALL THE COOL KIDS ARE DOING IT

Where did the idea and initial prototype for Facebook Moments begin? The service, which has now been used to share over 400 million photos, was born in a Hackathon, of course. What about GroupMe, the mobile group messaging startup that was acquired by Skype for $80 million less than a year after being founded? You guessed it, the company was born in a Hackathon. While the Hackathon technique is a fan-favorite among tech companies, it can be deployed to conquer nearly any creative challenge. Some unexpected examples:

- **British Parliament** holds an annual Hackathon called Accountability Hack in an effort to develop better citizen engagement. Billed as "your chance to impact the democratic process," it has become a running tradition for improving governmental accountability and fostering thoughtful public/private sector engagement.

- "On a mission to foster innovation around challenges affecting us at home and in space," **NASA** launched the Space Apps Challenge. This 48-hour event taps the minds of Innovation Hackers – both subject experts and enthusiasts – from across the country to advance the nation's space program.

- **The World Bank** has sponsored dozens of Hackathons, ranging from creative sprints to improve road safety in India, to a recently-held session to develop innovative approaches to agriculture in Uganda.

- **The U. S. Department of Veterans Affairs** recently held simultaneous Hackathons in Austin and San Francisco to develop brain health innovations for veterans.

In the words of Nolan Bushnell, the founder of Atari and grandfather of the video game industry, "the ultimate inspiration is the deadline."

HACK STARTERS

1. Take the Hackathon tactic out for a spin. To start, organize a single-day session using the best practices listed above. At first, take on a small or mid-level problem to generate momentum and post early results (later, once you're engaging in regular Hackathons, you can tackle the big stuff).

2. Layering the element of time into your creative process, what new ideas can you uncover with the following isolated timeframes:

a. What short windows of time could foster a successful new launch (seasonal, around a particular calendar event, etc.)?

b. If your new idea could only exist for a limited time, what might you consider (limited-time product offerings, sales promotions, internal bonus periods, hiring initiatives, etc.)?

c. If you're facing a longer-term challenge or opportunity, how could you break it down into focused **Agile Bursts** (2-14 days) to foster a more creative and ultimately productive process?

CHAPTER 11: THE REVERSE

The Target: United States National Security Agency (NSA)

The Hackers: The Shadow Brokers

The Technique: The Reverse

The story of a daring hack in which shadowy figures carry out criminal acts seems to hit the media on a daily basis. During the writing of this book, there's been no shortage of material. On August 13, 2016, just as I began this chapter, a rogue group calling themselves The Shadow Brokers stunned the cybersecurity world. The group revealed a successful hack into guarded national secrets and was now offering what they found to the highest bidder.

The NSA, in conjunction with their counterparts in Canada, Australia, New Zealand, and the United Kingdom, established an elite team to take on hackers. Bringing together the best minds across three continents, this five-country team is known as "The Equation Group" and also called the "Five Eyes." They collaborated to build a hacking toolkit specifically designed to enable the good guys to take on the bad: a sophisticated codebase that made it easy for governmental agencies to hack into the networks of terrorists, decode encrypted messages from cybercriminals, and disrupt rogue-states in order to keep the public safe.

Now if you're a hacker looking to generate illicit profits, your instinct may urge you to attack a bank, large corporation, or the financial system itself. But if you embraced the hacking technique of the **Reverse** – doing the exact opposite of conventional thinking – perhaps you'd set your targets on the Five Eyes. Well, that's exactly what The Shadow Brokers did. Preferring the road less travelled, they set out to pull of one of the biggest **Reverses** in history: to steal the hacking tools used by top governmental agencies and then sell them on the open market. To accomplish a breach of this magnitude, the group deployed oppositional approaches at every step. If convention said to penetrate in one fashion, The Shadow Brokers did the polar opposite.

Commenting on the crime, New York University computer security professor Justin Cappos told CNN, "This is dangerous. People who want to launch attacks but were not aware how to do it now have the tools and information available to do this."

Even their monetization strategy was unorthodox. Instead of secretly contacting likely buyers and conducting a clandestine negotiation, The Shadow Brokers are conducting a cyberweapons auction, selling their wares with eBay-like transparency. They have publicly posted some of the code so buyers can validate authenticity, and are now accepting bids. Their inelegant advertisement taunts, "Attention government sponsors of cyber warfare and those who profit from it!!!! How much you pay for enemies cyber weapons? We give you some Equation Group files free, you see. This is good proof no? You enjoy!!! You break many things. You find many intrusions."

The notion of such a powerful toolkit falling into the wrong hands sends chills down our spines. Yet these types of breaches occur with stunning regularity. To catch a hacker, we need to think like hackers. As this particular case unfolds, our best bet in thwarting the dangerous acts of these greedy criminals is to flip standard protocols upside down. It was a **Reverse** idea that led to this risky state of affairs, and it will likely be a **Reverse** approach by law enforcement that will restore our safety.

LEGIT FLIP

Doing the exact opposite of what's expected is a hallmark of hackers. Since hacking is nothing more than a methodology for creative problem solving, taking the **Reverse** approach is a powerful framework to unlock fresh ideas and foster innovation.

To deploy the **Reverse** in your own Innovation Hacking, force yourself to explore the complete opposite of what's always been done. When facing a challenge or new opportunity, I like making a list of how all the "experts" would generally attack it. I list what I've done in the past, what the industry norms are, and how everyone else goes about facing the same issue. Then, I draw a line down the page, the **Reverse** Line. On the other side of the line, I force myself to write the exact opposite of the list I just created.

Here's an example if you were considering getting into the auto business and opening a new car dealership:

Conventional Wisdom	The Reverse
Sell one brand of car	Sell many or all brands
Hours: 8am – 6pm M-F, open late Thursday	24 hours
Take delivery of new car at dealer	Home delivery
Once you buy it, it's yours	21-day risk-free trial
Local	National
Paperwork at dealer	Digital docs via your mobile device
Haggling salesperson	Set pricing
All cars sold from dealer	Facilitate peer-to-peer deals
Ketchup-stained polyester ties	Black turtlenecks
Cars, parts, and repairs	Many additional offerings (travel, insurance, apparel, etc.)
Slow career growth	Exciting job opportunities

These oppositional approaches enabled AutoNation to shake up the dealership business. Launched as the first national dealership offering dozens of brands, no-haggle pricing, and expanded hours, the company used the **Reverse** to become the most successful car dealership in history. They recently sold their 10 millionth car (no other dealership is even close), have 60,000 available cars to choose from, employ 26,000 people, and have a market value of over $5 billion on the New York Stock Exchange.

But that's old news. Everyone knows about AutoNation, but what about new entrants who are hacking their way to growth and success?

Carvana, a "dealership-free car buying experience," is using the **Reverse** to challenge every aspect of the car-buying process. Customers browse cars from their own living rooms, using advanced search features combined with HD virtual tours. As customers narrow their car search down to a few finalists, they can easily compare and contrast the respective features to make the best decision. The cars, which are all "Carvana Certified," pass a 150-point inspection to provide peace of mind for buyers.

Once a decision is made, buyers complete the entire process, financing, and all the paperwork online (current record is 11 minutes). And here's the really cool part: when it comes time to pick up your new ride, you visit the world's first Car Vending Machine. Imagine those matchbox car garages you played with as a kid, but in real-life size. You walk up to a glass structure the size of a large building, enter a code, and one of dozens of garage doors opens...the one containing your new car. Hop in and drive off, as easy as buying a Snickers bar at a hockey game.

With vending machines in Atlanta, Houston, Nashville, and Charlotte, Carvana is looking to expand their new model and make a serious dent in the $45 billion used-car industry. They've raised over $700 million of equity and debt and plan to be in 20 major markets by the end of 2017. The entire car-buying experience was upended to save customers money, provide better choices, ease the buying process, and create a memorable experience. All the while, the company is more profitable than a typical dealer staffed with salespeople and a support team. Designed by Innovation Hackers, the entire buying process involves zero human interaction.

Or take Beepi, billed as "the radical new way to buy and sell cars." Working both the supply and demand side, the company set out to create the largest peer-to-peer car marketplace in the world. Sellers simply list their cars online, and then a certified Beepi mechanic schedules a visit to perform a 240-point inspection. Once the car is ready for sale, Beepi guarantees they'll sell your car in 30 days or they will buy it from you directly, thereby eliminating any seller risk. Once the car is posted, buyers can check it out online, searching from an enormous list of options. When someone is ready to buy your car, it is delivered to them on a flatbed truck with a giant bow on top. According to the Beepi website, buyers get "10 magic days to fall in love" or they will refund the full purchase price, no questions asked. Here, they've eliminated all the risk for buyers as well.

Unlike Carvana, Beepi has no physical locations and a far lower inventory cost since most of their cars are still titled to previous owners. By eliminating risk on both sides of the deal, they've created a safe, transparent, and efficient marketplace for car sales. The 20-month old company has been valued at over $500 million, and is threatening to disrupt the old guard in a large, traditional industry.

In nearly every field, the industry stalwarts, who long for days gone by, and refuse to hack fresh approaches are in grave danger of being upended. No matter how staid your profession may be, embracing a **Reverse** may be instrumental to your very survival. In computers and business, it's hack or be hacked.

THE WONKAVATOR

When *Charlie and the Chocolate Factory* premiered back in 1971, the elevator that didn't only go up and down fascinated moviegoers. Now over 45 years later, German industrial conglomerate ThyssenKrupp is essentially bringing the Wonkavator to life.

Elisha Otis pioneered the modern elevator industry back in 1845, and not much has changed since. Sure, the cars are faster, and digital displays provide riders with news clips, but the elevator fundamentally still propels riders up and down a single shaft.

The talented hackers at ThyssenKrupp just weren't satisfied. What if they could create a system that moved in multiple directions? It could expand the uses of elevators completely and offer a new form of transportation altogether. Rejecting the established norms of the cable-driven elevator industry, they used a **Reverse** to invent magnetic-levitation technology, allowing an elevator car to travel with no cables at all. This breakthrough allows for previously impossible applications such as multiple cars sharing the same shaft, the ability to have a single ride include both vertical and horizontal travel, and even the ability to integrate with other means of transportation such as movable walkways or subway systems. It will liberate architects, who currently design buildings around core elevator shafts, to create new, unrestricted designs. It is also poised to offer a significant cost savings to construction companies and building operators.

The company is hoping their unorthodox approach will pay off, helping them grow their current 12.2% share of the worldwide elevator market significantly. The new technology represents the single biggest elevator breakthrough in over 160 years. Called The Multi, the first full-scale system is currently being installed in ThyssenKrupp's headquarter building in Germany and will be available for sale in late 2017.

Employing the **Reverse**, and the mindset that ***Every Barrier Can Be Penetrated***, the engineers shattered conventional wisdom by challenging the very foundation of their field. It was a "given" that all elevators operate with a shaft and cable system, like a giant yo-yo carrying passengers. Breaking free from this set belief allowed the team to explore new options and discover fresh possibilities.

WHEN THE SHARK BITES

When Chad Price told me all about the DMV he created in Holly Springs, North Carolina, I was stunned. I was about to end our conversation, but what he told me next was so unexpected I almost missed my impending flight because I just had to learn more.

"You think what we did at the DMV is cool?" he playfully taunts. "Then let me tell you about my *real* business.

"My buddies and I decided to start a business. We knew what we were looking for, but had no idea which industry or product offering to pursue." Using a **Compasses Over Maps** approach, Chad tells me that they decided to look at industries that were extremely hard to enter. Ideally, they sought a huge barrier to entry and only a couple incumbents with enormous market shares.

Who in the world would want to enter a tough field with giant barriers and dominant, established market leaders? This **Reverse** approach, Chad told me, was not only counterintuitive, it was ideal. "We assumed that an industry that met these criteria would be controlled by sleeping giants who were deeply complacent. We wanted to do something really challenging, and this would be a perfect scenario for disruption."

After studying a few different sectors, they landed on medical laboratories. The field was difficult to enter, and required regulatory licensing in every state. Further, it was controlled by two giants, LabCorp and Quest Diagnostics, which together controlled over 90% of the market. What if Chad and his team could completely reimagine every aspect of the medical lab business, in the same way he upended the traditional DMV?

This ragtag team started with zero healthcare experience and no funding. Believing that **Every Barrier Can Be Penetrated**, they began by studying the industry. The crew travelled the country, visiting labs and talking to customers. They sat down with healthcare professionals, patients, lab techs, insurance companies, and even the original founder of one of the two entrenched giants. Chad and his partners first needed to **Deconstruct** the entire process so they could discover opportunities for transformation.

Next, they had to raise capital. Chad and his team crafted a business plan very quickly, and within a few weeks they were pitching investors. While none of them had ever raised money before, their fresh approach combined with their conviction to serve others helped them to raise over $2 million from local investors in less than 30 days. While many of us readily accept delays, Chad's timeline showcases his hacker hustle:

May 2014: An idea at a pancake house

June 2014: Raised $2.0 million

November 2014: Licensed in all 50 states

December 2014: First lab operational

After learning the landscape, Chad decided to pull the ultimate **Reverse**. He systematically looked at every aspect of the business, and instead of complying, he pursued the opposite. Many existing labs have outdated and inefficient equipment, so Chad built his own state-of-the-art facility. Since the competitors already have deep investment in existing methods and couldn't afford to make a system-wide change, Chad gained ground by leveraging advanced robotics, cloud computing, automation, and artificial intelligence. The entire company was built around innovation, allowing healthcare professionals and patients alike to securely access test results from a mobile app.

More interesting than technology, they challenged every deeply-held industry assumption. The competition uses 1099 "reps" to sell their services (alongside other wares they sell). Chad opted to hire his own highly-trained sales force that truly understood the company's value proposition. It turns out, the doctors who make decisions prefer knowledgeable experts to pushy salespeople. Other companies rely on FedEx or UPS for transporting lab samples, so Chad hired his own drivers and logistics team to ensure faster, more reliable pickup and delivery.

In addition to their offering, Chad built his corporate culture to be different by design. His competitors' leaders have fancy titles, corner offices, wear $8,000 power suits, and fly corporate jets. Meanwhile, Chad and his leadership team have no titles on their business cards (no one in the company does), take the smallest cubes in their building in the worst locations, wear surgical scrubs (all employees do), and fly coach. The fat cat competitors line their own pockets while Chad and his team give back to the community through volunteering, donations, and sponsoring military families throughout the world.

"We all wear scrubs because we want to honor the industry, and honor those we serve," Chad tells me. "Even our CFO and General Counsel suit up." The attitude of service permeates the organization, as leaders are required to come in early and cook breakfast for the team at least once a month.

Chad also embraces an unorthodox leadership style. He demands that the newest employees share their ideas for disruption, before they get comfortable in their ways. In other lab companies, it would take an Act of Congress to shut down the business flow, but Chad empowers any employee at any level to shut down the entire lab if they feel something is wrong. Most organizations have decision-making log-jams for even the pettiest choices, but every single employee at Chad's shop has $2,000 of authority to make any decision they believe is in the best interest of the customers, company, and/or community.

Even the company name and logo balked tradition. "Clothing companies use an animal as a logo – a polo horse, an alligator, a whale," Chad explains. "So I decided to **Borrow** that approach and name our company Mako Laboratories, after the Mako shark. It symbolizes our hunger for results, around-the-clock intensity, power, grace, and intelligence. A lot better than a test tube logo!" The company now has tricked-out "shark cars" for deliveries and even has a Mako shark mascot that visits children's hospitals, helping to distract the kids from the clinical aspects of their visits.

Working at warp speed, Mako beat their five-year forecast in the first four months of operation. They won the Healthcare Heroes Award and the LifeScience Award in their first year of operation, an unheard-of honor for a new company, beating Bayer and other giant healthcare conglomerates. When they closed the books on year one, the company had delivered $51 million in revenue, demonstrating the inherent value of innovation hacking. The company – now with 185 employees in seven states – is on track to double each year, and there's no doubt this once-closed industry has now been forced to confront a fresh, predatory competitor.

"If anyone tells you they can't become a success...well that's just BS," Chad tells me with a warm Southern drawl. "I was born dirt poor. I never got above C in school, and took the SAT four times just to get a 900. Today, I take care of my adult sister with special needs, making me like a single parent. But I always believed that if I out-worked and out-created my competitors, I could achieve at the highest levels." Chad just described **Competence Is the Only Credential That Matters**, to a tee.

Despite having no coding expertise, it turns out Chad Price is a hacker extraordinaire. By **Deconstructing** and then **Reversing**, he was able to achieve incredible success in two completely different and seemingly unchangeable arenas (the DMV and medical labs). He leveraged the hacking mindsets of **Compasses Over Maps, Every Barrier Can Be Penetrated**, and **Competence Is the Only Credential That Matters** to better serve customers and create two wildly successful businesses.

Talk about taking a bite out of the universe.

THE REVERSE GOES FASHION FORWARD

If the **Reverse** technique could be turned into a brand, it would be Rebecca Minkoff. The designer and her eponymous lifestyle brand have defied tradition at just about every turn. When fashion is going one way, you can pretty much count on seeing Rebecca wave as she speeds past in the opposite direction. But her approach isn't just an iconoclastic one-fingered gesture toward mainstream fashion. On the contrary, she is incredibly in-touch with where fashion is headed and what her customer wants. The difference is, she is willing to follow those instincts even when they challenge all the conventional wisdom, which they usually do.

Minkoff's line, which launched in 2005, made its first **Reverse** with the price point of her now ubiquitous Mini M. A. C. handbag. The original price was $495 for the clutch-sized cross-body purse. Stores carrying the line quickly weighed in, saying that they wouldn't continue carrying the line with a purse selling for that amount. Drastic price reductions aren't generally the way to go about increasing profits, but when they re-launched the bag at $195, they opened up a window of opportunity for high fashion at more reasonable prices, timed perfectly in conjunction with the recession. Minkoff listened to what her customers wanted, and before long, her Mini M. A. C.s were everywhere.

High fashion was a reluctant participant in the advent of social media. Designers, worried about maintaining their elite cache and label purity, scoffed at social media. Unfazed, Minkoff was the first designer on Snapchat, and from the beginning, has been engaged with her shoppers on social media. She takes it so far as to personally interact with some of her customers via social media. Minkoff ignored warnings about "dirtying" her brand, and followed her instinct – she did the **Reverse** because she saw social media as a compelling way to stay in touch with her customers and their needs.

Just as the fashion world was reluctant to embrace social media, it also isn't the first place you tend to see tech innovations. Store experiences are often heavy on service but low on gadgets. Ever discontent with the status quo, Minkoff pulled another **Reverse**. Visit a Rebecca Minkoff flagship store, and you'll be greeted by a tech display. The futuristic starting point includes interactive photos of the current runway collection, styling suggestions from Minkoff herself, and it even takes drink orders. Then, when you go to the fitting room, each item contains an RFID chip that is registered by the room. The next-gen mirror in the fitting room will then show you images of other accessories to compliment the pieces you've brought with you. And it's not just a cool toy – since implementing these mirrors, 30% more shoppers have brought items into the rooms, leading to a threefold increase in sales.

Minkoff's next **Reverse** came earlier in 2016 when she flipped the runway supply chain model. Traditionally, fashion shows tease the upcoming collections a full six months before they're available to shoppers. In the meantime, fast-fashion companies have time to copy the trends and mass-produce their copycat designs in low-cost overseas factories. So while the looks that hit the runways are fresh and innovative, by the time they reach the stores, customers are already a little bored.

For the Spring/Summer 2016 New York Fashion Week show, Minkoff released a new collection, in conjunction with a social media campaign: #SeeBuyWear. Instead of using overseas factories, Minkoff planned ahead to have items made domestically and ready for sale immediately following the runway show. After she announced her plan, major designers like Tom Ford, Burberry, and Tommy Hilfiger said they would follow suit.

This supply chain shift was announced in December 2015, and had to be implemented well in advance of the February 2016 runway show. As a result, in December and January, as temperatures on the East Coast plummeted well below normal wintery lows, Minkoff was able to see trending social media searches, and release two indoor jackets to meet the demand immediately. Instead of reacting to trends over the last six months, Minkoff and her line are adapting in real time.

The result of Minkoff's series of **Reverse** executions is not only the reputation of being a disruptive fashion innovator, but these hacks have translated into booming sales and strong customer relationships. I can only imagine what she has in store for us this year.

CRAZINESS, CLIMBING, CHOCKS, AND COTTON

Most companies fear someone else coming along and drying up the sales reservoirs of their best sellers or core products. Smart companies innovate so they can be the source of disruption, rather than having it thrust upon them. But what kind of crazy company contacts its own customers and tells them to stop buying their own best-selling, core product?

That type of oppositional thinking is next-level, Innovation Hacking in action. And it's just what Yvon Chouinard and Chouinard Equipment did in 1972.

Chouinard had been an avid climber since his early teenage years, often living for extended periods of time in national parks. He and his friends idolized the likes of great American thinker and naturalist, Henry David Thoreau and John Muir, the legendary outdoorsman and Sierra Club founder. To support himself, Chouinard began making some of his own climbing equipment, specifically pitons. He had been inspired after meeting dedicated climber John Salathé, who made pitons from the axles of old Model A cars.

Pitons are hard metal spikes that are hammered into the mountain to aid in climbing and forcibly removed afterward. In order to make pitons from scrap metal, Chouinard taught himself blacksmithing and began to sell the pitons out of his car. After years of peddling his wares this way, demand increased enough for Chouinard to partner up with fellow climber, and aeronautical engineer, Tom Frost to form Chouinard Equipment in 1965.

They continuously evolved pitons and other climbing equipment utilizing a design principle borrowed from French aviator and author Antoine de Saint Exupéry that culminates in: "perfection is finally attained not when there is no longer anything to add, but when there is no longer anything to take away."

Five years later, they were the largest supplier of climbing hardware in America.

Despite being dedicated outdoorsmen that were committed to enjoying and preserving nature, their main product – the piton – was decimating the landscapes they most loved. As climbing gained in popularity, certain particularly well-traveled mountain passes began to show the destruction from each climber's pitons being hammered in and scraped out.

So, in their first catalog in 1972, Chouinard Equipment pulled the **Reverse** of a lifetime. Their catalog didn't feature a fine print warning, but opened with an editorial explaining the detrimental effect of pitons on the landscape. They weren't crazy, they just weren't afraid to radically innovate – to hack – in order to preserve the value that was most important to them: preserving nature. What makes this a hack and not business suicide is that they were prepared. Before launching the catalog, they developed a new product: chocks. Chocks are also reusable, but part of what is called a "clean" climbing strategy, one that leaves no trace of the climber after a climb; one that preserves the beauty of the climb for the next adventurer. Instead of ignoring the problem, waiting for a better solution, or passing the blame, they faced the problem head on and tossed their own biggest product in the trash.

It worked. Within a few months of the catalog going out, demand for pitons dried up and chocks were flying out the door. Chouinard Equipment began expanding into outdoor clothing the following year and decided to split the company – Chouinard Equipment remained the go-to for climbing hardware and the clothing was turned into a new brand: Patagonia.

The hacking that made Chouinard Equipment a mainstay in climbing was continued at Patagonia. They continued to innovate with fabrics, colors, and products that didn't fit into industries but created them.

In 1985, Patagonia was experimenting with two new fabrics: Capilene polyester and Synchilla fleece. These products could replace their older fabrics – polypropylene and bunting – and with properties that would be more durable for their customers. They could have tried introducing one garment in each of the new fabrics to see how it did, especially because the garments made of polypropylene and bunting accounted for 70% of their sales. But they didn't. Though their motivations were different this time – a better product not environmental protection – the **Reverse** they pulled off in 1985 was a throwback to their piton takedown in 1972. In one fell swoop, they replaced all the polypropylene and bunting products with

Capilene and Synchilla in the fall catalog. It didn't take long for customers to see why they'd made the change and embrace the new fabrics.

Ten years later, they would do it again. After realizing that the dangerous and harmful pesticides used on cotton were the most environmentally detrimental component among their top fibers, they knew they had to change. This time, instead of keeping the changes behind the scenes, they used **Brute Force** via Rapid Experimentation – t-shirts were an easy place to start with organic cotton, so they started there. As they continued to learn, refine, and grow on their educational journey, they decided to wage war on conventional cotton. They committed to improving the world, and realized that the longer they waited to fully embrace the change to organic cotton, the more damage they'd be foisting on the environment. So, to keep themselves accountable, in the fall of 1994, they committed to making their cotton sportswear 100% organic by 1996, 18 months away.

So far so good. Until they found out they had committed to the impossible. The infrastructure for organic cotton wasn't ready to do that volume; the brokers simply didn't have it to sell. In true hacker form, there was no motivator for Patagonia like being told something wasn't possible. So embracing the mindset **Every Barrier Can Be Penetrated**, they tried **Working Backward**: knowing how much cotton they needed to come up with, how could they get it? They worked back from their desired outcome through organic certifiers, spinners, and ginners, contacting each group of people to figure out how to get them to accommodate the needs of this project – like needing them to clean their equipment when switching from a conventional cotton order to a smaller organic cotton order. Finally, they **Worked Backward** to the very source: the farmers. They had to find and gain the commitment from farmers who were utilizing organic methods, long before such a thing became standard fare.

Although industry experts lambasted Patagonia's ambitions as farfetched, these creative hackers made their deadline. Every piece of cotton Patagonia clothing has been 100% organic cotton since 1996. When the supply chain they needed didn't exist, they **Worked Backward** and literally created their own.

Patagonia has shown the ethical and financial benefits possible for both hacking and sustainability. They set the bar for big companies to commit to real environmental changes, and showed that doing so can be satisfying and very profitable. Tools of the trade: the **Reverse**, **Working Backward**, and **Brute Force** via Rapid Experimentation tactics.

HACK STARTERS

1. Make a list of the sacred beliefs of your field and company. What are the things you've always done, the things that are taken for granted? Next to each item, write the polar opposite. You're not looking for a finished work product here, but rather sparks that can be nurtured and adapted into a fresh approach or an innovative break-through.

2. When facing a pesky problem, consider "Judo flipping" the situation. Instead of seeking incremental solutions or looking how others currently solve similar challenges, ask what would happen if you completely flipped the problem upside down. Think about conventional approaches – the way you've always done it – and then flip them upside down in order to yield better results. What would happen if you Judo flipped your problem, opportunity, threat, weakness, or challenge?

3. Create a mantra – "Flip it," "Reverse it," "Do the oppo-site." It could be spoken, displayed in a mobile app, written on index cards, printed on signs in conference rooms, or included in your company's email signature. Ingraining oppositional thinking as a core tenet of your business philosophy will help you uncover innovative approaches to complex problems.

CHAPTER 12: THE MASHUP

 John felt a burst of adrenaline course through his veins. This was no drill; it was a legitimate, real-life red alert. For the next 45 minutes, he poured himself into his work with absolute focus and intensity – it was all on the line and he had to perform. Right. Now.

No, John isn't a firefighter or fighter pilot. He is the Chief Information Officer of a regional institution with over $13 billion in assets that is publicly held on the New York Stock Exchange. While the emergency at hand wasn't life or death, billions of dollars and thousands of jobs were at stake. His company was under attack and the systems had been compromised.

During the crisis, John maintained a steely demeanor as he and his team shored up the intrusion. They quickly identified the breach in their systems and then "sandboxed" it by fully containing the infected software and "detonating" it in a controlled environment. Due to their ability to leap into action, John was once again able to thwart an attack and protect the security of his company.

"Comfort is your biggest enemy," John told me once the dust had settled. "The only way to protect against hackers is to stay one step ahead of them. The hackers are constantly changing up their approach, which means there is no such thing as a static state."

You would think that to prepare to battle the toughest of hackers, John would be a reformed criminal himself. Or possess an advanced degree in cybersecurity. But instead he came from a non-traditional background, with his undergraduate work in Liberal Arts. To a great extent, he saw an opportunity to lead in the cybersecurity field and hacked his way into the job. He studied the mindset and techniques of the most notorious hackers and has risen to the challenge to protect his organization against them.

John lights up when discussing the hacker mindset, in the way a musician enthusiastically describes her new keyboard: "Hackers have a real disdain for conventional wisdom. They reject established protocols in favor of discovering new ones," he tells me. "Hacking is akin to complex problem solving, and hackers love the challenge. They assume the existing way of doing things is wrong; that a better way is out there to be discovered."

Describing the hacker techniques John protects against, he shares vivid examples of **Social Engineering**, **Exploit**, and **Reverse** tactics. But the attack that concerns him the most? The **Mashup**. Combining two things into one is very difficult to defend against. A barrier designed to withstand attacks of a certain nature cannot possibly be ready for a combination of multiple efforts. The fusion of multiple techniques at once is one of the most dangerous hacking approaches, yet one of the most powerful tactics for business innovators with legitimate objectives.

"One year from now, if you're doing things the way you are today you'll be mocked," John says with a knowing grin. In the same way hackers are constantly trying new combinations and mixing together seemingly unrelated ideas to form new ones, John is surely doing the same to thwart their criminal attacks. He lives in a state of heightened awareness, saying he "feels most anxious when there's no sign of a problem." Knowing that fresh and increasingly inventive attacks will continue to threaten the company he protects, John remains vigilant by embracing the hacker mindset and using their favorite techniques against them. It may very well be his own **Mashup** of multiple security measures that prevents the most devious attacks from hitting their target.

LEGIT FLIP

Combining two ingredients to create a brand new substance has been a source of innovation for many of our favorite things – products, services, recreational activities, music, medical advances, and culinary delights. Here, your role is "fusion artist" – mashing two or more concepts together to create something entirely new.

Hotels provide shelter for guests. Department stores provide clothing for customers. But what would happen if these two divergent worlds collide? The St. Regis Hotel in Washington, DC decided to find out. In an effort to better serve their high-end customers, differentiate from their competitors, and make a couple bucks along the way, the luxury hotelier partnered with high-end retailer Neiman Marcus to create one haute combination. And this **Mashup** isn't just a service-sandwich – it meets the needs of luxury travelers who are pressed for time and expect to be wowed by fresh ideas and curated solutions.

Before guests arrive at the 5-star hotel, they are asked to complete a quick online survey. Customers are surveyed about their fashion styles, sizes, and who will be staying in the room. Upon arrival, guests discover a fully stocked closet, courtesy of Neiman Marcus. Garments are hand-selected according to the survey results. In other words, I may find a Hugo Boss suit while a female exec may discover a gorgeous new pair of Jimmy Choo pumps, in her size and favorite color, of course. Fusing fashion and retail with luxury travel, the novel concept makes it easy for customers to discover new wares. They are welcome to try it all on, and then just keep what they want. Upon checkout, any items that are removed by the guest are automatically billed to their master account.

Neither luxury hotels nor expensive fashion retail are new concepts, but the intersection of the two created a unique and compelling option for customers: in-suite customized apparel shopping. When fused together, something new was born. A powerful approach to discovery, innovation, and progress.

WHERE'S THE BEEF?

There are few industries more fiercely competitive than fast food. With over $200 billion of revenue in the U. S. alone, and 250,000 domestic locations, this is one super-sized industry. But it also has deep challenges including razor-thin margins, complex supply chains, and a highly transient workforce. A slight advantage could yield millions in profit, while a setback can send stock prices tumbling. In the last three years alone, McDonald's stock price has yo-yoed up and down, sending the market cap down by over $20 billion from high points and then back up again.

Fighting to stay competitive in a burger-dominated industry, Taco Bell turned to a **Mashup**. CEO Greg Creed challenged his team to reinvent the crunchy taco, the company's 50-year-old staple. Considering hundreds of ideas, ranging from different ingredients to bold new packaging, the one that got the team excited was the **Mashup** of a Doritos chip with the classic Taco Bell mainstay. The fusion is known as the Doritos Locos Taco®, and it became a gigantic hit. In the first year, over 600 million units were sold, generating extra spicy profits for both Taco Bell and Frito-Lay – the owner of Doritos – who joined forces for the launch. It has gone on to become one of the most successful products in fast food history. Taco Bell has expanded the **Mashup** to now offer several Doritos flavors on their tacos and other Mexican offerings (care for a Doritos Ranch Cheesy Gordita Crunch, anyone?).

In the highly competitive fast food arena, Taco Bell is standing out by mashing it up. But to really shake up this old-school field, nothing would cause more disruption than taking on the very foundation of the industry: the hamburger itself.

Your mouth waters as you stare at the plate in front of you. You size up a sizzling, juicy burger, grilled to perfection. Charred top, juicy center, enchanting aroma. That first bite sends your taste buds into a state of pure bliss. Truly one of the best burgers you've ever tasted.

The catch? It isn't a burger at all. This "burger" is grown, not fed. Meet the Impossible Burger.

Stanford biochemist and entrepreneur Patrick Brown is now serving up an incredible burger substitute. Brown's company, Impossible Foods, has spent five years working at the molecular level to craft the best darn plant-based burger in the world. So good you won't even miss the real thing.

Making plants taste like a juicy burger is no small feat. Industry experts said it couldn't be done, sentencing healthy eaters to an endless stream of cardboard-flavored substitutes. But Brown knew he could crack the code. He wanted to protect the environment, help people live healthier lives, launch a successful company, and of course, build one hell of a burger. "If people are going to be eating burgers in 50 years, they're not going to be made from cows," said Brown. "We're saving the burger." Talk about biting off more than he could chew.

But with his eye squarely on the prize, he refused to accept conventional wisdom and set out to hack the burger. He scientifically attacked every aspect of the burger, from the raw-to-cooked color change to the red juices that ooze out when pressed into a fresh bun. He reverse-engineered a plant-based patty that is indistinguishable to the untrained eye...and mouth. His burger has more protein, fewer calories, and less fat than a traditional lean-cut burger, while being much more ecologically sustainable.

The success came as a **Mashup**. By fusing together different ingredients in a creative way, he was able to innovate something totally new. The building blocks here are simple things you already know: wheat, potato protein, coconut oil, yeast extract, water, and beets. But they were assembled in a way that created something entirely new. The final **Mashup** is indistinguishable from its original ingredients – you'd immediately think it was a fresh, old-fashioned burger patty.

Brown has since turned down Google's offer to buy the company for nearly $300 million since he feels his work to make the world a better place is still incomplete. It sounds clear-cut, now that he's enjoying delicious success. But in those days before he proved out the model, it took intense determination and some serious hacker chutzpah to keep his dream alive. What was his secret sauce?

Too often, we focus on the barriers, the roadblocks and brick walls that hold us back. The zillion reasons that we can't achieve our vision. And even if we have the guts to chase a dream, it's easy to become dissuaded when facing early obstacles. Brown did the opposite: each setback simply fueled his commitment. He realized that every failed experiment was a step closer to an elegant solution. He employed the hacker technique of **Brute Force** (via Rapid Experimentation) along with the mindset that **Every Barrier Can Be Penetrated** to stay on track throughout his darkest days.

If Brown can convince carnivores that his plant products are as good as their beloved meat-based masterpieces by using the **Mashup** technique, imagine what you can do when applying this approach to your own challenges. If you deploy hacker mindsets and tactics, and you're unwilling to accept anything less, even the seemingly impossible can become your reality.

YOUR MASHUP LAB

As you tackle your own challenges and opportunities, consider the many ways that a **Mashup** can be deployed. Here are some examples of how mixing together various elements (trends, experiences, ingredients, technology, people) can blend together in fresh, innovative ways:

- **Related Concepts**: Combine professional boxing with martial arts, and you get a brand new sport: MMA (Mixed Martial Arts). Over the last decade, MMA has taken off as a premier sport, drawing fans from 156 countries. The UFC league was just purchased in 2016 by talent conglomerate WME for $4.0 billion.

- **Emerging Trends**: An aging population requiring an increasingly complex and complicated handful of daily meds and vitamins led TJ Parker to invent PillPack. The trend of shifting demographics, the need for complex medication bundles, and customers' increasing willingness to buy prescriptions online led Parker to start an online pharmacy that delivers individual per-dosage packets of patients' medications instead of single-drug bottles. Started at a 2012 MIT medical hackathon, his company is now licensed in 49 states, employs over 200 people, and has raised $62 million in venture backing.

- **Customer Experience**: What would happen if you combined golf, competitive video games, and a modern, luxury entertainment venue? You'd end up with a powerful fusion called TopGolf. Visitors rent out luxury suites – the kind you'd find in a stadium – that are tricked out with food, drinks, and comfy couches. Just outside the suite is an unparalleled driving range. Using their favorite clubs, players whack balls not only for distance but to earn points and rewards in a giant video-game-like experience. Over 10.5 million people visited TopGolf venues across 24 U. S. cities as this hot **Mashup** company rapidly expands into new markets.

- **Geographic Preferences**: African rhythms and European harmonies are among the elements blended to create a unique new style of American music: jazz. Blending together influences and ideas from various cultures can be a hotbed of innovation.

- **Unrelated Ingredients**: A torn shirt may buy a short reprieve with a seam stitch, but in most cases, a hole in fabric means the end of that garment. Researchers at Penn State University discovered a different idea by fusing unlikely ingredients – bacteria and yeast – to create a biodegradable liquid that helps fabric bind to itself. When applied to fabric, the new substance self-repairs. Still in early development, the team is experimenting with a wide variety of **Mashups** – including squid protein and exotic bacteria – to find fresh solutions for pesky problems.

- **Cultural Diversity**: Israeli scientists are solving a humanitarian problem in Peru with a technique developed in ancient India. Jugaad is an ancient Hindi word meaning "a clever way to solve a problem" (i.e. Hindi for "hacking"). Borrowing this frugal approach to problem solving, researchers at Technion University (Israel's version of M. I. T.) attacked the desperate clean water supply problem in rural Peru. They developed a low-cost, easy-to-build machine that harvests moisture from the air and converts it into safe drinking water. The **Mashup** here was blending a diverse set of ideas, people, and approaches to solving a pressing issue in a novel way.

THE ARCHITECT, THE PROGRAMMER, AND THE ENTREPRENEUR

Adam Somlai-Fischer was frustrated. First trained as an architect before expanding his work as an artist, he started to gain international acclaim and was often asked to present his work to audiences. His angst was due to the restrictive nature of available presentation software. Both Power-Point and Keynote were linear, page-after-page approaches. As an architect and artist, he realized that presenting ideas made the most impact when you could show the relationship between one concept and another – the lower level bathroom needed to be understood in the context of the adjacent family room to fully understand the space. After finding no available solutions to allow him to show his work and tell a non-linear story, he decided to cobble together a crude alternative himself. Using the metaphor of an artist's canvas and then zooming in and out of concepts to show idea relationships and detail, he was able to finally communicate in the way he wanted.

This completely new concept – the **Mashup** of presentation software, an artist's canvas, and the zooming feature of a camera – offered a better way to tell stories. But Adam just made it for his own use, he never envisioned building a tool for others. Enter Peter Halacsy, a computer science professor and software developer, who happened to see Adam present his clunky, homemade presentation concept. After the talk, Peter approached Adam and suggested they collaborate to take the idea of a canvas-based, zooming presentation and turn it into simple software that could be used by others. The two began working around the clock to build a whole new kind of presentation tool.

Unfortunately, once an early prototype was ready, Adam and Peter realized they didn't have any business skills. So they turned to Peter Arvai, a proven entrepreneur who had the skills and experience to build a company. The team was an unlikely **Mashup**: an entrepreneur, an architect, and a computer scientist? But the result was no joke, it was Prezi. The *zoomable user interface*, or ZUI, was born.

For the next 18 months, this haphazard trio toiled away, spending 100% of their energy for zero pay. They set out to build a software application that could be used by millions to tell better, more memorable stories. They also set out to build a company that could scale, one that would help put their home of Budapest on the map as a birthplace of great startups.

Fast forward to today: Prezi's 75 million customers have created over 260 million presentations. In the presentation software space, there are four major players: Microsoft, Apple, Google, and...Prezi – this small Hungarian startup used a **Mashup** to defy the underpinnings of what presentation tools can and should be. I recently caught up with Peter Arvai, CEO and co-founder of Prezi, to learn more about how these Innovation Hackers used hacker approaches to take on the industry giants.

"Our goal in the beginning wasn't to disrupt PowerPoint. It was to help communicate ideas in better ways," Peter told me. "We invented the canvas metaphor instead of the pagination approach that was used by everyone else. By fusing that with the ability to zoom in and out, we could show the relationship between content rather than just a series of unrelated slides."

It turns out this insight wasn't just cool – it was more effective. Brain science studies show that humans learn and retain more information when they understand the spatial relationship between concepts. "Let me do an experiment with you," Peter urges. "Name your five favorite kitchen appliances." I begin to rattle off my stove, toaster, espresso machine, and so on. "So how did you come up with the items? You probably did a mental walkthrough your own kitchen, you didn't envision a bullet point list," he chuckles. He goes on to tell me that the relative location of one item to another is critical in human comprehension: "Those visual cues make for much stronger learning. Which is why audience retention rates are 30% or higher when Prezi is used over PowerPoint."

The Prezi team has not only built a great product, they've built a culture of innovation. "Today, a company's success is directly proportionate to their ability to foster creative thinking," Peter tells me. "It is taking a shorter and shorter time to reach scale in today's global, technology-driven age. If you're going to survive, you need to build a culture of continued innovation."

Co-founder Adam Somlai-Fischer agrees: "We will always be a startup. Being a startup is a cultural question. For us, it is more about how fast can you react when you need to change? How much ownership does an individual engineer have? How much flexibility do we offer to our people? And not only when it comes to deciding what time they come to the office, but also how an issue gets solved." Hacking philosophy in action.

The company continues to gain ground against their Herculean competitors by staying connected to their sense of purpose: "We want to empower people to share ideas in better ways." This big vision which fuels the team was brought to life by a series of **Mashups** – of ideas and people, technology and culture, art and science. **Mashups** have since helped them attract $72 million in capital, disrupt the sleeping giants, and enable better communications across the 1.6 billion Prezi presentations that have been viewed by audiences to date. Color me im-PREZed.

HACK STARTERS

1. Take a look at your current products and services. What could you fuse into them to offer something completely different? Play around with lots of combinations to discover your Reese's-peanut-butter-cup moment.

2. If you're facing a problem or dealing with a setback, explore which two solutions could be combined to create a new and more powerful approach.

3. Examining your internal processes, are there any that could be combined to improve performance, increase quality, or drive efficiency? What could you take from outside the current process and combine with existing efforts to create a new, better path forward?

CHAPTER 13: WORKING BACKWARD

 English poet John Dryden wrote, "Beware the fury of a patient man." His sentiment was soon followed by playwright William Congreve's oft paraphrased declaration that "hell hath no fury like a woman scorned." In *Titus Andronicus*, Aaron rages, "Vengeance is in my heart, death in my hand, Blood and revenge are hammering in my head." Clearly, we humans are obsessed with revenge.

From the ancient Greek philosophers to Taylor Swift, it seems everyone has something to say about it. Because nothing stings like betrayal, like the wound of being wronged. Revenge has been the motive for crimes, wars, and literature for centuries. The human desire to get even has driven conflict and caused suffering. So it's no surprise then that cybercrime, too, has been fueled by this age-old motive.

Driven partially by disdain for infidelity, a hacker group who called themselves The Impact Team sought to expose cheating and deception. Angered by the casual nature in which husbands and wives betray each other, the hackers decided to use their skills to take on what they believed was an epidemic. How could they make the biggest impact on cheating spouses, while deterring future affairs and exposing what they deemed to be fraudulent business practices? Two words: Ashley Madison.

Ashley Madison, a website specifically developed to facilitate extramarital affairs, boasted over 47 million members. The site guaranteed privacy and captured millions in fees for enabling confidential hookups among its married users. The Impact Team hackers felt that Ashley Madison mocked the sanctity of marriage, and were further angered that the company was reportedly earning $1.7 million a year on "deletion fees," charges that members paid to wipe their accounts. When the site guaranteed absolute privacy and informed members that their identity was absolutely secure and could never be revealed, this was all but taunting the hacker mindset that *Every Barrier Can Be Penetrated*.

In July 2015, The Impact Team reported to the world that it had successfully hacked into Ashley Madison and made off with confidential user records, financial data, and more. The group threatened to publicly release the records unless Ashley Madison permanently shut down the site. Now here's a business dilemma – shut down a business that is raking in huge profits or wreak havoc on the millions of customers that trust the company. Since Ashley Madison is, in fact, in the business of betrayal, maybe that made the choice easier. The site continued on as the identities and confidential personal information of millions of customers were released to the world.

The damage was significant. Marriages were ended, millions were humiliated, and more than a dozen suicides were tied to the leak. The only real beneficiaries were divorce attorneys, who probably enjoyed a huge boost in business. While Ashley Madison still exists, it undoubtedly (and rightfully) lost the trust of the majority of their customers.

The Impact Team was never caught or brought to justice for their crimes, so the true details of their plot remain a mystery. Based on their public statements and anonymous interviews, The Impact Team had been gathering data from Ashley Madison for at least a few years. This wasn't a dash-and-grab, or the publication of a lucky exploit, but an approach called **Working Backward**. By starting with the end in mind (exposing cheaters, both marital and financial), the hackers then reverse-engineered their scheme. The technique of starting with a desired outcome and then systematically building a plan of attack in reverse order is a common approach used by hackers of all varieties.

LEGIT FLIP

In his book, *The Seven Habits of Highly Effective People*, Stephen R. Covey embraces the **Working Backward** approach. Habit #2 – Begin with the End in Mind – is based on the identical principle:

> *It's based on imagination – the ability to envision in your mind what you cannot at present see with your eyes. It is based on the principle that all things are created twice. There is a mental (first) creation, and a physical (second) creation. The physical creation follows the mental, just as a building follows a blueprint.*

Covey must have embraced the theory himself when crafting his best-selling book. The title has sold over 25 million copies in 40 languages since being published in 1989 and has been named by *Time* as one of the "25 Most Influential Business Management Books."

What sounds like an obvious truism is easier said than done. Most of our mental energy is spent on incremental change to existing products, services, or processes. This is especially the case in more established organizations. It's much easier to consider changing from brown raisins to yellow ones if you're the brand manager for Kellogg's Raisin Bran Crunch®, than it is to ask a different question altogether: "What is the ideal breakfast our customers truly want?" We toil away at making small tweaks to what already exists (working forward) as opposed to beginning with the vision of an ideal state and reverse-engineering from there (**Working Backward**).

DON'T KNOW SHIT FROM SHINOLA

The familiar phrase became popular in the 1940s during the rapid growth of American industrialism. Nothing was more patriotic than making something by hand, right here in the U – S – of – A. In the decades that followed, terms such as "low-cost countries" and NAFTA signaled a new era in which the notion of locally handcrafted goods became a quaint relic of the past. The actual product from the saying, Shinola shoe polish, fell on hard times as well, going out of business in 1960.

Enter Tom Kartsotis, the founder and former CEO of Fossil, which he took public in 1993. Today, the company boasts over $3 billion in revenue and employs over 10,000 people worldwide. After incredible success in the watch business, Tom had the desire to go upscale. He envisioned a handcrafted watch, made in America, which represented quality craftsmanship and national pride. Despite a crowded market dominated by foreign manufacturers, he believed customers would be enamored by the nostalgic connection to American manufacturing. So with the wacky vision of upscale customers buying watches handcrafted in the United States, Kartsotis could've started with his previous experience and contacts in the watch business and built up from there. Instead, he pursued the hacker approach of **Working Backward**, reverse-engineering his ideal state.

It started with his brand name. He could have cooked up a new name, just like he did with Fossil. But he sought to license the name of an iconic brand that represented the heyday of American Manufacturing. Exploring many possibilities, he landed on the defunct Shinola Shoe Polish Company. It was a brand name that everyone knew, a connection to the past. The name already conveyed a sense of humor, a head-tilting curiosity, and the implication that it could be something other than what's expected.

With name in hand, he needed to choose just the right location to craft his watches. **Working Backward**, he assembled focus groups to get customer feedback on different hometowns. He tried Shinola USA. He tested Shinola Los Angeles. There was a Shinola Chicago test. But when he tested Shinola Detroit, the results were off the charts. The "brand" of Detroit perfectly connected with the vibe he was trying to create. It was a symbol of grit and determination, of American ingenuity. Like the Shinola brand, Detroit had fallen on hard times and was fighting hard for a rebirth. It would have been easy to build the company near his home in Texas, but Tom's **Working Backward** approach led him to headquarter his new company in a city where he had no ties or connections. Shinola was (re)founded in 2011 in downtown Detroit, Michigan.

And the Shinola team continued to **Work Backward** from their idea of what Shinola could be – this tricky combination of grit and luxury. For the luxury element of the brand, their research revealed that the best way to build watches – the starting point for the brand – would be to bring in the highest quality components from Switzerland and use well-trained workers to assemble them in the U. S. So Shinola partnered with Ronda AG to acquire the top-notch watch pieces, and receive training on the assembly of the parts. Shinola hadn't just chosen Detroit because of its gritty public image; the Motor City is also the home of the automobile, the moving assembly line, and, after the recent recession, it was also the home of many highly-skilled factory workers who were looking for jobs. Shinola brought together the existing skillset of this pool of workers with the training and luxury components that would allow them to make beautiful, precision timepieces.

The quirky company intertwined its brand with my hometown of Detroit, and both have been on the rise over the last five years. The Shinola team now crafts handmade upscale bicycles, leather goods, and of course, American-made watches. In fact, Shinola is the only handmade watch being made in the country today. In the digital and disposable age, Shinola's high quality and simple design stand out. Tom didn't just build a watch company, he built a luxury American lifestyle brand. You don't just wear a Shinola because it looks nice or is high quality, customers line up around the world because of what it says about them – the watch represents tenacity and resilience, simplicity and durability.

Today, you may spot a Shinola on the arm of President Obama or any number of public figures – President Bill Clinton bought 14 – and the brand is featured in high-end retailers like Nordstrom, Saks Fifth Avenue, and Barney's New York. The Shinola team reverse-engineered their approach, first establishing their desired outcome of being an American manufacturer with the cache of the past. Only then, did they begin charting their course. Charting it by **Working Backward**, of course.

WORKING BACKWARD OUT OF A BIND

Working Backward is not only helpful when looking to drive growth and innovation – it can also help you get out of a jam. All of the Innovation Hacking techniques included in the book are applicable to both positive change and also overcoming adversity. The target may be different, but the methodology holds.

As I was building ePrize, I instituted a company-wide bonus program to align the team's efforts and give everyone a stake in the outcome. I built the model with my CFO, took it to my Board of Directors, and got it ratified as we approved our annual budget for the year. Sounds great, right? Well, I'm sure I'm not the first one to craft a well-intentioned plan that had a whopper of a flaw.

The flaw? That great, company-wide bonus was completely tied to our sales target: $40 million that year. The wildly imperfect plan was binary – if we beat the $40 million target by a dollar, all 500 people got a juicy bonus. If we missed it by a nickel, everyone got absolutely nothing. I know, deeply flawed. It did drive behavior, though. Large digital scoreboards illuminated our various offices around the world. Sacrifices were made, plans were crafted, and clients were wooed. This number was front-and-center for the entire company that year, all of us gunning hard to reach it.

On December 31, I got a call from my head of sales. "Josh, great news!" he exclaimed. "We made it! I just got in the final order of the year and we reached $40,200,000. We hit the goal!!"

In that moment, I was ecstatic. I patted myself on the back for our clear targets, thoughtful planning, and precise execution. I was proud of the hard work and commitment to results my team had demonstrated. So I immediately sent a heartfelt congratulatory note to the entire company.

"Great job everyone. We made it as a team! Everyone will share in this accomplishment together!"

Or so I thought.

According to our written compensation plan, the bonus was to be paid on Feb 15 of the New Year, or 45 days after my celebratory email. Based on the expected bonus, team members placed deposits on summer vacations, ordered new furniture for their homes, and planned their financial lives accordingly. I was all smiles myself, until my CFO walked into my office on Feb 2. "Hey Josh, you know that $40 million target we made for last year?" he said grimly. "It turns out we didn't just *make* it; we actually just *missed* it." He went on to explain that we double counted one order and didn't account for a client cancellation earlier in the year. Our grand total ended up around $39,989,000. Just short. Legally, no one in the company was entitled to a single cent of bonus.

I went to my Board and explained the situation. The financially-driven Directors, realizing we had no contractual obligation, emphatically refused to pay any bonuses. The company was not obligated and the team didn't earn it, they argued. Super Bowl championships aren't won by *almost* making it into the end zone, after all. The team wasn't comprised of children; these were all professional adults who understand how the world works. Even if we did pay the bonus, or part of it, we would be sending a terrible message – instead of rewarding performance we'd be rewarding the lack thereof.

Talk about a tough spot. In total, the bonuses added up to over one million dollars. We were successful at the time, but we didn't have millions in extra cash just lying around either. My board was very clear in their position, which I fully understood and appreciated. I had to do some real soul-searching to decide how to proceed. For me, I started thinking about the kind of company we were. The culture and philosophy that we stood for. How could I tell my team they were losing an already promised bonus based on a technicality? Sure I cared about the money in the short term, but I cared more about our value and legacy in the long-term.

Working Backward, I played out each scenario in my mind. If I didn't pay the bonus and saved a million dollars, I would undermine the trust I'd built over the last seven years. I determined I'd lose more than that amount in the form of apathy, employee attrition, broken trust, and damaged morale. I determined the money was already spent, no matter what I did. On the other hand, if I had already spent the money in one form or another, I might as well put it to good use. An investment in our team and culture was better than the penalty tax of perceived betrayal.

I fought and argued with my Board for a week straight. They insisted no bonus was to be paid, but I also refused to relent. It was a painful standoff, the business equivalent of the Cuban missile crisis. I felt bruised, battered, and exhausted.

Once a resolution was finally reached, I gathered my entire team together and explained the situation in great detail. I shared that we just missed the mark, rather than surpassed it as previously believed. I talked in great length about our commitment to results as a company and that we'd never reach our collective goals by rewarding the misses. The team understood, and I felt they were with me since they knew I was being genuine and transparent.

But then I dropped the bombshell. I said that while results are paramount, the one thing that trumps performance is trust. I said that we are a company that believes in keeping our word, and that I couldn't expect people to run through fire for me if I wasn't willing to do the same in return. I shared my philosophy of service, caring for each other, and making a positive impact for our team members as well as our clients. You could hear a pin drop until I announced that we were going to pay the bonus. In full. Every penny. On time.

Team members leapt to their feet. Cheers and clapping exploded; some people laughed while others cried. I couldn't count the hugs I received, many from grown men. As the meeting ended, the enthusiasm carried forward. Because of my demonstration of trust and commitment, the team paid it back ten-fold in the coming months and years. Morale was sky-high, turnover was low, and we over-delivered as a family. The story became known in the community, and was often told back to us by new people applying for a job. I'm convinced that my million-dollar payout that day was one of the best investments I ever made. The normal linear decision process of moving from one square to the next would have led to a saved bonus and a shattered team. Only through the **Working Backward** approach was I able to make the right call, turn a difficult situation into a positive one, and ultimately create the most possible value.

UNDERWEAR, EMPOWERMENT, AND SAVING THE WORLD

If you were brainstorming on how to make a product that could help empower women and increase opportunities for them, lingerie is not the first place you would go to. In fact, lingerie ad campaigns are often lambasted for objectifying women, not empowering them. But that's the beauty of **Working Backward** – you can find unexpected solutions because you're starting with the desired outcome and not getting bogged down by *expected* solutions. And that's exactly how Renata Mutis Black ended up building a foundation and a profitable business that are changing the world, one brief or thong at a time.

Renata was born in Colombia, but after being orphaned as a young child, she was raised by extended family in Miami. As a teenager, she began a journey to find herself – first going back to live in Colombia, then to an oil rig to serve as a translator. After pursuing a degree at the University of North Carolina, she traveled around the world, including helping small communities rebuild after the 2004 Indian Ocean Tsunami. While rebuilding in India, she was approached in the street one day by an impassioned woman. Renata suspected the woman was offended by her bare shoulders, but the woman's real motivation was very different: "I don't want your money," she said, "can you teach me how to make money?"

That was Renata's turning point. She had the painful realization that she couldn't help this woman. Despite her advantages and hard-won experience, Renata was crippled by student loans and didn't really know how to make money for herself. The woman's request inspired Renata to go to Bangladesh and reach out to Muhammad Yunus – the economist who was awarded the Nobel Prize for his work on microfinance.

Renata studied under Yunus for three months before returning to India. Excited by her new knowledge, she told a local village woman about what she had learned, and the woman asked her to come speak to some others about microfinance. Renata was humbled to go to the town square and find 800 eager women, ready to learn about how to build their own businesses.

Black spent two years with those women, doing accounting for them so that they would be creditworthy in the eyes of the government. That achievement would allow them to obtain loans and begin businesses. After returning to the U. S., Renata started the Seven Bar Foundation to help create awareness around microfinancing. From the beginning, the foundation was centered on an unlikely product: lingerie. And not accidentally.

During her time in India, women told Renata how terrible it must be in the U. S., where women had to use their hair and bodies to attract men – a reality that was unfathomable to them. But to Renata, living day-to-day bound up in a sari was equally unfathomable. When she returned to the U. S., Renata was watching the Victoria's Secret fashion show when she remembered the words of those women. She saw women in lingerie being used as tools of seduction, and she wondered, "What if we use the power of lingerie and fashion to empower women instead?"

From the beginning, Black was committed to the mindset that **Quantity Is a Force Multiplier**, and with microfinance, you need as many people as possible. So the Seven Bar Foundation started as a partnership with major designers like Agent Provocateur – Black hosted huge lingerie shows, to generate awareness and funding for microloans to help impoverished women achieve self-sustainability through entrepreneurship. And from the get-go, Black drew major attention – Eva Longoria and Sophia Vergara were both early supporters. Renata even reached out to Deepak Chopra, who was so impressed by her innovative vision for breaking the cycle of poverty that he came to speak at the first show and has dedicated a book chapter to her.

From her time in India, Renata was **Working Backward** from her vision: a world where women are empowered wage earners in their families and communities, and cycles of poverty are a thing of the past. First, she was providing on-the-ground help rebuilding the communities after the tsunami. That was fine, but she realized that just wasn't enough. Through her fateful encounter with the inquisitive woman, she worked backward to empower woman to make money. That quickly proved a compelling channel for change. So she started with those 800 women – what did they need to start businesses? Loans. What did they need to get those loans? Credit. What did they need to get credit? Records of their creditworthiness. Okay, done. So she stayed for two years to build that.

Bolstered by her first attempts at fostering microfinance for women, she decided that was the route for her. So she needed to find a way to make microfinance viable – visible to people with money, and able to generate enough money to finance the many needed loans. She was convinced from the beginning that social enterprise, not charity, is the future of global change. But what product was going to allow her to reach the ends that she wanted?

When she had her epiphany during the Victoria Secret fashion show, she saw the potential – on many fronts – for lingerie to bring about change. She saw this as her next step in **Working Backward** to create a sustainable way to alleviate poverty. By using lingerie to empower instead of objectify women, she would be challenging societal expectations about women, sexuality, and power. She wasn't making women choose between being sexy *or* empowered, she was giving them an opportunity to do both, and help each other in the process. Additionally, fashion shows in general, and lingerie shows in particular, had the tendency to draw big crowds and big names, which could help her drum up the awareness – and dollars – she sought.

Finally, for someone committed to creating long-term, lasting changes, what better product than underwear? After the success of the initial shows, Black expanded the Seven Bar Foundation into a social enterprise, the for-profit lingerie company, Empowered By You. Renata spent two years in R&D to create the perfect, "seamless panty," and made this clothing stable both a fashion necessity and a catalyst for social change. The underwear comes in a thong or a brief in a variety of colors, and by partnering with major brands like Rebecca Minkoff and Alice & Olivia, the underwear is also available in patterns that are extensions of brands shoppers already love.

Empowered By You has major pull with Millennials, a demographic Black has intentionally appealed to because she knows her model resonates with them. As she put it to *Forbes*, "74% of [Millennials] are more likely to buy a product if the proceeds go to something they believe in." In Black's case, twenty percent of all her profits go to funding microloans, the underwear is made in a Sri Lankan factory that adheres to UN's Women Empowerment Principles, and the packaging and website both contain testimonials of women who have received the microloans, from the U. S. to India. Black has shown not only that you don't have to sacrifice ethics to build a successful fashion business, but that by **Working Backward**, you can generate innovative new ideas that drive both business and world change.

HACK STARTERS

1. Leaving incremental advancement aside for the moment, take one situation you're facing and start by envisioning your ultimate desired state. What is the ideal product, solution, service, approach, or process for this challenge? Instead of being restricted in your thinking based on the resources at hand, envision the ultimate outcome. Once you are clear on your vision, what would the last step before completion look like? What about the step before that? And so on. Start with an unfettered and bold vision and then reverse-engineer the necessary steps to achieve it.

2. Pick a current problem or setback. Instead of digging yourself out of the hole one step at a time, imagine the obstacle completely eliminated. How would you feel? What would you do next? With this renewed energy, **Work Backward** – step by step – thinking up a plan in reverse order, leading all the way back to your current circumstance.

Part 3
HACKING MASTERCLASS

MASTERCLASS INTRODUCTION

Now that we've had the chance to examine each of the five hacker mind-sets and ten hacker tactics, it's time to take a look at how the principles can be applied in combinations to yield next-level, breakthrough performance.In the same way a professional boxer conquers his opponent by throwing a series of interconnected punches, you will enjoy the biggest leap forward by combining several tactics, all built upon the foundation of the core philosophies.

The following five stories give us a real-life view of how the Innovation Hacking model was able to drive stunning performance in completely un-related areas. As you embark on these five adventures, keep your own struggles and opportunities in the back of your mind. Look for ways to borrow the approaches of these innovators and apply similar winning strategies directly to the biggest challenges you face.

CHAPTER 14: MASTERCLASS 1 – A LEVER AND A ROCK TO MOVE THE UNIVERSE

It was an uncharacteristically hot June evening. There had been record-breaking temperatures across the country all month, and Ms. Lever was cursing her luck for being in one of the offices without air conditioning. Luckily, temperatures cooled as the night wore on, aided by a few fans, so she grabbed another cup of coffee to keep her energy up and got to work.

Alone in the office, she returned to the same piece of code she and her colleagues had been working on unsuccessfully for weeks. She tried Adding and Subtracting different combinations into the code, but nothing worked. Maybe it was the heat, or the freedom of being alone in the office in the middle of the night, maybe it was just sheer frustration over this infuriating bit of code. Whatever it was, she completely disregarded the parameters her boss had set for dealing with the code and experimented, following a hunch. She **Deconstructed** the elements of the code, putting them back together in different ways, including ways that had been ruled out by the project parameters.

It was like a switch had been flipped. Suddenly, miraculously, the pieces of the code started to come together, and she could see each bit working, understanding it in a way she never had before. By morning, she had completed this section of code and saved the day. In spite of, or rather, because of breaking all the rules.

Ms. Lever is not a computer programmer at a hip Silicon Valley startup, however. She was Mavis Lever, a student of German romantic literature who was one of the codebreakers at the top-secret Bletchley Park in Britain during World War II. And the code she was working on was not a programming language, but part of the Italian Naval code. This solution and those she worked on in the months following led to the British victory at the Battle of Matapan.

The similarity between Mavis's story and that of many successful start-ups and businesses is no coincidence. The operation at Bletchley Park during World War II is an incredible example of hacking in action. Also no coincidence? The fact that Bletchley Park is also the birthplace of Alan Turing's breakthrough – the bombe machine – that has led him to be called the father of modern computing. Turing's creation, which was used to crack German Enigma code at Bletchley Park, is believed to have shortened the war by two years and saved 14 million lives.

When you think of the winning of World War II, you probably picture young men storming the beaches of Normandy, fanfare in the streets of Europe, Allied troops liberating concentration camps, or a young sailor dipping a pretty nurse back for a spontaneous kiss in Times Square. These brave and celebratory actions are worth remembering, but they're far from the whole story. In fact, these famous pictures in our collective memory, and the many victories that led up to them, would not have been possible if not for a very unlikely group of people.

What do you get when you bring together students and professors of German, Latin, and the classics; a smattering of mathematicians and bank employees; a few chess players and actresses; crossword puzzle enthusiasts; some military men and women; and a bunch of teenage girls into a few tin huts? Surprisingly, it's not the opening of a joke, but a description of the ragtag team responsible for doing some of the soberest work in modern history. These were the men and women of the Bletchley Park operation, responsible for breaking Enigma, and bringing in most of the Allied intelligence during the war.

When Britain set out to fill positions in Bletchley Park, their approach utilized multiple hacking tactics. The first step of recruitment – targeted largely at universities – was to **Crowdsource** capable and trustworthy recommendations from government officials and top professors. Details of the work and positions were not disclosed, just that it was important work for King and Country. One of their most famous **Crowdsourcing** solutions was to put at ad in the paper. Well, sort of.

Readers of the *London Daily Telegraph* complained in 1942 that the puzzles had become easy enough to be solved in minutes. So a private citizen issued a contest to put the puzzles to the test, offering a reward for anyone that showed up and solved the next puzzle in 12 minutes or less.

The day after the contest, the puzzle was printed for everyone else to try their hands. The catch? The War Office was watching, and it reached out to participants and set up interviews for positions at Bletchley.

The War Office clearly wasn't looking for recruits where we would expect them to. Many of the employees were non-military, and though they did bring in mathematicians like Turing, they were generally unsure of the utility of mathematics in codebreaking and thought mathematicians were a bit too eccentric to be useful.

Another surprise? Bletchley Park employees were mostly women. Though men like Turing, Dilly Knox, Gordon Welchman, Stuart Milner-Barry, and Hugh Alexander have the headlines in most of the accounts of Bletchley, of the 10,000 or so total people who worked there during the war, about 75% of them were women. In addition to the daily transcription, data entry, and filing work these women did – which was indispensable to the whole of the operation – many major breakthroughs and breaks in code can be attributed to the women of Bletchley. Bletchley was the primary hub of intelligence for the British and Allied forces. To put this important work, and by extension the fate of the nation, in the hands of a bunch of young women, was, in the 1940s, certainly a **Reverse**.

But their unusual recruitment methods and hodge-podge roster worked to their advantage. Dilly Knox is one of the best-known names from Bletchley Park. In addition to being a code-cracking savant, Knox was also a classics scholar and papyrologist at King's College, Cambridge. Knox was responsible for devising an early method for cracking Enigma, called "rodding." Rodding was the method Mavis Lever used, and Knox the boss whose guidelines she disregarded when she cracked the Italian codes used to win Matapan. Knox had been working as a cryptanalyst since WWI, and near the end of that war he had a breakthrough that a mathematician or military officer simply couldn't have had.

While trying to break a piece of code, his well-trained ear detected the meter of poetry among the encoded gobbledygook. Through overlaps in the encryption and stressed syllables, he was able to make out the ends of 5 words. He took his suspicion to a German professor down the hall who quickly turned his 5 syllables into two lines from a German poem by Friederich Schiller. This gave them an "in" to crack the remaining code. They didn't need to execute a Different Lens (**Borrow**) tactic the way we might, by asking "How might a German solve this" or "How might a poet encode this," because with their diverse staff, they were able to view through Different Lenses in real time, and **Crowdsource** solutions. During the next war, Bletchley continued to embrace what we might now call neural diversity. Gordon Welchman, one of the mathematicians at Bletchley admitted, "The work did not really need mathematics but mathematicians tended to be good at it" (ATD 105).

And it wasn't just hacking tactics that helped the Bletchley hackers win the day, hacker mindsets dominated their work and attitudes.

Every Barrier Can Be Penetrated – Codebreaking in itself is a defiance of barriers. Granted, those at Bletchley had significant motivation – the code HAD to be cracked to win the war and preserve their way of life – but their ability to break the codes over and over came from believing in the possibility of cracking everything.

Compasses Over Maps – For the codebreakers, their work changed literally every day. Now, that doesn't mean they threw everything out each morning, but they only kept what worked. Because of all this fluidity, maps were a no-go at Bletchley, unless they were being used to chart Axis troops. Compasses were the only way they could guide their movement and not be held back by crippling assumptions.

Nothing Is Static – This mindset was unavoidable at Bletchley. Their codes came in multiple languages (which they often didn't speak), they came from locales around the world, each code bore the individual quirks of the operator who sent it, and to top it all off, the message encoding changed daily. With all these changing variables, the codebreakers didn't have the luxury of falling in love with any particular solution because at best, each one had only a 24-hour shelf life.

They kept Turing's bombe machine, but the "menu," or decoding key put through it, changed multiple times per day. They watched for patterns that they had seen before, but they didn't insist or expect to see them used in a particular way. And sometimes, they had to throw out just about everything they knew – like Mavis Lever did – to find a new solution.

Quantity Is a Force Multiplier – This was true, not only in the total number of people working at Bletchley. As they applied **Brute Force** to the codes, trying one decryption after another, it was often dumb luck as to who would get a break in the code for the day. And as excited as they would be to crack a code, they understood the process was more important than who happened to be announcing the breakthrough. Bletchley codebreaker Derek Taunt explained that "[Who] was irrelevant: everyone recognized that all successes were due to the team, not to individuals" (84). Even the seemingly solo successes like Lever's were built upon the successes and failures of others. When one person had a breakthrough, they all won. The more individual pieces of codes they cracked, the closer they were to winning the war.

 Competence Is the Only Credential That Matters – Bletchley wasn't perfect. Many of the roughly 7,500 women who worked at Bletchley have been forgotten to history. During the war, many of the gifted women who worked as codebreakers during the war were not given the same opportunities to advance as their male counterparts, and we will never know what that cost the war effort. But some leaders, like Dilly Knox, were known for valuing competence over everything, including gender.

Knox's ability to foreground the work over individual titles or egos may have come from a hard-learned lesson at the beginning of the war. In 1939, Britain's Government Code and Cypher School (GC&CS), the department that ran Bletchley Park, was working on figuring out exactly how the physical Enigma machine worked, so that they could crack it. It had a number of lettered rotors, a typewriter-like keyboard, and wires that connected that two, which had to be correctly placed to read a message (think of the old-school telephone operators plugging and unplugging wires to connect calls through their giant switchboards).

Mrs. B.B. (whose full name has been lost to history) was a codebreaker at GC&CS and she suggested that the wiring might be alphabetical. Without testing her idea on a crib (sample decoded message), the suggestion was written off as too simple. Later, at a meeting with Polish codebreakers, Knox found out that the Polish had beaten the British in figuring out the wiring – which was alphabetical. With frustration, Knox realized the lost opportunity of capitalizing on Mrs. B.B.'s solution.

Later, speaking of Mavis Lever and Margaret Rock, who worked with Knox to break the *Abwehr* code, he not only gave them sole credit for breaking the code, but he said, "Give me a Lever and a Rock and I will move the Universe" (308). He didn't care about their credentials or gender, he cared about their competence. And together, they helped hack the war.

Chapter 15: Masterclass 2 – Everything Is Awesome

Their spouses and families have no idea what they do at work. But then, very few people do. Their clandestine offices are hidden away from prying eyes and access is screened through multiple ID checkpoints. Only this small group and the most senior management can get into their hidden lair.

But today, this group of diverse and highly-trained operatives is working on a mission from outside the office. They've descended upon the swanky Hotel Trias in the town of Palamós, Spain. As the Mediterranean sun warms the gentle seaside breezes, they gather in one of the hotel's meeting rooms, where a tall, unassuming man waits for everyone to get situated before beginning their briefing. He lays out the work ahead of them in the coming days, before they assemble their tactical teams and get down to business.

So what is their business, exactly? Assassination? Weapons? Corporate or governmental espionage?

Toys.

That's right. The unassuming man at the front of the room is Erik Hansen and the super-secret group he is briefing is LEGO's FutureLab. They are on a weeklong getaway to bring together research, innovation, and play, to build the future of the company. LEGO makes a physical product in an increasingly virtual world, so innovation is not a buzzword or fanciful experiment for the FutureLab, it's a matter of survival.

In 2003, LEGO was nearly lost into the annals of toy history. The company was deferring to a purported expert, with no toy experience, who was arranging the corporate bricks from another country. They were reliant on licensing deals with major movies for surges in income, putting them at the mercy of film release schedules. And the previous Christmas season had left retailers in possession of too much of their LEGO stock.

Experts said that LEGO would be facing rapid obsolescence as video games and virtual worlds expanded. So they were dumping all of their resources into digitally-minded ventures that were out of sync with customer needs. Instead of approaching new products playfully, the company had quick, fear-based reactions. For example, trying to satisfy potential buyers who wanted less construction, they made kits with more molded pieces that required virtually no assembly. But the buyers they were trying to appease didn't really want to build at all, they wanted pre-built toys; and the builders that made up their base no longer recognized their once beloved, block-based toys. Jørgen Vig Knudstorp took over in 2004 and steadied the LEGO ship, helping LEGO and FutureLab to reach their full potential. But FutureLab isn't the first time LEGO embraced the hacker mindset, it was actually already in their injection-molded plastic DNA.

Ole Kirk Christiansen set up shop in the little village of Billund, Denmark as a carpenter. By the early 1930s, as a result of the Great Depression, people had little interest in buying furniture. So Christiansen did a **Mashup** of his well-honed craft – woodworking – and something he thought would be easier to sell: toys. He began making small wooden toys and officially founded the LEGO Toy Company in 1934.

About ten years later, Christiansen learned about injection-molded plastic. While talking with a supplier, he saw a selection of things that could be made with these machines. The item that captured his imagination was a small plastic brick, then being sold by a British company called Kiddicraft. He bought a machine, took a brick, and got to work.

Christiansen didn't just steal the Kiddicraft brick; he used the **Deconstruction** tactic to take apart the design of the brick and figure out how to make it work better. The result was a stud-and-tube design that could bind with other bricks strongly enough to withstand kids at play, but still come apart easily. The result is what LEGO calls "clutch factor" (it's what makes that satisfying popping noise when you attach and detach the bricks).

Christiansen's process is one that is frequently repeated by the FutureLab. During their weeklong annual retreats, the highlight is the **Agile Burst** tactic – a 24-hour Hackathon. During the hackathon, the teams use **Brute Force** via Rapid Experimentation to quickly test and cycle through ideas. And where does the FutureLab originate these ideas? They hack them, of course.

LEGO doesn't just make colorful bricks, pirate ships, and teeny-tiny Harry Potters, they're also a research hub. Through independent research and partnerships with major universities and institutions, LEGO **Crowdsources** information about play from the experts: kids. Equipped with data about how kids think and play, the FutureLab comes to the Hackathon ready to create. One such creation was LEGO Fusion, a **Mashup** which allowed kids to integrate physical and digital realities. **Crowdsourcing** ideas has become a major boon for them in recent years, but years ago, LEGO almost shut off this valuable pipeline of ideas.

In 1998, as part of their attempt to fend off the looming fate of extinction-by-electronics, LEGO partnered with MIT to release Mindstorms – a computerized yellow brick module that allowed kids to turn their LEGO bricks into rudimentary robots. Though we're probably still a few years away from the robot takeover, the Mindstorms did take on a life of their own.

The first Mindstorm surprise was who was using them. Designed, like all LEGO products, for kids, the company was shocked to learn that roughly half of all sales were to adults, for adults. The second Mindstorm surprise was how they were being used. A LEGO fan at Stanford hacked the code in the Mindstorm module and began writing new code for it, and within three months, over 1,000 hackers were creating codes for Mindstorm robots.

LEGO's initial response was defensive – their product had been violated and was being misused – they called in senior management and legal teams to decide how to deal with the situation. As Tormond Askildsen, Senior Director of Community Engagement & Events, explains, the company had two available reactions. They could either be "aggressive, protective, controlling" or they could say, "Wow...this is interesting." The traditional model is to circle the wagons and draw up the lawsuits, but the hacker model challenges us to explore, question, and experiment. And that's exactly what LEGO did; Mindstorm has had various iterations and is still in production. This opened LEGO up to entertaining the power of **Crowdsourced** ideas, which led them to execute a major **Reverse** tactic in 2007, when they did something that had previously been unthinkable – they released a line of their toys just for adults.

When Chicago-based architect Adam Reed Tucker lost his job, he channeled his frustration in an unexpected way: he began to carefully construct human-sized landmark buildings, entirely out of LEGO. Tucker reached out to LEGO executive Paal Smith-Meyer about the potential for adult LEGO kits. Smith-Meyer was in agreement, but knew he needed more to take to management before they would sanction breaking their business model. Smith-Meyer wasn't even sure the project was feasible, but he sent Tucker the bricks to see what he could come up with. Tucker used the **Working Backward** tactic to create 200 kits in his home, complete with instructions, box art, and packaging. Now convinced that the project had potential, LEGO took a gamble and released the first of the adult Architecture series. Not only did the initial series sell well, but it did so at twice the price point of the kids' kits.

But these tactics can't be sustained or used to bring about real change without embracing the hacking mindsets that nurture them. Let's look at LEGO's spin on our core hacking mindsets.

Every Barrier Can Be Penetrated – From children to adult markets, from the physical to virtual worlds, from boys to girls, scientists to Harry Potter enthusiasts, and everything in between, LEGO has created products that appeal to people across many demographics. But, arguably the biggest barrier in reaching people around the world is language. LEGO learned that you can create a product that transcends even this greatest of communication barriers. LEGO has created something that people intuitively get. Every product isn't going to have this effect, but don't assume that an obstacle – even something as profound as language – is an insurmountable one.

Compasses Over Maps – LEGO always had a general course set, but by not being tied to a map, the company has been able to make unexpected detours, like veering away from their primary children's toy market to delight adults with the Architecture series. But this mindset isn't just about going in new directions; it's about being able to retrace your steps when something has gone amiss and then course-correct. With some of their digital projects and overly-molded, mostly-assembled products, LEGO was able to see that they didn't like the lay of the land, and choose a new direction.

Nothing Is Static – Ole Kirk Christiansen knew this from the start – from wooden furniture, to wooden toys, to plastic toys, through three separate factories burning down, from the Kiddicraft brick to the LEGO stud-and-tube – Christiansen was always willing to shake things up. The company has never stopped challenging itself and its users to imagine what may be possible with those innocuous little bits of plastic. They've also added countless shapes, figures, accessories, and other plastic pieces throughout the years.

 Quantity Is a Force Multiplier – Even though the Future-Lab work is top-secret, even this hush-hush R&D team is a collaborative effort. The activities on their annual team retreat are team-oriented and show just how important it is to pool ideas and resources. And after Mindstorms, LEGO embraced the potential of collaboration outside the company, particularly with their customers. One such effort is their Japan-based Cuusoo project, which allows users to submit their dream LEGO kits to a website for consideration. Those that get over 10,000 user likes are considered for the annual, special-edition Cuusoo kit. The competition to become the next Cuusoo kit is just as popular as the kits themselves. As LEGO's Tormod Askildsen brilliantly puts it, "We need to be aware that 99.99% of the smartest people in the world don't work for us."

 Competence Is the Only Credential That Matters – Who do you consult to test your ideas, plans, products? Even though LEGO has plenty of savvy, well-educated, well-credentialed employees, when it comes down to deciding what's ahead for everyone's favorite plastic bricks, they hand the reins to kids. Business plans and market projections are fine and dandy, but as any parent knows, kids tend not to adhere to adult expectations. So LEGO isn't afraid to do the research by taking toys to kids and seeing how they play, what they really want, and adjusting accordingly. It may feel reassuring to get an opinion from someone with a lot of letters after their name or the fanciest framed piece of paper in their office, but those things don't necessarily translate to the experience or real-world knowledge needed to get a job done.

The hacking at the heart of LEGO has trickled down to its millions of users. Today, LEGO embraces that, despite having thought of themselves as a children's toy company, some of their most avid and enthusiastic users are adults. And many LEGO fans are tapping into their inner children to use LEGO for very grownup projects, from fully functional cars to livable houses, from recreating ancient Greek technology to public and private art installations.

Architects use LEGO to mock up building plans, researchers at MIT use scale LEGO cities to explore city-planning efforts. Studies out of the Yale School in New Jersey have even shown that a LEGO-based therapy can improve social outcomes for autistic children. One of NASA's California offices has a room filled with LEGO bricks, where they dream up space missions and spacecraft. One such creation was the Juno mission to Jupiter, which included specially-made LEGO mini figurines, made out of space-grade aluminum, mounted to the outside of the craft.

LEGO has now released a blockbuster movie of their own and no longer relies on licensing deals to hit their margins. By embracing hacking – in their overall operations, through a dedicated group of high-intensity hackers, in interactions with customers – LEGO has not only defined the childhood of millions, but they're also defining the future of toys. And with their generations of customers, they're hacking the future of architecture, space, and in many ways, the human imagination.

Chapter 16: Masterclass 3 – The Tour de France, Giant Puppets, and Rock 'n' Roll

These aren't the results of a Rorschach inkblot test, but milestones for a company that has integrated hacking into the waterproof fiber of their company, year after year, innovation after innovation.

But first, we have to start with plastic heart implants. That's what Gore (W.L. Gore & Associates) engineer Dave Myers was working on. In fact, that is one of his specialties, inventing plastic heart implants. Luckily, Gore encourages its associates to regularly play with new ideas.

As a side project, Dave was tinkering with his mountain bike, trying to improve the transition between gears. As a possible remedy, Dave used the **Borrowing** tactic – he tried applying a thin coat of plastic, like the plastic he uses to make implants. Myers' side project eventually resulted in the Gore cycling cables called Ride-On, which became an instant favorite with cyclists, including Andy Schleck who had them on his bike when he won the 2010 Tour de France.

Most people would be pretty satisfied with having developed a game-changing product in an industry completely unrelated to their own. But not Dave, and not at Gore. With his last **Borrow** being such a success, Myers considered where else this idea of coated strings may be useful. Naturally, he thought of giant puppets. And a new **Mashup** was born.

Beginning what I can only imagine was a visually curious R&D journey, Myers began studying the small-gauge cables that were used in huge animated puppets, like those you might see at Walt Disney World. Struggling to find materials with a small enough diameter, he tried using guitar strings, after coating them with plastic like his cycling cables. I don't know if Dave's puppet revolution ever panned out, but his makeshift solution got him thinking about guitars, and he wondered if these strings would be useful to musicians.

Not knowing anything about guitars, Dave checked with Chuck Hebestreit, a colleague and fellow engineer who confirmed that the notorious fickleness of acoustic guitar strings could potentially benefit from such a revamp. Then came two years of **Brute Force** via Rapid Experimentation. And waiting.

Eventually, another colleague, John Spencer – who had been working on Glide dental floss – joined the team when he wasn't working on medical inventory management systems. The guys then inspired a few others to join the team and tinkered with the strings in their spare time until they thought they had a viable product. The company agreed, but they still faced a major obstacle: how do you go about getting into a market in which your company has no experience? The answer: hack your way in, of course.

The tactic of choice for Gore's hack into the music industry was a **Social Engineering** and **Exploit** combo, a **Mashup**, if you will. These new guitar strings, named Elixir, cost three to five times as much as standard strings; so, as a company with no foothold in that marketplace, marketing them was going to take some doing. When retailers refused to carry the high-priced newcomers, Gore turned to the experts and sent 20,000 samples to major guitar magazines' subscribers. They hoped to **Social Engineer** a fan base, and then **Exploit** that foothold in the market. And it worked – within a few years, they were leading the market for acoustic guitar strings.

You probably already know Gore from one of their most famous inventions. Clothing made from the revolutionary waterproof, breathable GORE-TEX fiber has become standard for workouts and outdoor adventures. Innovative products like the Ride-On cables, Elixir strings, and GORE-TEX fiber are all the result of hacking tactics and mindsets, but they aren't the trendy attempts of an older company to catch up to the whippersnappers in the startup world; they're the fruits of over 50 years of dedicated hacking labor.

Bill and Vieve Gore founded W.L. Gore & Associates in 1958. To start this new venture, Bill left his job at DuPont because he was convinced that polytetrafluoroethylene (PTFE), a polymer discovered in 1938, had potential far beyond what had been harnessed. Despite the fact that the company was founded on Bill's belief in this new material, it was actually Bill and Vieve's son, Bob, who had the company's first breakthrough. A college lab experiment of Bob's turned into Gore's first patent and major product: a coated electronic cable.

In the early years, the Gore family and a small group of employees worked out of the basement of the Gore's home, sourcing tools from the kitchen and assembling products on the lawn. Today, Gore is a privately-held global company that has also become known for being an early adopter of a lattice-structure culture. With the exception of a CEO and a few division heads, employees (they prefer "associates") are accountable to their teams, not a looming supervisor. In hacking terms, the whole culture is **Crowdsourced** – ideas, innovations, internal changes come from the group; even raises are determined by a committee, based on past and present performance combined with future ideas.

Gore doesn't just use many of the classic hacking tactics in its operations, the 5 Core Hacker Mindsets are also visible across the company. Let's take a closer look.

 Every Barrier Can Be Penetrated – At Gore, they don't allow themselves to get bogged down by limitations – employees work together across teams and traditional department boundaries, and they openly cross in and out of different industries and even roles. They go beyond penetrating barriers, and just assume there aren't any to begin with; it's *"how* will I solve this problem," not *"can* I solve this problem?"

 Compasses Over Maps – Because they focus on solving problems and playing with solutions and materials, Gore avoids being overly committed to any particular solution or product. By directing their associates to spend some of their time regularly on interest-based projects, they encourage their staff to think in new directions and actively explore in the workplace. The result? Gore goes anywhere it wants to. That doesn't mean every idea will pan out, and Gore understands and celebrates this. Failed ideas are given a beer or champagne celebration, because a failure represents ideas explored, as well as lessons and experience gained.

 Nothing Is Static – The beauty of Gore's commitment to exploration and play is that it is continuous and fluid – just because you found a solution doesn't mean it's the only solution, or the last one. Gore continuously improves their own products and works to develop better ways of solving the problems they already solved. This goes for internal processes, too. After doing employee focus groups, Gore realized that to meet the needs and expectations of younger team members, they needed to update their methods of communication and use of technology. So they started making changes. They value their tradition, and make decisions thoughtfully, but they're not afraid to make change a constant.

 Quantity Is a Force Multiplier – In a **Crowdsourced** environment like Gore's, they know the value of more heads. From product development to revamping their internal communication, they actively seek out more ideas, different ideas, to make things better. Teams are ad-hoc and associates are encouraged to reach out to bring new people and expertise to the team. This practice began early – Gore started as a family affair, with Bill and Vieve at the helm, bolstered by their son, Bob, and a small group of employees. Their initial funding relied on this principle as well. The seed money for Gore didn't come from a major bank or fancy VC firm, but from the Gores' bridge club.

 Competence Is the Only Credential That Matters – Without the traditional organizational charts and alphabet soup job titles, Gore associates have to find other ways to determine who is getting the job done. From forming product teams to evaluating raises, these things are done not based on your titles or degrees, but what you do. To encourage the creation and exploration of new ideas, future prospects are part of the raise-evaluation process at Gore; so it's not just what have you already done, but what are you willing to explore and try out going forward.

And Gore's hacking works.

While Steve Jobs was still playing on the swings, Bill and Vieve Gore began the diligent work of building a hacking and innovation empire. Since then, Gore products have run city infrastructures, powered electronics from computers to calculators to microwaves, they were at the moon landing, they've been on the backs of soldiers and mountaineers, and they pulse with the heartbeats and organs of millions of patients. They've flossed your teeth, delivered the sound of your favorite songs, powered space stations, and helped protect your cellphone.

Their employees are happy, challenged, and fulfilled – Gore regularly appears on international lists of the best places to work, and also ranks highly on regional lists around the world. And when so many companies are battling the financial and morale costs of turnover, Gore enjoys an incredibly low full-time voluntary turnover rate of around only 3%.

Oh, and their annual sales are about $3 billion. Need I say more?

Chapter 17: Masterclass 4 – The Entrepreneur, the Nerd, the Soccer Mom, and the Rock Star

We humans have always had a fascination with flying. For at least hundreds of years before the Wright Brothers' first voyage, we longed to soar through the clouds with heavenly grace. Today, many of us rely on commercial aircraft for our livelihood – racing off to give that big presentation in Munich, zipping to New York to meet the marketing agency, or shipping hundreds of packages from an e-commerce website to serve eager customers' demands worldwide.

Those of us who find ourselves in more airports than we'd like, can quickly become accustomed to the hassles of commercial flight. Hour-long security lines, frequent delays, last minute cancellations, lost luggage, horrible airline customer service, that sneezing seatmate whose cold will surely be yours by the end of the flight. We road warriors often dream of a different path: a marvelous existence that involves the convenience and luxury of private aircraft. No more racing to the airport, since your plane accommodates your schedule. No wasted time, inconvenient schedules, or screaming babies. You'll finally be able to make it home in time to catch your kids' baseball games.

The fantasy ends abruptly as the flight attendant crudely orders you to stow your laptop for arrival. Looking up at his condescending gaze, you realize you'll be flying commercial forever. The impenetrable barrier you face: cost.

Flying private is wonderfully convenient, extremely efficient, wildly glamorous, and stupidly expensive. A Delta flight from New York to San Francisco may set you back $450, but that same flight in a Gulfstream could run $65,000. These jets can cost upwards of $40 million to purchase, burn thousands of dollars of fuel per hour, require a highly trained crew, and have maintenance costs in the hundreds of thousands per year.

Despite a huge market of travelers willing to pay a premium to avoid the big airlines, the cost barrier has just been too big to cross. But several bold companies are now trying to hack the friendly skies. These four renegades are applying hacking techniques and mindsets to tackle the extremely difficult challenge of making private aviation affordable. Here you'll see how the innovators I affectionately call the Entrepreneur, the Nerd, the Soccer Mom, and the Rock Star each took radically different approaches to hack the same problem of making private aviation more accessible.

THE ENTREPRENEUR

"Life is short. There is no time for things that do not completely move you," David Loury told *Business Insider*. Loury is the visionary CEO behind Cobalt, a company taking a Silicon Valley approach to private aviation. His new aircraft, the Co50 Valkyrie looks like a science fiction spacecraft, ready to shoot lasers as it defends the galaxy. The design is essentially a **Mashup** of a fighter jet and a single-engine propeller plane. Everything about the aircraft, in fact, is unorthodox for private aviation. Instead of entering through side doors, a giant 320-degree glass bubble canopy opens and passengers can enter like Goose and Maverick. A single propeller powers the aircraft, but it is placed at the back instead of the front, pushing the plane instead of pulling it (in hacker parlance, a **Reverse**). Instead of boring white, this new plane stands out on the runway in jet black or matte dark platinum. Instead of a single tail wing, the tail has two wings on an angle, resembling an F-16 fighter. Inspired by companies like Apple that want their products to be beautiful as well as functional, the design of this bold new aircraft is something you'll probably see one day at the museum of modern art.

But Cobalt didn't just hack a super-sexy exterior. The plane travels at up to 300 mph, at the very high end of speed for single-engine propeller planes. It is also extremely fuel-efficient, burning only 20 gallons per hour (compared to roughly 250 gallons per hour for a light private jet). **Working Backward**, Loury set out to make the plane not only beautiful but also affordable and safe. In addition to the hyper-efficient engine, the design team fought hard to keep construction costs low. They scoured the world for low-cost parts and reverse-engineered many facets of the aircraft to support lower-cost (yet still safe and FAA-approved) assembly. As a result of their hacking approach, the cost for a brand new Co50 Valkyrie starts at

$595,000, roughly 70% lower than the cost of a similarly-performing private jet. More importantly for flyers, the all-in cost per mile is only $0.65, compared to approximately $3.00 per mile in a small jet.

On the safety front, the unorthodox wing design makes the plane easier to land and helps avoid stalling in various conditions. The plane also **Borrowed** an idea from skydiving by providing a full-aircraft parachute that can safely float the craft and its passengers to the ground in the event of a catastrophic failure.

How does one go about funding a new aircraft company with a bold idea? Loury hacked that as well, with large amounts of startup capital coming from customers instead of banks or investors (i.e., **Crowdsourcing**). Within 90 days of the aircraft's announcement, $50 million in orders were received online. Eager customers plunked down $15,000 deposits with the same ease as ordering a book from Amazon. Once the first customers eagerly made deposits, the company followed the gold and was able to enjoy the benefits of an **Exploit,** seizing customer demand as a mechanism to fund continuing growth.

THE NERD

Michimasa Fujino had been at it for 29 years. Trained as an aeronautical engineer at Tokyo University, he wanted to fuse his love of air travel with the keen eye of an engineer, to create something entirely new. Faced with the same challenges as others in the industry – cost, aerodynamics, safety, passenger comfort, baggage capacity, speed, and range – Fujino dreamed of inventing a breakthrough.

It took a prolonged and persistent **Brute Force** approach to eventually deliver the answer. For years, he toiled away with experiments, computer simulations, and trials. Employed by Honda, who wanted to expand beyond cars, motorcycles, and generators into the aircraft market, Fujino and his team tried just about everything. They experimented with **Deconstruction** and Substitution, taking apart a propeller plane and rebuilding it with a jet engine to see what would happen. Rapid prototypes yielded hundreds of failed results, but the team forged ahead nonetheless.

In his effort to break the mold, Fujino tried every possible change he could think of. In the middle of the night one on fateful evening, he jumped out of bed with an exciting new idea – he thought he may have finally discovered his breakthrough. Without any nearby paper, he tore the calendar off his wall and crudely sketched his idea. The inspiration was a **Reverse** – instead of putting the engines under the wings, as is the case with every other jet on the planet, what if he mounted the engines on top of the wings?

When running computer simulations of his new idea back at the office, the results were highly disappointing. It appeared that his clever idea created more drag and made the aircraft less aerodynamic. But using the hacker mindset that **Every Barrier Can Be Penetrated,** he persisted: maybe it was the specific placement of the engine on top of the wing that was the problem. Through ongoing experiments and deep exploration into the world of aerodynamic science, he realized that if he raised the engines up rather than placing them directly on top of the wings, it actually created *less* drag than placing the engines in the traditional below-wing position.

As Fujino and his team continued to challenge conventional wisdom, they refined and optimized each aspect of their new aircraft. The final result: the HondaJet. The plane, with its two jet engines positioned at just the right height *above* the wings, has reinvented the small business jet. Compared to directly competitive aircraft, the cabin is 20% larger and provides an extra 14" of legroom, per passenger. Honda says their jet flies higher and faster than any other jet in its class, and is about 15% more fuel-efficient. Fujino's creativity has paid off – Honda has a long list of customers waiting to take delivery of the $4.5 million aircraft. **Working Backward**, the nerdy engineer reimagined every aspect of the small business jet and hacked his way to a best-in-class product.

THE SOCCER MOM

Private aircraft are generally built to target the business traveler. "Save time, take in more meetings, and make it home for dinner," the promise goes. Instead of crafting yet another business plane in a crowded field, the leaders at Cirrus Aircraft pulled a **Reverse**. Where David Loury at Cobalt set out to craft the flying version of a Ferrari, Cirrus engineers set out to build a flying minivan. Instead of targeting the machismo of male business travelers, why not aim for the safe, functional desires of families?

The Cirrus Vision Jet isn't the prettiest thing you've ever seen. In fact, it has about the same sex appeal as a station wagon. **Borrowing** from the success of family automobiles, Cirrus crafted their plane to prioritize function over form. If you think of the Cobalt as a two-seat convertible that's great for a night out, but not so comfortable to drive cross-country; versus your not-so-sexy, but oh-so-spacious sedan, you'll understand the comparison to the Vision Jet. With a respectable range of 1,500 miles, a speedy pace of 350 mph, and comfortable seating for a family of five, it may be the perfect aircraft for a family getaway.

While a flying minivan is nice, the coolest innovation of the Vision Jet comes from **Deconstruction** and Substitution. Jets the world over have at least two engines. Until now. The creative team at Cirrus tore apart prevailing wisdom, examining every component and interrelation of an aircraft. By using a specific type of jet engine and placing it in on top of the plane's aft (as opposed to the typical placement under each wing), they were able invert and invent an entirely new approach. Engines are the most expensive equipment on a plane in every aspect – purchasing, maintenance, and usage. By building a plane with a single jet engine, Cirrus is able to sell the plane for 50% less than competitive aircraft and operate at a 40% savings.

THE ROCK STAR

Sergey Petrossov looks the part of the rock star for our misfit quartet. Dashingly handsome, dressed to the nines, and sporting the elegant accent of his native Moscow, Sergey oozes success. Pictured in $6,000 suits boarding $60 million jets, you'd think he was the son of a shipping magnate or a model for a men's luxury lifestyle magazine. But when you speak to him, you find a passionate hustler, a whip-smart business hacker that is ready to leave a big mark. A Warren Buffett or Bill Gates kind of mark.

Seeing a giant industry ready for disruption, Sergey has an audacious goal: to make private aviation accessible to as many people in the world as he can. Unlike the hackers above who applied their creativity to remaking planes themselves, Petrossov is hacking the entire business model of flying.

"I met a private jet operator and saw how clumsy and difficult it was to book a private flight," Sergey told me. "It felt a lot like a stock market transaction back in the 1980s. 'Why hasn't this been digitized?' I thought. I saw a huge segment that was desperate for a better solution."

In March 2013, Sergey launched a radically different approach: JetSmarter. "Once I got into my research, I realized there were major inefficiencies on the supply side. As planes are repositioned from one location to another, there are over 1.5 million hours of unoccupied private air travel each year. I felt like there were billions of dollars of dormant value."

Setting out to unlock that value, Sergey **Deconstructed** the traditional approach. "The average private plane flies only 250-300 hours per year, but the economics are optimized closer to 1,000 hours," he told me. "I saw a massive market to provide more efficient service to those who already fly privately, but more importantly to serve the five million high-end commercial flyers that could afford to use our service."

So Sergey started **Borrowing**. He borrowed the notion of an on-demand transportation service with total transparency, accessed from a mobile app. As a result, his company has been named the "Uber of Private Jets" by over a dozen major publications. Sergey borrowed his economic model from that of a country club, having members pay an initiation fee and annual dues to participate.

Petrossov also uses **Social Engineering** to propel his company to higher altitudes. Members gain the excitement and exclusivity of nightclubs and high-end networking functions by flying with celebrities and other influential travelers. Alerts such as "Fly with Jamie Foxx from NYC to Miami" produce a flurry of excitement and help spread the word to both members and prospects. When you see who is part of this rock star club, how could you *not* want to join? With each new member becoming a spokesperson to help recruit others, the mindset of **Quantity Is a Force Multiplier** is helping spread the word.

Today, the company offers scheduled routes between major cities and allows members to hop on open flights for free. If members need to schedule a guaranteed flight on their own terms, they can reduce their cost by offering extra seats on the trip to other members. If a standard charter is needed, JetSmarter offers the only mobile app that searches over 1,600 planes in a matter of seconds, provides a real-time quote, and allows a member to confirm and pay for the flight with a single tap.

Sergey embraced **Compasses Over Maps**, setting out to transform an industry rather than beginning with a specific product idea in mind. He's since raised over $56 million in venture capital from A-list investors including Jay Z, the Saudi Royal Family, and Twitter. In 2016 alone, the company grew 400% providing over 30,000 private flights to its members.

"We are going to disrupt planes like Uber disrupted taxis," Sergey tells me with rock star bravado. "We are going to be *the* company that people associate with accessible private jet travel."

In a highly regulated industry with daunting complexity, enormous costs, and deeply-held traditions, our Entrepreneur, Nerd, Soccer Mom, and Rock Star each enlisted hacking techniques and mindsets to discover new and exciting innovations. While many competitors stay mired in the quicksand of obstacles, these hackers enjoyed rarified success. If you're feeling stuck in your own company, industry, or community, recognize that these four innovators are exactly like you. They dreamed of a better way and relied on an internal set of resources to bring their ideas to life.

By leveraging hacking mindsets and tactics, you can reach unprecedented heights of success. And your flight is now boarding and ready for departure.

CHAPTER 18: MASTERCLASS 5 – A HACK-IN-PROGRESS

As someone who loves learning and professional development, I was increasingly frustrated with the existing options. I've spoken at hundreds of conferences and events that miss the mark, conducted in dingy hotel ballrooms with bad florescent lighting. Ferns and flags on the stage, business conferences are often loathsome. If you tell a friend you're going to a concert, they say, "Wow...how cool!" If you tell the same friend you are going to business event, they say, "Bummer...sorry to hear that."

My long-time business partner, Jordan Broad, and I decided there had to be a better way. We decided to hack professional development and business conferences in an effort to make a positive impact in the world. We hoped to raise individual and corporate performance while building a fun new company. On September 1, 2014, I launched my fifth company: Fuel Leadership, LLC.

Since then, we've had more setbacks than successes, and the ultimate fate of this fledgling company is still unknown. By the time you read this, we may be enjoying booming success or we may have failed spectacularly. The writing of this book will come to an end far before the Fuel Leadership story has been completed, but I wanted to give you a personal account of how I put the hacking mindset and tactics to work to launch our new company.

The original premise was a bold one: to disrupt the tired and boring business event world with something completely different. We set out from the beginning to shake things up. First, we **Deconstructed** what was good and bad about business events. On the positive side, there was professional learning, inspiration, and networking. Events were a great way to grow and interact, especially in a digital world. On the negative front, they were tiresome. Typical formats were lengthy, boring, poorly orchestrated, expensive, and flat-out draining. What if we kept the pros and shaved off the cons?

Next, we **Borrowed** a format from music tours. In the same way a Lady Gaga tour is designed once and then replicated in various cities around the world, we thought it made sense to build an unbelievable experience and then transport it to various cities. Most business events are destinations, so we pulled a **Reverse** – bringing the event to the audience. Instead of bland staging, we decided to do a **Mashup** – combining the energy, set design, and vibe of a rock concert with the business value of the best leadership event imaginable. We started with a blank page and let our creativity unfold to imagine the ultimate business event. We ditched all conventional wisdom and sought to do something remarkable. Knowing that **Nothing Is Static**, we set out to discover a better way.

We landed on the format of a single-day event that would tour from city to city. The events would have unprecedented production quality, with lighting and staging rivaling A-list musical acts. We then stacked the line-up with celebrity entrepreneurs, business titans, and irresistible leaders. Our premier event – FUEL: Detroit – featured Jessica Alba, Magic Johnson, bestselling author Seth Godin, Ford Motor Company CEO Mark Fields, and Navy commander Michael Abrashoff. With an energetic vibe and a killer program, what could possibly go wrong?

Leading up to the event, we struggled. Selling tickets was immensely more difficult than we expected, even though our price point was comparable to other events and our content was infinitely better. Our sponsorship sales goals fell woefully short and we were looking down the barrel of a huge loss. **Brute Force** efforts at the last minute – the entire team scrambling and doing whatever we could to sell sponsorships and fill the arena – paid off, but barely. We broke even on the event, only by a hair.

Despite our economic disappointment, people loved the event. We heard from attendees and sponsors alike that it was the best business event they'd ever attended...by far. Emboldened by the positive feedback and passionate about our cause, we pressed on. We figured each event would improve and we'd "crack the code" sooner rather than later. Filled with optimism and entrepreneurial fire, we began planning our next event – FUEL: Cleveland.

We doubled down and sought to outdo ourselves. We booked expensive speakers including former NBA commissioner David Stern, Olympian Jackie Joyner-Kersee, and former Apple exec and bestselling author Guy

Kawasaki. We rented a theater that held 2,500 people and set out to fill every seat.

What sounded great in theory turned out to be disastrous in reality. Sponsorship sales paled in comparison to our mediocre-at-best results in Detroit. Ticket sale were horrendous, even after several price drops and special offers. In the end, we gave away many tickets and still only had a half-full house. The Cleveland event was an economic catastrophe, losing nearly $750,000.

My team and I were feeling depressed, ashamed, and immensely frustrated. We knew we had a great product – even the attendees in Cleveland loved the event – but we were battered and bruised economically, facing a highly unsustainable model.

Refusing to give up, we tried again. We thought we could capitalize on the enthusiasm from our previous Detroit effort, so we set out to make FUEL: Detroit an annual event. Learning from our mistakes, we brought in new talent to the team and a new approach to ticket sales and sponsorships. The production quality would once again be over-the-top, and we brought in more famous presenters. FUEL: Detroit 2016 featured Martha Stewart, men's fashion and retail legend John Varvatos, astronaut Mark Kelly, bestselling author Marcus Buckingham, and NFL hall-of-famer and TV personality Michael Strahan. We cut ticket prices in half to make it more accessible, and carefully orchestrated every detail from the gourmet food to the special staging effects.

The result? Another financial setback. The event enjoyed rave reviews, but our checkbook told a different story. Despite intense dedication, hard work, and what we believed to be a disruptive model, the economics just didn't work. It's dark moments like these that require painful soul searching. Should we give up? Are we wasting our time and money chasing a dream that can never be?

While many people would throw in the towel, we decided to pivot instead. My close friend Dave Zilko – who had just sold his previous company, Garden Fresh, to Campbell's Soup for $231 million – joined the team full-time as our CEO. The title of his bestselling book is *Irrational Persistence*, a mindset that allowed him and his partner to build an incredible company and an approach that we decided to embrace for Fuel Leadership. With the hacking mindset that **Every Barrier Can Be Penetrated**, we forged ahead.

Taking a step back, we focused on what mattered most. We wanted to be part of people's daily lives. We wanted to deliver both inspiration and practical learning to help people boost performance in their jobs, in turn, driving better performance in our economy. We wanted to make the world a better place and do something that had artistic integrity. And yes, we needed to have a business that was sustainable.

We also had the insight that Millennials – who will soon represent over 50% of the global workforce – were facing an even bigger professional development gap than previous generations. This new group who grew up as technology natives were increasingly frustrated with professional development options. They didn't necessarily want to take an 8-week course, read a 12-hour book, or even attend a full-day event. They love TED talks, but even those are too long...who has extra 18-minute blocks readily available on a daily basis?

Embracing the hacker philosophy of **Compasses Over Maps**, we fell in love with the problem instead of our solution. In other words, we didn't care *how* we made the world better through professional development, we just cared that we delivered. Accordingly, it wasn't hard for us to let go of our existing solution – breathtaking business events – because we didn't define ourselves as an event company. We were in the business of modern professional development and helping improve performance.

With all this in mind, Dave, Jordan, and I **Worked Backward** and reverse-engineered a solution. How could we deliver high quality and inspiring professional development insights to Millennials on a daily basis?

Our new invention: The Daily Fuel.

In the same way millions of people guzzle their Starbucks each morning to fuel their bodies, we set out to fuel their minds and careers. We wanted to be the Starbucks of professional growth and learning. The Daily Fuel is a video series that features close-up interviews with compelling people. Shot with cinematic beauty, every segment is two minutes or less, allowing them to be easily consumed and shared. Delivered for free every workday, subscribers enjoy what feels like a personal conversation with some of the most fascinating people in the world. We envisioned variety that one day may be a celebrity entrepreneur like Elon Musk, or a captain of industry like Warren Buffet. Another day may be a trailblazing exec like Sheryl Sandberg, a world-class trauma surgeon talking about leading through a crisis, or a 28-year-old craft brew maker, sharing his struggles in an authentic and informative way. **Competency Is the Only Credential That Mat-**

ters when a single week may feature household-name celebrities followed by dreamers and doers of whom no one has ever heard. Each segment is both inspiring and practical, but never canned. Every day, subscribers discover someone new, learn a fresh insight, or embrace an unexpected tip or technique.

The content is in line with the hacking philosophy that **Quantity Is a Force Multiplier**. Instead of reading the book of one author or attending a university course from one professor, learners gain insight and perspective from a wide and diverse group of minds. Subscribers hear right from the source, not someone else retelling their stories. As a digital content company, we are not relying on our own team to write stories, but selecting inspiring and informative storytellers from around the world.

To arrive at our conclusion and launch the Daily Fuel, we didn't only rely on our own ideas. Embracing the **Crowdsourcing** tactic, we sought input and guidance from a large variety of people. A senior executive at a major media conglomerate and an 18-year-old theater major each contributed to the concept. We spent time with a filmmaker, the head of an ad agency, digital media planners, and fresh college grads. In the end, the idea we shaped and refined was a collective effort rather than the more singular approach we took when launching live events.

The new business model is another **Borrow,** this time going with two proven revenue streams: advertising sales and premium subscriptions. Advertisers are desperate to connect with Millennials, authentically, in the context of their professional lives. To serve this need, we offer tasteful sponsorship opportunities to progressive brands that want to stand out as thought-leaders. While most Daily Fuel subscribers will enjoy their Fuel for free, a small percentage of innovators and go-getters want more. For a nominal monthly fee, subscribers are able to upgrade to a premium subscription that is ad free; provides full access to our Daily Fuel archives, extended interviews, webinars, podcasts and other content; and allows for an immersive community experience with likeminded professionals.

It all sounds good and we're pumped, but this cake is still in the oven. Early beta results have been strong, but we haven't yet invested heavily in scale. We will continue **Brute Force** via Rapid Experimentation to further refine the offering, and once we find what's resonating most with our audience, we'll double down and **Exploit** the best approach.

Our intentions are noble – we truly want to make the world better by helping people boost their professional performance. We are producing high-quality, original content and distributing it in a novel way that is on-trend. Yet, the business may never take off.

No matter the eventual outcome, my view is that even if we tank the business, we will not have failed. Instead of "you win some, you lose some," my partners and I share the belief that "you win some, you learn some." Whether we build the next global phenomenon or end up falling short, I'm proud of our work and our hacking approach. The Fuel Leadership experiment ended up using all five hacker mindsets and all ten hacker tactics. Time will tell the outcome, but no one can deny the boldness and creativity that enabled the journey so far.

Stay tuned, and I hope you're rooting for us.

CHAPTER 19: HACKING AHEAD

It was the 2015 Cyber War Games simulation in Silicon Valley where I got to know Samir Kapuria. The head of a 1,000-person elite security team for Symantec, Samir may just be the world's top cybersecurity defender. Symantec is on the leading edge of cyberdefense worldwide, and Samir is the one responsible for their most important threat prevention clients. Before selling his company to Symantec, Samir was the co-founder of @Stake, a cybersecurity consulting firm which was paid by top corporations and governments around the world to hack into their systems to expose – and ultimately correct – vulnerabilities. Today, he is leading the charge of the most elite minds in cybersecurity, protecting the most sensitive corporate and governmental assets.

I was invited to present the closing keynote after the annual Cyber War Games concluded. The event, which was Samir's brainchild, brings hundreds of cybersecurity professionals together from around the globe for one of the most sophisticated simulations on the planet. Divided into teams, participants are given their assignments in James Bond-esqe dossiers. Each team has 48 hours to complete various levels of a sophisticated hack; the team who completes the most levels is declared the champion, the ultimate hacking team.

The exercises are tough and designed to push the teams' creative and technical skills to the max. Throughout their 48-hour sprint, they are subject to a variety of unexpected distractions and twists. One year, real FBI agents "raided" the lab, forcing the teams to discard their work and start anew. Another year, the mission and assignments changed midstream, requiring participants to adapt and pivot under the intense pressure of competition. Winning teams enjoy some perks and rewards, but they crave recognition and bragging rights far more. It is the hacker equivalent of winning a Super Bowl ring.

As enthralled as I was in the games themselves, I was even more impressed with Kapuria, Symantec's Senior Vice President and General Manager of Cyber Security Services. The intellect of a scholar combined with the grit of a street fighter, I admired the work and the man instantly. We became friendly, and he was kind enough to take time away from his special ops teams to share his perspective on hacking innovation.

Samir affirmed the hacker mindsets we've covered. "Hackers fundamentally examine a system or process to look for ways to make it do things it was never intended to do," he explains. "They refuse to live within the confines of what something is supposed to do. Instead, they look for novel ways of transforming the ordinary."

When I asked what would happen if a reformed hacker took over a Fortune 500 company and applied her skills for legitimate purposes, Samir's already fast words increased in pace and enthusiasm. "She would immediately attack the three variables that can create the most leverage: people, technology, and processes," he says without missing a beat. "She would question each system and seek to upend the current approaches.

"Starting with people, she'd explore how to boost the human factor. She would view employees, customers, suppliers, investors, the media, and other stakeholders as valuable resources that could be hacked and optimized. Next, she'd explore the technology and look for gaps. Most companies don't have tech that is fully integrated, so creative inefficiency and vulnerabilities abound. Our hacker would streamline and integrate the tech to boost value and impact. Finally, she would attack the processes, seeking dormant opportunities to accelerate growth and reduce friction."

By applying the same creative rigor that a hacker would use to bring down an oil company, the Innovation Hacker here would systematically attack each aspect of a business with the objective of disrupting the status quo. "Hacking is about deconstructing a system and then rebuilding it in a new way," Samir continues. "It is a way of reverse-engineering a desired outcome. Using curiosity to explore the possibilities, and then pulling on a thread once it's discovered."

Fundamentally, that's what this whole book has been about. In these challenging times, we are all looking for new models to enable growth, innovation, and ultimately sustainable success. The hacking mindsets and subsequent tactics are simply a framework for complex problem-solving – a methodology for creative disruption. And I sincerely hope that they become a powerful tool for you as you continue on your own Innovation Hacking journey.

As I closed my conversation with Samir, I asked him how might organizations defend against hackers? "The only way to defend against hackers is to think like a hacker," he states emphatically. "If someone wants to break in, they only need two things: time and intent."

As you think about the competitive threats in your industry, and the hungry business hackers they employ to steal your market share, Samir's words ring true. Your competition certainly has time and intent. You must proactively choose to outwit them, to be the source of disruption rather than having it thrust upon you.

Hacking is our most important tool for growth, and our most powerful system of defense. Your job is to protect much more than your data files; with the velocity of change at unprecedented levels, the job has been elevated to protecting our very existence.

The art of hacking is our primary weapon to surviving the dramatic shifts of the modern business climate. As change and complexity increase, we need a system as fluid as the competitive environment itself, and to that end, Innovation Hacking is our collective imperative.

Now is the time to embrace this new model of growth.

Now is the time to reimagine what's possible.

Now is the time to stretch the boundaries of our imagination and ring in a new era for ourselves, our companies, and our communities.

Now is the time to hack innovation.

Hack away....

CHAPTER 20: QUICK REFERENCE GUIDE

THE MINDSETS

EVERY BARRIER CAN BE PENETRATED: This mindset can be summed up in the name of Mick Ebeling's philanthropic hacking group – Not Impossible. Approach every problem, every step of a system, every obstacle with the understanding that it can be overcome; the question is not *if*, but *how*. But assuming a problem can be solved is where the assumptions end. To triumph over barriers, hackers assume nothing, take nothing at face value. When approaching any task or problem, proceed as if everything is up for debate – no information is set in stone, no system is infallible, no solution is fixed, no problem is ever permanently solved. This mindset also favors simplicity – the easiest, laziest solutions can be the most elegant.

COMPASSES OVER MAPS: Hackers have a lot in common with history's great explorers – they have a general idea of where they're headed, but they go off into uncharted territory and maybe draw up a map later. This mindset is about curiosity and exploration. Using a map is perfunctory and it presupposes both the destination, and the best way of getting there. Using a compass admits a general direction, but surrenders playfully to the realities of the landscape, allowing the traveler to adjust course based on the lay of the land. A mountain is an opportunity, not an obstacle. Fall in love with the problem, not the solution, constantly re-navigate the problem based on the current landscape, instead of carefully retracing the mapped-out routes of previous solutions.

NOTHING IS STATIC: This mindset isn't about fearmongering or the quicksand-like nature of life, but maintaining a constant thirst for knowledge and self-improvement. For computer hackers, technical knowledge is obsolete almost as soon as it's learned, so hackers are committed to constantly expanding and updating their skills and knowledge bases. Complacency is simply not an option. Embrace, don't fear, change. Instead of waiting for someone else to corner you into change, constantly initiate change – actively court and choose change instead of running from it. From systems to solutions, nothing lasts forever, so relish learning, growing, and exploring new possibilities.

 QUANTITY IS A FORCE MULTIPLIER: Two heads are better than one. This mindset isn't new, hackers just apply it more consistently and universally than the rest of us. Do away with the romantic notion of the singular genius in the attic (or the C-suite) in favor of diverse and democratized ideation. Let go of the fantasy of the midnight stroke of brilliance for the hard work of rapid experimentation. Replace VC investment with crowdfunding. Pool knowledge, resources, ideas; and be as open and excited about the ideas of others as about your own.

 COMPETENCE IS THE ONLY CREDENTIAL THAT MATTERS: Computer hacking is literally a science, but in the hacking community, it is also something of a performance art. A hallmark of hacker culture is anonymity, so hackers can't rely on "real-world" credentials or distinguishers. All that matters is what you can do, what you can demonstrate. In the "real world," we take comfort in degrees, credentials, and familiarity to vouch for someone's capabilities, taking them as symbols of capability. Challenge how you interact with others – take risks on people based on what they do, not who they are on paper, or what they say they can do; find brilliant people who look and think totally differently than you. Challenge yourself – don't rest on the laurels of your degrees, credentials, or past achievements, but measure yourself on what you're doing *now*. Expertise may be found in the unlikeliest of places. Balk authority, get scrappy, get results.

THE TACTICS

BRUTE FORCE: The best example of this tactic is Rapid Experimentation. This is about using a battering ram, or three, not a picking a lock. Try lots of solutions to narrow down the best options quickly.

SOCIAL ENGINEERING: Let others do the work for you. Customers, fans, happy employees – they can be the most powerful form of endorsement or advertisement. Make sure you are utilizing them, authentically, to their full potential.

CROWDSOURCING: Stop waiting for one genius to have a lightbulb moment. Bring together people from diverse backgrounds, experience, departments, even industries. Two heads are better than one, three are better than two...you get the idea.

THE EXPLOIT: How do you climb a mountain? One step at a time. This tactic is about focusing on a small win and then leveraging that to create bigger, longer lasting wins. Think of your problem as a wall – look for the tiniest hole, figure out how you can wiggle through, and then expand the hole until the whole wall is gone.

BORROWING: Stop looking in the usual places for solutions and inspiration. Look outside of your industry, look to nature, look anywhere that is totally unrelated. Find things that work really well somewhere else. Ask yourself why and see if it could translate to your work. Pretend to be someone else and approach your problem freshly, through a Different Lens.

DECONSTRUCT: If something isn't working or you're sure it could do better, take it apart. Break it into its smallest elements, seeing how the parts works together. Then put it back together, but differently. Add, Subtract, or Substitute elements for improved variations.

AGILE BURSTS: Hackathons are a great example of this tactic. Agile Bursts are about speed – attack a problem hard, intensely, even completely, in a short span of time. A few hours, one week, set a short deadline and commit 100% of your attention.

THE REVERSE: How should you solve a problem? Do the opposite. Whether it's flipping your first inclination upside down or following that inkling when it's the opposite of what you're supposed to do. This tactic is all about thumbing your nose at expectations and daring to do things totally differently.

THE MASHUP: Sometimes the best solution isn't a new one, but existing solutions combined and reimagined. Maybe you combine two strategies into one, maybe you take one of your strategies and combine it with something from another industry. The result is one elegant solution you can't imagine having lived without.

WORKING BACKWARD: Don't get hung up on your favorite solution. This tactic is about starting with your ideal outcome, in vivid detail, and then going backward to imagine a new solution. If you want to do something that's never been done, you probably need to go about it in a new way, too; so, start at the finish line.

REFERENCES

CHAPTER 1

"10 Alarming Cyber Security Facts That Threaten Your Data." *Heimdal Security Blog.* 12 May 2016. https://heimdalsecurity.com/blog/10-surprising-cyber-security-facts-that-may-affect-your-online-safety/

"2014 IC3 Annual Report." *FBI: Internet Crime Complaint Center.* Web. 1 Oct. 2016.

Ensha, Azadeh. "Audi and BMW Engage in Billboard Battle." *New York Times Blogs.* 23 Apr. 2009. http://wheels.blogs.nytimes.com/2009/04/23/audi-and-bmw-engage-in-billboard-battle/?_r=0

"Company Overview of Facebook, Inc." *Bloomberg.* 30 Sept. 2016.

Magid, Larry. "Mark Zuckerberg's Letter to Prospective Facebook Investors." *Forbes.* 1 Feb. 2012.

"Not Impossible Labs." *Not Impossible.* N.d. http://www.notimpossible.com/#notimpossible

Pagliery, Jose. "Half of American Adults Hacked This Year." *CNN Money.* 28 May 2014. Web. http://money.cnn.com/2014/05/28/technology/security/hack-data-breach/index.html

Pagliery, Jose and Charles Riley "Target will pay hack victims $10 million." *CNN Money.* 19 Mar. 2015.

"Project Daniel: 3-D Printing Prosthetic Arms for Children in Sudan." *Not Impossible Now.* 14 May 2014. http://www.notimpossiblenow.com/labs/project-daniel

Raymond, Eric S. "Cracker." *The Jargon File.* N.d. http://www.catb.org/jargon/html/C/cracker.html

Raymond, Eric S. "Hacker." *The Jargon File*. N.d. http://www.catb.org/jargon/html/H/hacker.html

Stenovec, Timothy. "Myspace History: A Timeline Of The Social Network's Biggest Moments." *The Huffington Post*. 29 Aug. 2011.

"The Target Breach, By the Numbers." *Krebs On Security*. 16 May 2014.

"What are crackers and hackers?" *PC Tools by Symantec*. N.d. http://www.pctools.com/security-news/crackers-and-hackers/

Vijayan, Jaikumar. "90% of Companies Say They've Been Hacked: Survey." *Computerworld*. 22 Jun. 2011. Web. 1 Oct. 2016.

CHAPTER 2

"14 Jeff Bezos Quotes That Show Why Amazon's Boss Is A Total Genius." *Business Insider, India*. N.d. http://www.businessinsider.in/14-Jeff-Bezos-Quotes-That-Show-Why-Amazons-Boss-Is-A-Total-Genius/On-complacency-A-company-shouldnt-get-addicted-to-being-shiny-because-shiny-doesnt-last-/slideshow/24104411.cms

"Amazon Dash." *Wikipedia*. N.d. https://en.wikipedia.org/wiki/Amazon_Dash

Boyd, Clark. "Mine Kafon: Wind-blown landmine clearance." BBC Future. 18 Nov. 2014. http://www.bbc.com/future/story/20120503-blowing-in-the-wind

Buchanan, Leigh. "An Entrepreneur Who Never Runs Out of Energy." *Inc.* 20 May 2016. http://www.inc.com/leigh-buchanan/jessica-matthews-will-never-run-out-of-energy.html   [http://www.inc.com/leigh-buchanan/jessica-matthews-will-never-run-out-of-energy.html]

Cornish, David. "Watch Pablos Holman's Wired 2012 talk: why hackers need to do more than hack." *Wired*. 11 Dec. 2012. http://www.wired.co.uk/article/pablos-holman

Couric, Katie and Gabriel Noble. "Deaf singer 'hears' music with help from 'Not Impossible' tech-hackers." *Yahoo! News.* 12 Nov. 2015. https://www.yahoo.com/katiecouric/deaf-singer-experiences-her-own-music-with-help-151205934.html

Crown, Judith and Glenn Coleman. *No Hands: The Rise and Fall of the Schwinn Bicycle Company, an American Institution.* New York: Henry Holt & Co., 1996.

Fenn, Donna. "This Company Has Come Up With a New Alternative Energy Source: Kids." *Inc.* 24 May 2016. http://www.inc.com/donna-fenn/2016-30-under-30-uncharted-play.html

Goodin, Dan. "'NASDAQ is owned.' Five men charged in largest financial hack ever." *arsTECHNICA.* 25 Jul. 2013. http://arstechnica.com/security/2013/07/nasdaq-is-owned-five-men-charged-in-largest-financial-hack-ever/

"Handbook for New Employees." *Valve,* 2012. http://www.valvesoftware.com/company/Valve_Handbook_LowRes.pdf

Harvey, Mandy. "Home." *Mandy Harvey.* N.d. http://www.mandyharveymusic.com/

Hough, Jack. "Amazon Could Be Largest U.S. Company by 2020." *Barron's.* 2 Jun. 2016. http://www.barrons.com/articles/amazon-could-be-largest-u-s-company-by-2020-1464866783

"John Dillinger." *Wikipedia,* N.d. https://en.wikipedia.org/wiki/John_Dillinger

Keith, Clinton. "Valve's Culture, Self-Organization and Scrum" *Front Row Agile.* 11 Mar. 2016. https://www.frontrowagile.com/blog/posts/27-valves-culture-self-organization-and-scrum

"Kevin Bull at the American Ninja Warrior 2014 Venice City Finals." *Esquire.* 8 Jul. 2014. http://tv.esquire.com/videos/71287-kevin-bull-at-the-american-ninja-warrior-2014-venice-city-finals

Linkner, Josh. Interview with Massoud Hassani. 29 May 2015.

Linkner, Josh. Interview with Yony Feng. 14 Jun. 2016.

Maeterlinck, Maurice. *The Life of the Bee*. New York: Dover Publications, 2006.

Nuñez, Michael. "Pablos Holman Wants You To Break Your Gadgets." *Popular Science*. 9 Mar. 2015. http://www.popsci.com/pablos-holman-wants-you-break-your-gadgets

Pagliery, Jose. "What we know about the bank hacking ring – and who's behind it." CNN *Money*. 16 Feb. 2015. http://money.cnn.com/2015/02/16/technology/bank-hack-kaspersky/

Reeves, Martin and Johann Harnoss. "Don't Let Your Company Get Trapped by Success." *Harvard Business Review*. 19 Nov. 2015.

Soffel, Jenny. "These RoboBees could pollinate crops and save disaster victims." *World Economic Forum*. 27 Jun. 2016. https://www.weforum.org/agenda/2016/06/the-bees-of-the-future-that-can-pollinate-and-save-disaster-victims/

"Top hacker shows us how it's done." *TEDxMidwest*. 30 Aug. 2012.

CHAPTER 3

"Reese's Commercial." *The Hershey Company*. 1981.

"Crooks Steal, Sell Verizon Enterprise Customer Data." *Krebs on Security*. 24 Mar. 2016. https://krebsonsecurity.com/2016/03/crooks-steal-sell-verizon-enterprise-customer-data/

"Four Johns Hopkins Research Teams Win Funding to Combat Zika Virus." *Johns Hopkins University*. 10 Aug. 2016. http://hub.jhu.edu/2016/08/10/usaid-zika-challenge-grants/

"'Funtenna' Software Hack Turns a Laser Printer into a Covert Radio." *Ars Technica*. 6 Aug. 2015. http://arstechnica.com/security/2015/08/funtenna-software-hack-turns-a-laser-printer-into-a-covert-radio/

"James Veitch | Comedian and Scamp." *James Veitch*. 30 Sept. 2016. http://veitch.me/

McCandless, David. "World's Biggest Data Breaches & Hacks." *Information is Beautiful*. http://www.informationisbeautiful.net/visualizations/worlds-biggest-data-breaches-hacks/

Newcomb, Alyssa. "Pentagon Will Reward Hackers Who Find Security Problems on Its Websites." *Yahoo!*. 18 Apr. 2016. http://abcnews.go.com/Technology/pentagon-reward-hackers-find-security-problems-websites/story?id=38481413

"PS: I Love You. Get Your Free Email at Hotmail." *TechCrunch*. 18 Oct. 2009. https://techcrunch.com/2009/10/18/ps-i-love-you-get-your-free-email-at-hotmail/

"Reese's Peanut Butter Cups." *Wikipedia, the free encyclopedia*. 26 Sept. 2016.

Shontell, Alyson. "What Is GroupMe and How Did It Get Acquired for $85 Million." Business Insider. 22 Aug. 2011. http://www.businessinsider.com/what-is-groupme

Soderbergh, Steven. *Ocean's Eleven*. 2001. Film.

"Startup Weekend." *Wikipedia, the free encyclopedia*. 19 Aug. 2016.

Heidt, Frank. "Hacking 101." *TEDx Midwest*. 11 Mar. 2014. http://tedxtalks.ted.com/video/Hacking-101-Frank-Heidt-at-TEDx

"Temporary Tattoo Offers Needle-Free Way to Monitor Glucose Levels." *UC San Diego*. 14 Jan. 2015. http://ucsdnews.ucsd.edu/pressrelease/temporary_tattoo_offers_needle_free_way_to_monitor_glucose_levels

"The Columbia University Intrusion Detection Systems Lab." *Columbia University*. N.d. http://ids.cs.columbia.edu/users/ang.html

"Protection Mishap Leaves 55M Philippine Voters at Risk." *Trend Labs*. 6 Apr. 2016. http://blog.trendmicro.com/trendlabs-security-intelligence/55m-registered-voters-risk-philippine-commission-elections-hacked/

Veitch, James. "This Is What Happens When You Reply to Spam Email." TED Talks. Dec. 2015. https://www.ted.com/talks/james_veitch_this_is_what_happens_when_you_reply_to_spam_email?language=en

CHAPTER 4

"6 Million Password Attacks in 16 Hours and How to Block Them." *Wordfence.* 16 Feb. 2016. https://www.wordfence.com/blog/2016/02/wordpress-password-security/

"Berkshire Hathaway." *Wikipedia, the free encyclopedia.* 30 Sept. 2016. *Wikipedia.* Web.

Connor, Deni. "Five Things You Don't Know about EMC." *Computerworld.* 5 Jul. 2007. http://www.computerworld.com/article/2542376/data-center/five-things-you-don-t-know-about-emc.html

Ferdows, Kasra, et al. "Zara's Secret for Fast Fashion." *Harvard Business School.* 21 Feb. 2005. http://hbswk.hbs.edu/archive/4652.html

Fishman, Charles. "The Road To Resilience: How Unscientific Innovation Saved Marlin Steel." *Fast Company.* 17 Jun. 2013. https://www.fastcompany.com/3012591/marlin-steel-metal-baskets

"IBM." *Wikipedia, the free encyclopedia.* 29 Sept. 2016. *Wikipedia.* Web.

Loeb, Walter. "Zara's Secret To Success: The New Science Of Retailing." *Forbes.* 14 Oct. 2013. http://www.forbes.com/sites/walterloeb/2013/10/14/zaras-secret-to-success-the-new-science-of-retailing-a-must-read/#1da88b1e1332

"Meet Mafiaboy, The 'Bratty Kid' Who Took Down The Internet." NPR. 7 Feb. 2015. http://www.npr.org/sections/alltechconsidered/2015/02/07/384567322/meet-mafiaboy-the-bratty-kid-who-took-down-the-internet

"Melissa (Computer Virus)." *Wikipedia, the free encyclopedia.* 31 Aug. 2016. *Wikipedia.* Web.

"Pixar." *Wikipedia, the free encyclopedia.* 25 Sept. 2016. *Wikipedia.* Web.

"Pizzo (Extortion)." *Wikipedia, the free encyclopedia.* 29 Aug. 2016. *Wikipedia.* Web.

Rouse, Margaret. "What Is Brute Force Cracking?" *Tech Target*. N.d. http://searchsecurity.techtarget.com/definition/brute-force-cracking

Ruddick, Graham. "How Zara Became the World's Biggest Fashion Retailer." 20 Oct. 2014. *www.telegraph.co.uk* [*http://www.telegraph.co.uk*]. Web.

"Suzuki." *Wikipedia, the free encyclopedia.* 17 Sept. 2016. *Wikipedia*. Web.

"The Complete History of Instagram." *We Are Social Media*. N.d. http://wersm.com/the-complete-history-of-instagram/

"The Rise, Dominance, and Epic Fall – a Brief Look at Nokia's History." *GSMArena*. 12 Aug. 2015. http://www.gsmarena.com/the_rise_dominance_and_epic_fall__a_brief_look_at_nokias_history-blog-13460.php

Turkel, Dan. "Victims Paid More than $24 Million to Ransomware Criminals in 2015 – and That's Just the Beginning." *Business Insider*. 7 Apr. 2016. http://www.businessinsider.com/doj-and-dhs-ransomware-attacks-government-2016-4

"Usage Statistics and Market Share of WordPress for Websites, September 2016." W3 *Techs*. 30 Sept. 2016. https://w3techs.com/technologies/details/cm-wordpress/all/all

CHAPTER 5

"About Us." *Little Lotus*. N.d. Web. 30 Sept. 2016. http://littlelotusbaby.com/pages/about-us

Bukszpan, Daniel. "Infamous Hackers of the 80s and 90s: What They're Doing Now." *Fortune*. 18 Mar. 2015. http://fortune.com/2015/03/18/famous-hackers-jobs/

Chen, Jane. "A Warm Embrace That Saves Lives." TED *Talk*. Nov. 2009. https://www.ted.com/talks/jane_chen_a_warm_embrace_that_saves_lives?language=en

"Embrace." *Stanford University.* 2007. http://extreme.stanford.edu/projects/embrace

"Embrace Warmer | Infant Warmer." *Embrace Global.* N.d. Web. 30 Sept. 2016. http://embraceglobal.org/embrace-warmer/

Fawzy, Farida. "Ice Bucket Challenge Leads to Gene Discovery." CNN. 27 Jul. 2016. http://www.cnn.com/2016/07/27/health/als-ice-bucket-challenge-funds-breakthrough/

Fisher, Lawrence M. "Ricardo Semler Won't Take Control." *Strategy + Business.* 29 Nov. 2005. http://www.strategy-business.com/article/05408?gko=3291c

"How a Lying 'Social Engineer' Hacked Wal-Mart." CNN. 7 Aug. 2012. http://money.cnn.com/2012/08/07/technology/walmart-hack-defcon/

Greenberg, Andy. "Kevin Mitnick, Once the World's Most Wanted Hacker, Is Now Selling Zero-Day Exploits." *Wired.* 24 Sept. 2014. https://www.wired.com/2014/09/kevin-mitnick-selling-zero-day-exploits/

Liszewski, Andrew. "DHL Pranked UPS Into Advertising For Them." *Gizmodo.* 20 Feb. 2014. http://gizmodo.com/dhl-pranked-ups-into-advertising-for-them-1526964505

O'Connell, Justin. "10 Most Notorious Hackers of All Time." *Hacked.* 3 Sept. 2015. https://hacked.com/hackers/

Restauri, Denise. "A Personal Story: How Low Cost Technology Is Saving Babies' Lives." *Forbes.* 18 Nov. 2014. http://www.forbes.com/sites/deniserestauri/2014/11/18/a-personal-story-how-low-cost-technology-is-saving-babies-lives/#43e14d997dc5

Routson, Joyce. "Embracing a Way to Change the World." *Stanford Graduate School of Business.* 1 May 2011. https://www.gsb.stanford.edu/insights/embracing-way-change-world

Semler, Ricardo. "How to Run a Company with (Almost) No Rules." TED *Talk.* Oct. 2014. https://www.ted.com/talks/ricardo_semler_radical_wisdom_for_a_company_a_school_a_life?language=en

---. *Maverick: The Success Story Behind the World's Most Unusual Workplace*. Reprint edition. New York, NY: Grand Central Publishing, 1995. Print.

Shaughnessy, Dan. "The Amazing Pete Frates Story Continues to Inspire." *The Boston Globe*. 03 Mar. 2015. https://www.bostonglobe.com/sports/2015/03/03/the-amazing-pete-frates-story-continues-inspire/vDfnJSntd5Wjcx8urvsizL/story.html

"The Incredible History of the ALS Ice Bucket Challenge!" ALS Association. N.d. http://www.alsa.org/fight-als/edau/ibc-history.html

"Top 10 Most Famous Hackers." 27 Nov. 2009. *Telegraph*. N.d. http://www.telegraph.co.uk/technology/6670127/Top-10-most-famous-hackers.html

"WHO | Infant Mortality." WHO. N.d. Web. 30 Sept. 2016. http://www.who.int/gho/child_health/mortality/neonatal_infant_text/en/

Yakowicz, Will. "This Space-Age Blanket Startup Has Helped Save 200,000 Babies (and Counting)." *Inc*. 27 Apr. 2016. http://www.inc.com/magazine/201605/will-yakowicz/embrace-premature-baby-blanket.html

CHAPTER 6

Bercovici, Jeff. "A Biotech Lab in the Cloud, Backed by Peter Thiel." *Inc.com*. 26 Mar. 2015. http://www.inc.com/jeff-bercovici/emerald-therapeutics-peter-thiel.html

BrandIndex. "Crowdsourcing Campaign Appears to Boost Brand Perception for Lay's." *Forbes*. 11 Oct. 2104. http://www.forbes.com/sites/brandindex/2014/10/11/crowdsourcing-campaign-appears-to-boost-brand-perception-for-lays/#303842b95141

Buhr, Sarah. "A Look Inside Transcriptic's New Biotech Testing Facility." *TechCrunch*. 25 Mar. 2015. https://techcrunch.com/2015/03/25/a-look-inside-transcriptics-new-biotech-testing-facility/

"Emirates, Cathay, Air New Zealand Latest Airlines to 'crowdsource' New Products." *Airline Trends*. 26 Oct. 2010. http://www.airlinetrends.com/2010/10/26/airlines-crowdsourcing-new-products/

Empson, Rip. "WTF Is Waze And Why Did Google Just Pay A Billion+ For It?" *TechCrunch*. 11 Jun. 2013. https://techcrunch.com/2013/06/11/behind-the-maps-whats-in-a-waze-and-why-did-google-just-pay-a-billion-for-it/

Houston, Gillie. "We Got a Sneak Peek at Lay's New Flavor Contest." *Yahoo!*. 11 Jan. 2016. https://www.yahoo.com/style/we-got-a-sneak-peak-1340877996630070.html

Linkner, Josh. Interview with Mick Ebeling. 29 Jul. 2016.

"Rand McNally." *Wikipedia, the free encyclopedia*. 1 Sept. 2016. *Wikipedia*. Web.

"Rand McNally – Our History." N.d. Web. 30 Sept. 2016. http://www.randmcnally.com/about/history

"Samsung Strategy and Innovation Center." *Samsung*. Web. 30 Sept. 2016. http://www.samsung.com/us/ssic/

CHAPTER 7

"Bose Corporation." *Wikipedia, the free encyclopedia*. 21 Sept. 2016. *Wikipedia*. Web.

"Chinese Hacked U.S. Military Contractors: Senate Panel." *Reuters*. 18 Sept. 2014. http://www.reuters.com/article/us-usa-military-cyberspying-idUSKBN0HC1TA20140918

Porges, Seth. "Dr. Bose Tells All: Company Secrets, Why They Don't Publish Specs, And More." *TechCrunch*. 19 Sept. 2007. https://techcrunch.com/2007/09/19/dr-bose-tells-all-company-sercrets-why-they-dont-publish-specs-and-more/

Ferguson, Aaron J. "Fostering E-Mail Security Awareness: The West Point Carronade." *Educase Quarterly*. 1 Jan. 2005. http://er.educause.edu/

articles/2005/1/fostering-email-security-awareness-the-west-point-carronade

Scott, Bartie. "How Hillary Hooch and Trump Tonic Are Saving This 112-Year-Old Soda Business." *Inc.* 20 Jul. 2016. http://www.inc.com/bartie-scott/averys-beverages-trump-tonic-hillary-hooch.html

"The First 50 Years of Bose." *The complete history and future of Bose.* N.d. Web. 30 Sept. 2016. http://dreamandreach.bose.com/en_US

Zetter, Kim. "Kaspersky Finds New Nation-State Attack – In Its Own Network." *WIRED.* 10 Jun. 2015. https://www.wired.com/2015/06/kaspersky-finds-new-nation-state-attack-network/

CHAPTER 8

Alsever, Jennifer. "Finding Inspiration in Shark Tanks and Bee Hives." *Inc.* 18 Dec. 2014. http://www.inc.com/magazine/201412/jennifer-alsever/tipsheet-into-the-wild-shark-tanks-and-bee-hives.html

Althoefer, Kaspar. "How We Made an Octopus-Inspired Surgical Robot Using Coffee." *The Conversation.* 18 May 2015. http://theconversation.com/how-we-made-an-octopus-inspired-surgical-robot-using-coffee-41852

Baumeister, Dayna, and Toby Herzlich. "Why the Most Exciting Ideas in Leadership Are Coming From the Forest." *Inc.* 30 Nov. 2015. http://www.inc.com/dayna-baumeister/what-can-nature-teach-us-about-social-innovation.html

"Biology and Robotics Come Together." *Financial Times Video.* 16 Feb. 2015. http://video.ft.com/4051712926001/Biology-and-robotics-come-together/Companies

"Burn Therapy: An Award-Winning Regenerative Medicine Approach." *The University of Pittsburg.* 28 Oct. 2013. https://www.mirm.pitt.edu/news-archive/burn-therapy-an-award-winning-regenerative-medicine-approach/

Giammona, Craig. "LeBron-Backed Pizza Chain Aims to Top Chipotle." *Bloomberg.com.* 14 Apr. 2015. http://www.bloomberg.com/news/articles/2015-04-14/lebron-backed-pizza-chain-aims-to-top-chipotle-after-sales-surge

"Houston Car Hackers Arrested in Theft of More than 100 SUVs and Trucks." *Fortune.* 6 Aug. 2016. http://fortune.com/2016/08/06/houston-car-hackers/

Lutz, Ashley. "A Chipotle-Style Pizza Chain Endorsed by LeBron James Is Taking over America." *Business Insider.* 12 Feb. 2015. http://www.businessinsider.com/blaze-pizza-business-story-and-strategy-2015-2

National Geographic. *The Skin Gun.* Feb. 2011. https://www.youtube.com/watch?v=eXO_ApjKPaI

Novak, Matt. "The Untold Story of the Teen Hackers Who Transformed the Early Internet." *Gizmodo.* 14 Apr. 2016. http://paleofuture.gizmodo.com/the-untold-story-of-the-teen-hackers-who-transformed-th-1770977586

Palermo, Elizabeth. "Flying Machines? 5 Da Vinci Designs That Were Ahead of Their Time." *Live Science.* 19 Dec. 2014. http://www.livescience.com/49210-leonardo-da-vinci-futuristic-inventions.html

Petronzio, Matt. "26 Incredible Innovations That Improved the World in 2015." *Mashable.* 20 Dec. 2015. http://mashable.com/2015/12/20/social-good-innovations-2015/

Winslow, Timothy. "1980s Teen Computer Hacker Tells Story." CNN. 11 Mar. 2015. http://www.cnn.com/2015/03/11/tech/computer-hacker-essay-414s/

CHAPTER 9

"A Rich History." *Rust-Oleum Europe.* N.d. http://www.rust-oleum.eu/history

Linkner, Josh. Interview with Chad Price. 12 Sept. 2016.

Rethford, Wayne. "Robert Fergusson and Rust-Oleum Paint." *Scots Great and Small, People and Places*. 25 Jan. 2010. Web. 30 Sept. 2016. http://chicagoscots.blogspot.com/2010/01/robert-fergusson-and-rust-oleum-paint.html

"'The History of American Graffiti:' From Subway Car to Gallery." PBS *NewsHour*. 31 Mar. 2011. http://www.pbs.org/newshour/art/the-history-of-american-graffiti-from-subway-car-to-gallery/

CHAPTER 10

"About." *Sorry as a Service*. Web. 30 Sept. 2016. https://sorryasaservice.com/

Anderson, Nate. "Confirmed: US and Israel Created Stuxnet, Lost Control of It." *Ars Technica*. 1 Jun. 2012. http://arstechnica.com/tech-policy/2012/06/confirmed-us-israel-created-stuxnet-lost-control-of-it/

Cherry, Steven. "How Stuxnet Is Rewriting the Cyberterrorism Playbook." *IEEE Spectrum: Technology, Engineering, and Science News*. N.p., 13 Oct. 2010. Web. 30 Sept. 2016.

"Duke 101." *National Review*. 2 Nov. 2013. http://www.nationalreview.com/article/362692/duke-101-interview

Fildes, Jonathan. "Stuxnet Virus Targets and Spread Revealed." *BBC News*. 15 Feb. 2011. http://www.bbc.com/news/technology-12465688

Kushner, David. "The Real Story of Stuxnet." *IEEE Spectrum: Technology, Engineering, and Science News*. N.p., 26 Feb. 2013. Web. 30 Sept. 2016.

Linkner, Josh. Interview with Martin McGloin. 20 Sept. 2016.

Nakashima, Ellen and Joby Warrick. "Stuxnet Was Work of U.S. and Israeli Experts, Officials Say." *Washington Post*. 2 Jun. 2012. https://www.washingtonpost.com/world/national-security/stuxnet-

was-work-of-us-and-israeli-experts-officials-say/2012/06/01/gJQAl-
nEy6U_story.html

Odineca, Marija. "Sorry as a Service Admitted to TechStars London."
ArcticStartup. 8 Jul. 2015. http://arcticstartup.com/article/sorry-as-a-
service-admitted-to-techstars-london

Pagliery, Jose. "The inside Story of the Biggest Hack in History." CNN
Money. 5 Aug. 2015. http://money.cnn.com/2015/08/05/technology/
aramco-hack/

Savage, Adam. "Under the Gun: When Less Time Can Mean Better
Problem-Solving." *Wired*. 11 Feb. 2013. https://www.wired.com/2013/02/
under-the-gun/

"The Agile Manifesto for Software Development." *Agile Alliance*. 29 Jun.
2015. https://www.agilealliance.org/agile101/the-agile-manifesto/

Veluz, Danielle. "STUXNET Malware Targets SCADA Systems." *Trend
Micro*. 1 Oct. 2010. http://www.trendmicro.com/vinfo/us/threat-
encyclopedia/web-attack/54/stuxnet-malware-targets-scada-systems

CHAPTER 11

"About Us." *Beepi*. Web. 30 Sept. 2016. https://www.beepi.com/about

"About Us." *Carvana*. Web. 30 Sept. 2016. http://www.carvana.com/
about-us

Alessi, Christopher. "Thyssenkrupp Reimagines the Elevator as a Hyper-
loop for Buildings." *Wall Street Journal*. 19 Jul. 2016. http://www.wsj.com/
articles/thyssenkrupp-reimagines-the-elevator-as-a-hyperloop-for-
buildings-1468875762

"AutoNation." *Fortune*. N.d. Web. 30 Sept. 2016.
http://beta.fortune.com/fortune500/autonation-136

Biggs, John. "Everything You Need to Know about the NSA Hack (but
Were Afraid to Google)." *TechCrunch*. 16 Aug. 2016.

https://techcrunch.com/2016/08/16/everything-you-need-to-know-about-the-nsa-hack-but-were-afraid-to-google/

Hall-Geisler, Kristen. "Beepi Lets You Buy, Sell and Now Lease a Car with an App." *TechCrunch*. 21 Apr. 2016. https://techcrunch.com/2016/04/21/beepi-lets-you-buy-sell-and-now-lease-a-car-with-an-app/

Henry, Jim. "Carvana Used-Car Vending Machine Is Tip Of The Disruption Iceberg." *Forbes*. 29 Nov. 2015. http://www.forbes.com/sites/jimhenry/2015/11/29/carvana-used-car-vending-machine-is-the-tip-of-the-disruption-iceberg/#2c69710d9f80

Henry, Zoë. "Rebecca Minkoff on the Surprising Benefits of a Supply Chain Shift." *Inc.* 16 Feb. 2016. http://www.inc.com/zoe-henry/rebecca-minkoff-disrupting-new-york-fashion-week.html

"History of Patagonia – A Company Created by Yvon Chouinard." N.d. Web. 30 Sept. 2016. https://www.patagonia.com/company-history.html

Le, Vanna. "How Fashion Designer Rebecca Minkoff Uses Technology to Win Over Customers." *Inc.* 2 Oct. 2015. http://www.inc.com/vanna-le/fashion-designer-rebecca-minkoff-on-branding-technology-and-standing-out.html

Linkner, Josh. Interview with Chad Price. 15 Sept. 2016.

Ohikuare, Judith. "Rebecca Minkoff: Inspiration Is Closer Than You Think." *Inc.* 15 Apr. 2013. http://www.inc.com/magazine/201304/judith-ohikuare/inc-5000-profile-rebecca-minkoff.html

Pagliery, Jose. "Hacker Claims to Be Selling Stolen NSA Spy Tools." CNN *Money*. 15 Aug. 2016. http://money.cnn.com/2016/08/15/technology/nsa-spy-tools-stolen/

"Rebecca Minkoff on Selling Your Products at the Right Price." *Inc.* 1 Aug. 2016. http://www.inc.com/rebecca-and-uri-minkoff/how-to-sell-your-products-at-the-right-price.html

"This Startup Raised $160 Million For Its 'Car Vending Machines.'" *Fortune*. 10 Aug. 2016. http://fortune.com/2016/08/10/carvana-car-marketplace-160-million/

CHAPTER 12

Adams, Susan. "How Prezi's Peter Arvai Plans To Beat PowerPoint." *Forbes*. 7 Jun. 2016. http://www.forbes.com/sites/forbestreptalks/2016/06/07/how-prezis-peter-arvai-plans-to-beat-powerpoint/#3ea4ba176bdd

Burns, Mark J. "How Topgolf Flipped The Traditional Driving Range Model And Created A New Category Of Entertainment." *Forbes*. 2 Mar. 2015.   http://www.forbes.com/sites/markjburns/2015/03/02/how-topgolf-flipped-the-traditional-driving-range-model-and-created-a-new-category-of-entertainment/#5caa94e5fbbc

Carr, Austin. "Deep Inside Taco Bell's Doritos Locos Taco." *Fast Company*. 1 May 2013. https://www.fastcompany.com/3008346/deep-inside-taco-bells-doritos-locos-taco

Curda, Pavel. "Prezi: Building a Successful Startup From a Small Country." *The Next Web*. 27 Jun. 2014. http://thenextweb.com/insider/2014/06/27/how-build-globally-successful-startup-small-country/

Hoshaw, Lindsey. "Silicon Valley's Bloody Plant Burger Smells, Tastes And Sizzles Like Meat." *NPR.org*. 21 Jun. 2016. http://www.npr.org/sections/thesalt/2016/06/21/482322571/silicon-valley-s-bloody-plant-burger-smells-tastes-and-sizzles-like-meat

"Impossible Foods." *Impossible Foods*. N.d. Web. 30 Sept. 2016. https://www.impossiblefoods.com/

"Israeli Purification Technology Chosen By Peru To Clean Its Sewages." *No Camels*. 27 Apr. 2011. http://nocamels.com/2011/04/israeli-purification-techonolgy-chosen-by-peru-to-clean-its-sewages/

Kavilanz, Parija. "This Liquid Could Let Torn Clothes Repair Themselves." *CNN Money*. 10 Aug. 2016. http://money.cnn.com/2016/08/10/technology/self-repairing-fabric/

Linkner, Josh. Interview with Peter Arvai and Adam Somlai-Fischer. 11 Aug. 2016.

Messer, A'ndrea Elyse. "Self-Healing Textiles Not Only Repair Themselves, but Can Neutralize Chemicals." *Penn State University*. 25 Jul. 2016.

http://news.psu.edu/story/418507/2016/07/25/research/self-healing-textiles-not-only-repair-themselves-can-neutralize

Soller, Kurt. "The Impossible Burger Is Ready for Its (Meatless) Close-Up." *Wall Street Journal* 14 Jun. 2016. http://www.wsj.com/articles/the-impossible-burger-is-ready-for-its-meatless-close-up-1465912323

"Ultimate Fighting Championship." *Wikipedia, the free encyclopedia.* 30 Sept. 2016.

Weisul, Kimberly. "How This Startup Is Taking the Frustration Out of Multiple Medications." *Inc.* 24 May 2016. http://www.inc.com/kimberly-weisul/2016-30-under-30-pillpack.html

CHAPTER 13

Barbato, Lauren. "What Is The Impact Team? The Ashley Madison Hackers Delivered On Their Promises." *Bustle.* 19 Aug. 2015. https://www.bustle.com/articles/105183-what-is-the-impact-team-the-ashley-madison-hackers-delivered-on-their-promises

Congreve, William. *The Mourning Bride.* P. 45. London: Dodo Press, 2008. Print.

Covey, Stephen R. *The 7 Habits of Highly Effective People: Powerful Lessons in Personal Change.* Revised edition. New York: Free Press, 2004. Print.

Dryden, John. *Absalom and Achitophel.* Kessinger Publishing, 2010. Print.

Goodin, Dan. "Ashley Madison Hack Is Not Only Real, It's Worse than We Thought." *Ars Technica.* 19 Aug. 2015. http://arstechnica.com/security/2015/08/ashley-madison-hack-is-not-only-real-its-worse-than-we-thought/

Green, Dennis. "The Real Story behind the Detroit-Made Watch Obama Just Gave to David Cameron." *Business Insider.* 17 May 2016. http://www.businessinsider.com/the-real-story-behind-shinola-detroit-2016-5

Linkner, Josh. Interview with Jacques Panis. 21 Apr. 2016.

Restauri, Denise. "From Thongs To Briefs, This Self-Made Woman Sells Panties To Empower Women." *Forbes*. 28 Apr. 2015. http://www.forbes.com/sites/deniserestauri/2015/04/28/from-thongs-to-briefs-this-self-made-woman-sells-panties-to-empower-women/#963ca4e54de0

Shakespeare, William. *Titus Andronicus: The Oxford Shakespeare Titus Andronicus*. Ed. Eugene M. Waith. Reissue edition. P. 115. Oxford; New York: Oxford University Press, 2008. Print.

Ward, Mark. "Ashley Madison: Who Are the Hackers behind the Attack?" BBC *News*. 20 Aug. 2015. http://www.bbc.com/news/technology-34002053

"What to Know About the Ashley Madison Hack." *Fortune*. 26 Aug. 2015. http://fortune.com/2015/08/26/ashley-madison-hack/

"Who Hacked Ashley Madison?" *Krebs on Security*. 26 Aug. 2015. https://krebsonsecurity.com/2015/08/who-hacked-ashley-madison/

CHAPTER 14

Chivers, Tom. "Could You Have Been a Codebreaker at Bletchley Park?" 10 Oct. 2014. http://www.telegraph.co.uk/history/world-war-two/11151478/Could-you-have-been-a-codebreaker-at-Bletchley-Park.html

CNN, By Charlotte Lytton, for. "Lifting the Veil of Secrecy: Meet the Female Code-Breakers of WWII." CNN. 11 Nov. 2013. http://www.cnn.com/2013/11/11/world/europe/lifting-the-veil-of-secrecy-codebreakers/

Hollingshead, Iain. "What Happened to the Women of Bletchley Park?" 4 Sept. 2012. http://www.telegraph.co.uk/culture/tvandradio/9520807/What-happened-to-the-women-of-Bletchley-Park.html

Norton-Taylor, Richard. "Woman 'Opened up Enigma.'" *The Guardian* 15 Oct. 2001. https://www.theguardian.com/uk/2001/oct/15/humanities.highereducation

Smith, Michael. *Action This Day*. First edition & printing edition. London; New York: Bantam Press, 2001. Print.

CHAPTER 15

Davidson, Kief, and Daniel Junge. *Lego Brickumentary*. ANCHOR BAY, 2015. Film.

"Lego Architecture." *Wikipedia, the free encyclopedia*. 12 Sept. 2016.

"Lego Mindstorms." *Wikipedia, the free encyclopedia*. 28 Sept. 2016.

Ringen, Jonathan. "How Lego Became The Apple Of Toys." *Fast Company*. 8 Jan. 2015. https://www.fastcompany.com/3040223/when-it-clicks-it-clicks

CHAPTER 16

Deutschman, Alan. "The Fabric of Creativity." *Fast Company*. 1 Dec. 2004. https://www.fastcompany.com/51733/fabric-creativity

Roberts, Daniel. "At W.L. Gore, 57 Years of Authentic Culture." *Fortune*. N.p., 5 Mar. 2015. http://fortune.com/2015/03/05/w-l-gore-culture/

Safian, Robert. "Terri Kelly, The 'Un-CEO' Of W.L. Gore, On How To Deal With Chaos: Grow Up." *Fast Company*. 29 Oct. 2012. https://www.fastcompany.com/3002493/terri-kelly-un-ceo-wl-gore-how-deal-chaos-grow

"Timeline." *Gore*. N.d. Web. 30 Sept. 2016. http://www.gore.com/timeline/

"Tour de France Winning Bikes." *BikeRadar.* 29 Jun. 2012. http://www.bikeradar.com/us/road/gear/article/tour-de-france-winning-bikes-34375/

"WL Gore & Associates on the Forbes America's Largest Private Companies List." *Forbes.* N.d. Web. 30 Sept. 2016. http://www.forbes.com/companies/wl-gore-associates/

CHAPTER 17

Creedy, Kathryn. "HondaJet Is A Game-Changer For The Business Aviation Market." *Forbes.* 14 Dec. 2015. http://www.forbes.com/sites/kathryncreedy/2015/12/14/hondajet-the-one-to-beat-changes-the-business-aviation-aircraft-market/#7450c6a14d0f

Fierman, William. "This Radical Aircraft Design Is Already a Hit in Silicon Valley." *Business Insider.* 16 Feb 2016. http://www.businessinsider.com/this-radical-aircraft-design-is-already-a-hit-in-silicon-valley-2016-2

Green, Dennis. "This Tiny Private Jet Has Room For 7 – And Its Own Parachute." *Business Insider.* 5 Jan. 2015. http://www.businessinsider.com/cirrus-vision-private-jet-2015-1

Kamps, Haje Jan. "JetSmarter Puts a Jet in Your Pocket, and Is Happy to See You." *TechCrunch.* 23 Mar. 2016. https://techcrunch.com/2016/03/23/jetsmarter-expands-to-europe/

Linkner, Josh. Interview with Sergey Petrossov. 13 Jan. 2016.

Magee, Christine. "With $20M In The Bank, JetSmarter Is Building The Uber Of The Skies." *TechCrunch.* 23 Jun. 2015. https://techcrunch.com/2015/07/23/with-20m-in-the-bank-jetsmarter-is-building-the-uber-of-the-skies/

Muller, Joann. "How The HondaJet Took Flight: An Engineer's 29-Year Obsession." *Forbes.* 6 May 2015. http://www.forbes.com/sites/joannmuller/2015/05/06/how-the-hondajet-took-flight-an-engineers-30-year-obsession/#42b3cf9f14c1

"Private Jet Charter & Hire Costs | PrivateFly." N.d. Web. 30 Sept. 2016. http://www.privatefly.com/us/private-flights/how-much-does-a-private-flight-cost

"Vision Jet." *Cirrus Aircraft.* N.d. Web. 30 Sept. 2016. http://cirrusaircraft.com/aircraft/vision-sf50/

"Why I'm Kind of in Love with JetSmarter." *The Points Guy.* 22 Feb. 2016. http://thepointsguy.com/2016/02/why-i-love-jetsmarter/

Index

A

B

D

F

G

H

I

M

P

Q

R

S

T

U

V

W

Acknowledgements

There's an approach even more powerful than those covered in this pages: the mindset of gratefulness. I would not have been able to bring these ideas to life if it weren't for an amazing group of supportive people who helped and guided me at every step of the journey.

First, to my incredible wife, Tia. You are my inspiration and make all of the late nights and early mornings worthwhile. Thank you for you unwavering belief, too many sacrifices, and for being by my side no matter what. I love you with all my heart. And some.

In addition to Avi and Tallia – my brand new hacker twins who themselves are a miracle of life and for whom this book is dedicated – a big shout out to my bigger kids Noah and Chloe. I'm so proud of everything you've become, and even more proud to be your dad.

Thank you to my hilarious and amazing family: Renita Linkner, Ethan and Tara Linkner, Sarah and Nick Zagar, Michael Farris and Joe Wert, Constantin and Marcelle Kouchary, and Carla and Ryan Deisenroth. And to those I lost far too soon yet continue to provide incredible inspiration: Robert Linkner, Monica Farris Linkner, and Mickey Farris. I miss you dearly.

This book would have never come to life without the amazing research, prose, and editing of Andrea Nienstedt. Thank you for being my partner in crime on this enormous project, and learning to hack together with me. Your sacrifice, professionalism, enthusiasm, and sense of humor truly made this effort something special.

A huge thank you to my long-time business partner Jordan Broad, who has been an incredible friend and supporter for over 20 years. Thanks to my partners, colleagues and friends at The Institute for Applied Creativity and Fuel Leadership: Matt Ciccone, Dave Zilko, Jonathan Deisenroth, Carly Szydlowski, and Connor Trombley.

Special thanks to Dr. Caren Lipsky, Mallory Wooldridge, Shantel White, Dr. James Verrees, and the whole crew at Sunrise Hospital & Medical Center in Las Vegas, Nevada. You are amazing people that literally saved the lives of my beloved children and wife. Thank you for your incredible work and infinite compassion; I remain forever grateful.

To my friends that continue to provide inspiration and support: David Farbman, Craig Erlich, Jeff Davidson, Kathy Ciccone, Ashley Broad, Peter Sheahan, Jeremy Gutsche, Mel Robbins, Sally Hogshead, Mike Scott, and Wes Matthews.

Thanks to the amazing crew at FastPencil PREMIERE for having the courage to hack publishing and bring a far better model to the world of print.

And a special thanks to my three-pound dog, DaVinci, who brings joy and love to our home by the metric ton. For as much time as he spent on my lap while writing this book, the little guy deserves a Pulitzer.

HACKING TOGETHER

If your organization needs help embracing the Hacking Innovation mindsets and tactics, Josh Linkner and his team are ready to help.

SPEAKING ENGAGEMENTS

Josh brings his deep executive and entrepreneurial background to the stage, along with extensive keynote speaking experience. He's delivered thousands of inspiring and impactful speeches on four continents to over 250,000 people who are now better armed to meet the challenges they face. Clients range from large corporations and associations to high-growth startups, universities, and governmental agencies. Consistently ranked as a top innovation keynote speaker, he brings the perfect balance of an energizing performance blended with real-world experience and credibility. He not only inspires, but also moves audiences to action by offering practical and effective approaches to driving better business outcomes.

WORKSHOPS & SEMINARS

Often in conjunction with a keynote, Josh Linkner and his team conduct powerful workshops for corporate clients, ranging from half-day to three-day sessions. These hands-on seminars help participants build muscle memory and tackle real business challenges using proven innovation methodologies.Immersive and interactive, participants leave with fresh approaches to drive breakthrough creativity, innovation, and transformation.

CONSULTING

All organizations seek growth and sustainable success. However, delivering on those goals requires a fully growth-enabled organization that has the right culture, leadership, model, and relevance to consistently create new and untapped value in the market. Our teams of experts use proven diagnostics, methodologies, and thought-leadership to help organizations accelerate growth. We identify performance gaps and clarify what is needed, catalyzing the strategy to deliver sustainable results. By channeling energy and building clarity around the behaviors, attitudes, and structures needed to support sustainable growth, we help remove friction from the system, and in turn, drive maximum performance. Additionally, we embed the behaviors that are needed so that growth will continue over time – altering the DNA of the organization to be continually oriented towards growth, innovation, and ongoing transformation.

To learn more and explore a collaboration, please visit **JoshLinkner.com** or email **ask@JoshLinkner.com.**